THE FOUNDATION
OF BUDDHIST PRACTICE

THE LIBRARY OF WISDOM AND COMPASSION

The Library of Wisdom and Compassion is a special multivolume series in which His Holiness the Dalai Lama shares the Buddha's teachings on the complete path to full awakening that he himself has practiced his entire life. The topics are arranged especially for people not born in Buddhist cultures and are peppered with the Dalai Lama's unique outlook. Assisted by his long-term disciple, the American nun Thubten Chodron, the Dalai Lama sets the context for practicing the Buddha's teachings in modern times and then unveils the path of wisdom and compassion that leads to a meaningful life, a sense of personal fulfillment, and full awakening. This series is an important bridge from introductory to profound topics for those seeking an in-depth explanation from a contemporary perspective.

Volumes:

1. *Approaching the Buddhist Path*
2. *The Foundation of Buddhist Practice*

More volumes to come!

THE FOUNDATION OF BUDDHIST PRACTICE

Bhikṣu Tenzin Gyatso,
the Fourteenth Dalai Lama

and

Bhikṣuṇī Thubten Chodron

Wisdom

Wisdom Publications
199 Elm Street
Somerville, MA 02144 USA
wisdompubs.org

Library of Congress Cataloging-in-Publication Data
Names: Bstan-dzin-rgya-mtsho, Dalai Lama XIV, 1935– author. | Thubten Chodron,
    1950– author.
Title: The foundation of buddhist practice / Bhiksu Tenzin Gyatso, the Fourteenth
    Dalai Lama and Bhiksuni Thubten Chodron.
Description: Somerville: Wisdom Publications, 2018. | Series: The library of wisdom and
    compassion; volume 2 | Includes bibliographical references and index. |
Identifiers: LCCN 2017037684 (print) | LCCN 2018009580 (ebook) | ISBN
    9781614295457 (ebook) | ISBN 9781614295204 (hard cover: alk. paper)
Subjects: LCSH: Buddhism—China—Tibet Autonomous Region. | Buddhism—
    Doctrines. | Religious life—Buddhism. | Spiritual life—Buddhism. | Buddhist
    philosophy.
Classification: LCC BQ7604 (ebook) | LCC BQ7604 .B768 2018 (print) | DDC
    294.3/420423—dc23
LC record available at https://lccn.loc.gov/2017037684

ISBN 978-1-61429-520-4   ebook ISBN 978-1-61429-545-7

22 21 20 19 18

5 4 3 2 1

Photo credits: p. xii, Kenryun Ong; pp. 50, 230, Thubten Tenzin;
p. 130, Stephen Ching; p. 182, Libby Kamrowski; p. 340, Mike Novak
Cover and interior design by Gopa & Ted2, Inc.
Set in Diacritical Garamond Premier Pro 11/14.6.

Publisher's Acknowledgment

The publisher gratefully acknowledges the generous help of the Hershey Family Foundation in sponsoring the production of this book.

Contents

Preface

WELCOME TO THE second volume of the Library of Wisdom and Compassion that shares His Holiness the Dalai Lama's compassionate wisdom on how to practice the path to full awakening. The first volume of the Library of Wisdom and Compassion, *Approaching the Buddhist Path*, principally contained introductory material that set the context for Buddhist practice. It gave us a way to approach the Buddha's teachings: to "get our toes wet" without diving in. This volume, which can also be read as an independent book, takes the next step and describes the foundation of Buddhist practice—important topics that will help us to stay focused on what is worthwhile and to build a firm basis on which to establish a healthy Dharma practice.

As an individual who has studied and practiced the Buddhadharma since he was a small child, His Holiness the Dalai Lama is uniquely qualified to share with us what he has learned and how he implements it in his life. Occupying the office of the Dalai Lama, Bhikṣu Tenzin Gyatso is the spiritual leader of the Tibetan people, and until he resigned in 2011 he was also their political leader. From early on, he insisted that Tibetans develop democratic institutions in keeping with modern standards. Once the Central Tibetan Authority was established in Dharamsala, India, with functioning legislative, executive, and judicial branches, he followed his heart's yearning to retire from government service and devote his time to the Buddha's teachings. Looking back on his years as a political leader, he comments that the confluence of spiritual and political power in pre-1959 Tibet was influenced by feudalism. He relinquished the political power of the institution of the Dalai Lama in favor of a democratic government and believes that spiritual and political leadership should be distinct.

His Holiness is nonsectarian in his approach to the Dharma. He is not the leader of the Geluk tradition—that position is held by the Ganden Tripa and is a seven-year appointed position accorded to a former abbot of one of the two Geluk tantric monasteries. His Holiness refers to himself as a simple Buddhist monk who follows the Nālandā tradition—the teachings of the vibrant Buddhist monastic universities in classical India, one of which was Nālandā.

How the Library of Wisdom and Compassion Came About

As explained more extensively in *Approaching the Buddhist Path*, the first volume in the Library of Wisdom and Compassion, this series grew from the need for a presentation of traditional Buddhist teachings in a new format designed especially for people who did not grow up with knowledge of the Buddha's teachings. This audience—myself included—generally engages with Buddhism using a rational approach. We seek reasoned explanations and examine what we learn to see if it makes sense and is logically consistent. We try it out to see if it works before having faith or calling ourselves Buddhists.

With this in mind, in 1995 I requested His Holiness to write a short text that teachers could use for this purpose. He responded by saying that a larger commentary should be written first and, giving me transcripts of some of his talks, charged me with that task. Since I have been His Holiness's student since 1979, I also had a wealth of notes as well as English translations of many of the texts he has taught. With each new teaching I heard, more was added to the manuscript, and what began as one book quickly turned into a series of volumes. In addition, His Holiness said that he wanted this book to be unique and to include the perspectives of the Pāli and Chinese Buddhist traditions.

Every few years I would meet with His Holiness for a series of interviews to ask him questions that I had accumulated from my own studies and from my friends who were also Western Buddhists. Perhaps because of cultural differences or the way society is now structured, we often have questions and qualms that require in-depth explanations that are not found in the classical Buddhist texts. His Holiness enjoyed these discussions—he would often invite two or three geshes, his brother Ngari Rinpoche (Tenzin Choegyal), and the scholar and former Tibetan prime minister Samdhong Rinpoche to join us. There were serious philosophical debates and robust laughter during our sessions.

Much of the content of the two chapters on properly relating to a spiritual mentor came from these interviews as well as from gatherings of Western Buddhist teachers with His Holiness in 1993 and 1994, when we spoke frankly with him about difficulties that have arisen as Buddhism spreads in new lands. His Holiness discussed these topics openly and gave practical responses suitable for current issues.

Since the material for this series came from oral teachings, interviews, and written texts, which were translated by various interpreters who had different English translations of technical terms and different speaking and writing styles, one of my tasks as editor was to express the material in a consistent style and standardize the terms. At one point His Holiness insisted that the series be coauthored, although this was not my intent or wish. Although the series follows His Holiness's teachings, I have expanded on certain points that he covered briefly and mentioned some points that were omitted. He has been my spiritual mentor for nearly forty years, so whatever I have written has definitely been shaped by his perspective and guidance. Geshe Dorje Damdul and Geshe Dadul Namgyal also checked the manuscript.

Most of the series is written from the perspective of the Nālandā tradition, which stems from the monastic universities in ancient India, and the Sanskrit tradition in general. There are so many similarities between the Sanskrit tradition and the Pāli tradition of Buddhism that quotations from sūtras and commentaries in the Pāli tradition are freely intertwined in this book. In some places—for example, in the chapters on karma and its effects—some points from the Pāli tradition are added to expand our understanding. This is part of His Holiness's vision of our being twenty-first-century Buddhists with flexible minds who can understand and learn from a variety of perspectives.

His Holiness wants this series to address the spiritual needs of not only

Westerners but also people from traditionally Buddhist cultures in Asia and abroad, as well as the younger generations of Tibetans who are English educated.

Overview of "The Foundation of Buddhist Practice"

The "prelude" to the Library of Wisdom and Compassion was *Buddhism: One Teacher, Many Traditions*, which shared the Buddha's teachings in both the Pāli and Sanskrit traditions, showing the many similarities as well as the different perspectives. In our modern world, it is increasingly important that Buddhists from different traditions and countries learn about one another. In that way we will abandon old misconceptions that divide us and be able to speak as one voice on the Buddha's principal teachings on nonviolence, love, compassion, ethical conduct, and so forth—values that desperately need to be promulgated to counter the self-centeredness of individuals, groups, and nations.

His Holiness's teaching style is unique. He respects the intelligence of his audience and is not afraid to introduce profound concepts to beginners. While he does not expect us to understand everything the first time we hear or read it, he urges us to do our best and to come back to the material repeatedly over time and continue to deepen our understanding. He presents the path in a straightforward manner, without exaggerated claims of quick or easy attainments that require minimum effort and commitment, and urges us to exert joyous effort in learning, reflecting on, and meditating on the topics. He earnestly models this effort and commitment in his own life, living simply without any intention to become a celebrity. He also trusts that when we encounter difficult concepts, we will not give up but will persevere, gradually progressing according to our individual ability. By teaching in this way, His Holiness gives us a clear aim and path to get there as he compassionately encourages us to keep going.

The present volume begins with the four seals—basic premises that are accepted by all Buddhist schools—and the two truths, which are the basis of the path. Here we are introduced to key Buddhist ideas such as dependent arising and emptiness according to the view of the Prāsaṅgika Madhyamaka tenet system. We begin to understand that things—especially our own selves—do not exist as they appear. There is an ultimate reality to be discovered that does not negate the existence of the world but gives us a new, liberating way to see it.

Chapter 2 focuses on epistemology, how we know the phenomena that comprise the two truths. How do we discriminate reliable cognizers—awarenesses that accurately know their objects—from wrong consciousnesses that misperceive sensory objects or hold incorrect views? This topic keeps our spiritual exploration grounded in reason and is important to fulfill both our temporary and ultimate aims.

Knowing the qualities of correct and erroneous cognizers, we examine the objects of these cognizers in chapter 3—external objects that form the environment and internal ones that are the basis of the self, our body and mind. This chapter contains an extensive classification of phenomena that is helpful to keep in mind as we explore other topics on the path.

Chapters 4 and 5 discuss a subject that many people find confusing: how to choose a qualified spiritual mentor and form a healthy relationship with that person. Practicing under the guidance of excellent spiritual mentors is essential; without them we risk wandering in the spiritual marketplace, taking a little of this and a little of that and blending them together in a way that pleases us. Worse yet, an unqualified teacher may lead us on the wrong path. These chapters explain the different kinds of spiritual mentors, their requisite qualities, and how to relate to them in a way that benefits our practice. But for benefit to occur, we need to become receptive students. When difficulties arise in the mentor-student relationship, we need to address them skillfully. His Holiness is very practical in this regard.

Before actually embarking on the path, we also need to know the various types of meditations and how to structure our meditation session. This is covered in chapter 6. The preliminaries, such as proper sitting positions and calming the mind through observing the breath, facilitate meditation. Reciting verses that direct our minds to positive thoughts settles the mind. Doing these recitations while imagining that we are in the presence of the buddhas and bodhisattvas makes them especially heartfelt.

In chapter 7 His Holiness explains the mind, body, and rebirth in more depth, bringing in a scientific perspective while adhering to the Buddhist view that body and mind have different natures and different causes. He also introduces a meditation to help you get a sense of the clear and cognizant nature of the mind.

Chapter 8 begins the path in common with the initial-level practitioner. First we contemplate our precious human life, its meaning, and its rarity. This meditation is a wonderful antidote to depression and discouragement, for it emphasizes the good fortune and remarkable opportunity we have at present.

Chapter 9 asks us to look at what distracts us from practicing the path: our addiction to the pleasure that comes from other people and sense objects and our aversion to any pain or disappointment. The attitude that seeks only our own happiness of this life keeps us busy trying to make other people and the environment correspond with our current wishes and ignores the need to create the causes for fortunate future lives, liberation, and full awakening. Meditation on death helps us clear away our "rat race" mentality and set clear priorities. This chapter also includes advice for how to prepare for death and help someone who is dying.

Understanding the value of our lives and determined to use them to progress on the path to awakening, we want to learn how to create the causes for happiness and abandon the causes of suffering. This is covered in the final three chapters about karma and its effects. Here we find a comprehensive description of how our actions create our experiences. We learn to distinguish virtuous and nonvirtuous actions, giving us power to create the kind of future we want. A section on current ethical issues is a starting point for discussions on how to live an ethical life in a changing society. The four opponent powers set out a psychologically healthy way to remedy our misdeeds and begin anew. We also explore the deeper implications of causality. With this knowledge we can live in a healthy, wholesome, and meaningful way that enables us to accomplish our spiritual goals.

Please Note

Although this series is coauthored, the writings are primarily His Holiness's instructions. I wrote the parts pertaining to the Pāli tradition and some other paragraphs.

For ease of reading, most honorifics have been omitted, but that does not diminish the great respect we have for these most excellent sages and practitioners. Foreign terms are given in parentheses at their first usage and in the glossary. Unless otherwise noted with "P" or "T," indicating Pāli or Tibetan, respectively, the italicized terms are Sanskrit. Sanskrit spelling is used for Sanskrit and Pāli terms used widely (nirvāṇa, Dharma, arhat, and so forth), except in citations from Pāli scriptures and parenthetical technical terms in explanations from the Pāli tradition. For brevity, the term *srāvaka* encompasses solitary realizers (*pratyekabuddha*) as well, unless there is reason to specifically speak of solitary realizers. To maintain the flow of a passage, it is not always possible to gloss all new terms on their first use, so a glossary is included at the end of the book. Unless otherwise noted, the personal pronoun I refers to His Holiness.

Acknowledgments and Appreciation

I bow to Śākyamuni Buddha and all the buddhas, bodhisattvas, and arhats who embody the Dharma and share it with others. I also bow to all the realized lineage masters of all Buddhist traditions through whose kindness the Dharma still exists in our world.

Since this series will appear in consecutive volumes, I will express my appreciation of those involved in that particular volume. This second volume is due to the talent and efforts of His Holiness's translators—Geshe Lhakdor, Geshe Dorje Damdul, and Mr. Tenzin Tsepak. I appreciate Samdhong Rinpoche, Geshe Palden Dragpa, Geshe Sonam Rinchen, and Geshe Dadul Namgyal for their clarification of important points. I also thank Bhikkhu Bodhi for his clear teachings on the Pāli tradition, Geshe Dadul Namgyal for checking the manuscript, the staff at the Private Office of His Holiness for facilitating the interviews, the communities of Sravasti Abbey and Dharma Friendship Foundation for supporting me while I wrote this series, and David Kittelstrom and Mary Petrusewicz for their skillful editing. I am grateful to everyone at Wisdom Publications who contributed to the successful production of this series. All errors are my own.

Bhikṣuṇī Thubten Chodron
Sravasti Abbey

Abbreviations

TRANSLATIONS USED in this volume, unless noted otherwise, are as cited here. Some terminology has been modified for consistency with the present work.

ADK   *Treasury of Knowledge* (*Abhidharmakośa*) by Vasubandhu.

ADKB   *Treasury of Knowledge Autocommentary* (*Abhidharmakośa-bhāṣya*) by Vasubandhu.

ADS   *Compendium of Knowledge* (*Abhidharmasamuccaya*).

AN   Aṅguttara Nikāya. Translated by Bhikkhu Bodhi in *The Numerical Discourses of the Buddha* (Boston: Wisdom Publications, 2012).

BCA   *Engaging in the Bodhisattvas' Deeds* (*Bodhicaryāvatāra*) by Śāntideva. Translated by Stephen Batchelor in *A Guide to Bodhisattva's Way of Life* (Dharamsala, India: Library of Tibetan Works and Archives, 2007).

CMA   *Abhidhammattha Saṅgaha* by Anuruddha, in *A Comprehensive Manual of Abhidhamma*, edited by Bhikkhu Bodhi (Seattle: BPS Pariyatti Editions, 2000).

CŚ   *The Four Hundred* (*Catuḥśataka*) by Āryadeva. Translated by Ruth Sonam in *Āryadeva's Four Hundred Stanzas on the Middle Way* (Ithaca, NY: Snow Lion Publications, 2008).

DN   Dīgha Nikāya. Translated by Maurice Walshe in *The Long Discourses of the Buddha* (Boston: Wisdom Publications, 1995).

EPL   *Elucidating the Path to Liberation: A Study of the Commentary on the Abhidharmakosa* by the First Dalai Lama. Translated by David Patt (PhD dissertation, University of Wisconsin–Madison, 1993).

LC   *The Great Treatise on the Stages of the Path* (T. *Lam rim chen mo*) by Tsongkhapa, 3 vols. Translated by Joshua Cutler et al. (Ithaca, NY: Snow Lion Publications, 2000–2004).

MMA   *Supplement to the "Treatise on the Middle Way"* (*Madhyamakāvatāra*) by Candrakīrti. Hereafter *Supplement*.

MN   Majjhima Nikāya. Translated by Bhikkhu Ñāṇamoli and Bhikkhu Bodhi in *The Middle Length Discourses of the Buddha* (Boston: Wisdom Publications, 2005).

PDA   *Praise to Dependent Arising* (T. *rten 'brel bstod pa*) by Tsongkhapa. Translated by Thubten Jinpa. http://www.tibetanclassics.org/html-assets/In%20Praise%20of%20Dependent%20Origination.pdf.

PV   *Commentary on the "Compendium of Reliable Cognition"* (*Pramāṇavārttika*) by Dharmakīrti. Hereafter *Commentary on Reliable Cognition*.

RA   *Precious Garland* (*Ratnāvalī*) by Nāgārjuna. Translated by John Dunne and Sara McClintock in *The Precious Garland* (Boston: Wisdom Publications, 1997).

SN   Saṃyutta Nikāya. Translated by Bhikkhu Bodhi in *The Connected Discourses of the Buddha* (Boston: Wisdom Publications, 2000).

Sn   *Sutta Collection* (*Suttanipāta*). Translated by Bhikkhu Bodhi in *The Suttanipāta: An Ancient Collection of the Buddha's Discourses Together with Its Commentaries* (Somerville, MA: Wisdom Publications, 2017).

T.   Tibetan.

Vism   *Path of Purification* (*Visuddhimagga*) by Buddhaghosa. Translated by Bhikkhu Ñāṇamoli in *The Path of Purification* (Kandy: Buddhist Publication Society, 1991).

The Foundation
of Buddhist Practice

Introduction

Three Aspects of Buddhism's Contribution

OVER THE CENTURIES, Buddhism has made a powerful and valuable contribution to our human culture. When speaking of the contribution of the Nālandā tradition in particular, I place its contents in three categories: Buddhist science, philosophy, and religion. *Buddhist science* includes discussion of the nature of the external world and the subject, the mind, that cognizes it, as well as how the mind engages its objects through sensory and mental cognizers and through conceptual and nonconceptual consciousnesses. Buddhist science also discusses how the mind engages with objects by employing reasoning that helps establish facts about the world.

Buddhist philosophy includes discussion about the conventional and ultimate modes of existence of persons and phenomena, the four seals indicating a philosophy is Buddhist, the two truths, and emptiness and dependent arising. *Buddhist religion* describes the basis, path, and result of spiritual practice and emphasizes its liberating aspirations and goals. Buddhist religion relies on understanding Buddhist science and philosophy, in the sense that they provide the foundation and essential elements for the path to fulfill the spiritual aims of liberation and full awakening. Based on the assumption that every living being has the potential to become fully awakened, Buddhist religion stresses the path of mental development and transformation to attain these supramundane states.

Since we live in a multicultural, multireligious world, one of my aims is to present ethical conduct and compassion in a secular way, free of reliance on a specific religious doctrine, so that people of all faiths and of no faith can benefit. I also wish to give society access to the intellectual treasures in India's ancient texts and ensure that they are preserved in the body of world knowledge. In this light, I asked some of my foremost students, who are scholars in their own right, to form compendiums of the important points of Buddhist science and philosophy and translate them into a variety of languages. The series of these compendiums is entitled *Science and Philosophy in the Indian Buddhist Classics* and is published by Wisdom Publications.

Buddhist science and philosophy can be studied by all. However, Buddhist religion is for Buddhists and those interested in it. We respect each individual's choice regarding religion. The Library of Wisdom and Compassion deals with the spiritual and religious perspective of Buddhism's contribution to the world. It is for those who are interested in learning and practicing the path that frees us from *duḥkha*—the unsatisfactory conditions of cyclic existence (*saṃsāra*)—and enables us to actualize our full human potential. In this Library, you will find Buddhist science and philosophy presented as the basis and means for practicing the liberating path. You will learn how to engage with this liberating knowledge in a personal, transformative way.

A Good Attitude toward Learning the Dharma

Buddhist texts contain wise advice about how to approach learning the Buddha's teachings and explaining them to others. Since in this volume we will establish the foundation for Buddhist practice, it is especially helpful to touch on this now.

Reflecting on the value of learning the Dharma in my own life, I recall some verses in the *Jātaka Tales* (LC 1.56):

> Hearing (learning) is a lamp that dispels the darkness
>   of afflictions,
> the supreme wealth that cannot be carried off by thieves,
> a weapon that vanquishes the foe of confusion.
> It is the best of friends, revealing personal instructions,
>   the techniques of method.

It is the friend who does not desert you in times of need,
a soothing medicine for the illness of sorrow,
the supreme battalion to vanquish the troops of great misdeeds.
It is the best fame, glory, and treasure.

Due to the problems concerning Tibet's sovereignty that occurred during my youth, I had to accept the request of the Tibetan people and assume leadership of the Tibetan government. I was a mere teenager at the time, with little to no experience of my new duties and responsibilities that concerned the well-being of millions of people. Although anxiety was always beckoning, the Buddha's teachings gave me inner strength. They were the lamp that dispels the darkness of afflictions.

When I had to suddenly flee to India in March 1959, and leave almost all possessions behind and go forward to an unknown future, the Dharma was the friend who did not desert me in times of need. All the sūtras and scriptures I had memorized throughout the years came with me to India, providing guidance whenever I needed it. As I lived in exile and watched my homeland and its traditions, culture, and temples be destroyed, the Dharma was a soothing medicine for the illness of sorrow, giving me optimism and courage. In exile, the Buddha's teachings have been the best fame, glory, and treasure because they are always valuable in life and in death.

Seeing the benefits of learning the Buddha's teachings, we want to listen to and study them in an effective manner, without the defects of three faulty vessels. If we don't pay attention while at teachings or when reading Dharma books, we don't learn anything. Like an upside-down pot, nothing can go in. If we don't review what we have heard or read to make our understanding firm, we will forget the teachings, becoming like a leaky pot that can't retain the precious nectar poured into it. If we are closed-minded, opinionated, or have the wrong motivation for learning the Dharma, we become like a filthy pot; pure nectar may be poured inside and stay there, but because it is mixed with the filth in the pot it cannot serve its purpose to nourish us.

With this in mind, please set a wholesome altruistic intention when reading this book. Aspire, "May I read, reflect, and meditate on the Buddha's teachings so that I can become a kind, compassionate, and wise person.

Through this, may I be of benefit to all living beings, and in the long term, may I become a fully awakened buddha."

Bhikṣu Tenzin Gyatso, the Fourteenth Dalai Lama
Thekchen Choling

1 | The Buddhist Approach

Four Seals

THE ISSUE OF distinguishing Buddhists from non-Buddhists existed in olden times as it does now. In ancient India, this was usually done on the basis of philosophical views regarding the nature of the self and phenomena. A convenient and concise way to delineate Buddhist views is according to the four seals as found in the *King of Concentration Sūtra* (*Samādhirāja Sūtra*). People accepting the four seals are considered Buddhists by view,[1] and those accepting the Three Jewels as their ultimate source of refuge are considered Buddhists by conduct. The four seals are: (1) all conditioned phenomena are transient, (2) all polluted phenomena are duḥkha (unsatisfactory) in nature, (3) all phenomena are empty and selfless, and (4) nirvāṇa is true peace.

1. All conditioned phenomena are transient.

Conditioned phenomena are products of causes and conditions, and all of them undergo change, disintegrating from what they were and becoming something new. Change occurs in coarse and subtle ways. Coarse change occurs when the continuum of a thing ceases. Subtle change occurs moment by moment—it is a thing's not remaining the same from one instant to the next.

We can observe coarse impermanence with our senses: we see that after coming into being, things later cease. A chair breaks, a person dies, bottles are recycled. Understanding coarse transience is not difficult; we don't need logical arguments to accept this coarse level of change.

However, for something to arise and cease in this obvious way, there must be a subtler process of change occurring moment to moment. Without a seed changing moment by moment, a sprout will not appear. Without the sprout growing in each moment, the plant won't come into being. Without the plant aging and disintegrating moment by moment, it won't die. Without subtle, momentary change, coarse change could not occur. The fact that things end indicates they change subtly in each instant. They are transient or impermanent. In Buddhism, "impermanent" means changing moment by moment.

All the main Buddhist philosophical tenet schools (except for Vaibhāṣika, which has a slightly different understanding of the process of change and cessation) accept that the moment a thing comes into being, it contains the seed of its own cessation simply by the fact that it is produced by causes and conditions. It is not the case that one cause produces a particular thing, that thing remains unchanged for a period of time, and then another condition suddenly arises that causes its cessation. Rather, the very factor that causes something to arise also causes it to cease. From the very first moment of a thing's existence, it has the nature of coming to an end. The very nature of conditioned phenomena is that they do not last from one moment to the next.

Generally speaking, when we think of something coming into being, we look at it from a positive angle and think of it growing. When we think of something ending, we have the negative feeling that what existed before is ceasing. We see these two as incompatible and contradictory. However, if we reflect on the deeper meaning of impermanence, we see that its very definition—momentary change—applies to both the arising and ceasing of a thing. Nothing, whether it is in the process of arising or the process of ending, lasts into the next moment.

The present is insubstantial. It is an unfindable border between the past—what has already happened—and the future—what is yet to come. While we spend a great deal of time thinking about the past and planning for the future, neither of them is occurring in the present. The only time we ever live is in the present, but it is elusive, changing in each nanosecond. We cannot stop the flow of time to examine the present moment.

Scientists, too, speak of momentary change: subatomic particles are in continuous motion, and cells in our body undergo constant, imperceptible alteration. When we understand impermanence to mean momentariness, we see that arising and ceasing are not contradictory but are two aspects of the same process. The very fact that something comes into being means it will cease. Change and disintegration occur moment by moment. When we understand impermanence in those terms, we'll recognize the significance of the first seal, that all conditioned phenomena are impermanent.

Understanding impermanence is a powerful antidote to harmful emotions that plague our lives. Emotions such as attachment or anger are based on grasping: we unconsciously hold the view that the people to whom we're attached will not cease and that the problem or mood we're experiencing at present will continue. Contemplating impermanence shows us the opposite: since everyone and everything changes, clinging to people, objects, or situations as being fixed doesn't make much sense. Since our problems and bad moods are transient by nature, we do not need to let them weigh us down. Rather than resist change, we can accept it.

While the direct and complete antidote to attachment is the realization of selflessness, an understanding of impermanence will prepare our mind to gain insight into the meaning of selflessness. But understanding impermanence will not harm beneficial qualities such as love, compassion, and altruism because those emotions are not based on unrealistically grasping impermanent things to be permanent. Contemplating impermanence gives us confidence that our disturbing emotional habits can change and that excellent qualities can grow in us.

2. *All polluted phenomena are duḥkha—unsatisfactory by nature.*
Polluted phenomena are those produced under the control of ignorance and its latencies. Because all things in cyclic existence—including our body and mind—are polluted in this way, they are said to be *duḥkha*, unsatisfactory by nature. They are not capable of providing the enduring happiness and security that we seek.

How are the unsatisfactory circumstances in our lives related to our minds? In the *Sūtra on the Ten Grounds* (*Daśabhūmika Sūtra*), the Buddha said, "The three realms are only mind." The Cittamātra (Mind Only) school says this means the external physical world that we perceive is nothing but a projection of our mind. The Prāsaṅgika Madhyamaka school understands this statement differently, saying that it indicates there is no absolute, independent creator and that the source of our experiences lies in our minds—our virtuous, nonvirtuous, and neutral minds—and the actions, or karma, that these mental states motivate.

From the Buddhist viewpoint, many universes exist simultaneously at different stages of development—some are beginning while others are devolving. Before a particular universe begins, the potential for material substances exists in the form of space particles. Changing moment by moment, these space particles are not absolute or independent entities.

How is the physical evolution of a universe related to sentient beings—their mental states and their experiences of pain and pleasure, happiness and unhappiness? This is where karma comes in. Karma is intentional actions done by sentient beings.[2] As the potencies remaining from these actions ripen, they shape the evolution of the external world and condition our experiences in it.

Sentient beings create karma physically, verbally, and mentally. Our motivation is principal, for it fuels our physical and verbal actions. Destructive actions are motivated by afflictions such as attachment, anger, and confusion, which in turn are polluted by and rooted in ignorance, an erroneous belief in inherent existence.[3] Even when sentient beings act with kindness, the karma they create is still polluted by the ignorance grasping inherent existence. So whether the actions are constructive or destructive, they produce rebirth in cyclic existence. Because unawakened cyclic existence is a product of the undisciplined mind, it is said to be duḥkha, unsatisfactory by nature. Secure peace and happiness cannot come from ignorance. For this reason, the second seal of Buddhism is that all polluted phenomena are in the nature of duḥkha.

The first truth, the truth of duḥkha, consists of two factors: those in the external environment, such as our environment, tables, and oceans, and those internal to sentient beings—our bodies and minds. Within the latter, the feeling aggregate, the primary consciousnesses and mental factors that accompany them, and the cognitive faculties that cause these consciousnesses are all unsatisfactory by nature. Both the external and internal objects are true duḥkha because they come into being due to the polluted karma and the afflictions of ordinary sentient beings.

Once someone has eliminated afflictions and karma, she becomes an arhat, someone liberated from cyclic existence. Even so, she may continue to live in the external world, which is true duḥkha. In other words, the criterion for being in cyclic existence is not the environment in which a person lives but her state of mind.

The first two seals are related. We can use the transient nature of functioning things as a reason to show that all polluted phenomena are unsatisfactory in nature. Functioning things are products of causes and conditions, thus they are under the control of other factors. Polluted things, such as our ordinary bodies and unenlightened minds, are under the power of polluted causes—the undisciplined mind, at the root of which lies ignorance. As long as our minds remain under the control of ignorance, we live in an unsatisfactory state where the cause of suffering is always present.

3. All phenomena are empty and selfless.
4. Nirvāṇa is true peace.

The third and fourth seals are closely related. The explanation of the third seal accepted by almost all Buddhist tenet schools glosses the term "empty" as the absence of a permanent, unitary, independent self or soul and "selfless" as the absence of a self-sufficient, substantially existent person. According to the Prāsaṅgika Madhyamaka school, which is considered the most accurate view, "empty" and "selfless" both refer to the absence of inherent, true, or independent existence. Unless otherwise noted in this book, explanations will be according to this school.

The root of our cyclic existence is the ignorance that grasps phenomena as possessing some sort of independent existence, selfhood, or self-existence. The word *ignorance* conjures up the image of something inauspicious or undesirable, and it is indeed so. Just as whatever grows from a poisonous seed will be poisonous, everything that arises from ignorance will be undesirable. As long as we remain under the control of ignorance and erroneous views, there is no possibility for lasting joy.

According to Prāsaṅgikas, ignorance is not simply a state of unknowing. It actively grasps or conceives things to exist in a way that they do not. Superimposing inherent existence on persons and phenomena, it apprehends what is contrary to reality. Whereas persons and phenomena do not exist inherently, under their own power, ignorance grasps them as existing in that way.

As we investigate how phenomena actually exist, our conviction that ignorance is erroneous increases. By seeing and familiarizing ourselves with the wisdom knowing reality, we gradually erode the force of ignorance and the undisciplined mind. When the cause, ignorance, is completely uprooted by its counterforce, wisdom, its resultant duḥkha is likewise extinguished. This state of freedom is nirvāṇa, lasting peace and true freedom. Therefore the fourth seal of Buddhism is that nirvāṇa is true peace.

Knowing the evolution of afflictions such as attachment and anger helps us understand the necessity of employing analysis to gain the wisdom realizing the selflessness of persons and phenomena that eradicates ignorance. If we examine emotions such as attachment and anger, we see that they are rooted in grasping at inherent existence. The stronger our grasping at an independent I, the stronger our attachment to the concerns of that self. We cling to whatever is seen as important to the self and are hostile toward whatever impedes fulfilling its interests.

For example, we may see a beautiful item that we are very attracted to in a store, and we crave to possess it. After we buy it, we call it mine and become even more attached to it. Behind the label mine is the belief in a self whose happiness is extremely important. If someone else then takes or breaks the article, we become angry because the happiness of this I has been adversely affected. Here we see the relationship between our grasping at an inherently existent I and our attachment to the article and anger at whatever interferes with our enjoying it. Refuting the inherent existence of this I eliminates the basis of our attachment and anger, which subsequently diminish and eventually are totally eradicated.

The distinguishing mark of being in cyclic existence is the mere I being under the control of ignorance and karma; that is, when the aggregates that are the basis of designation of the I are produced by these polluted causes, the person designated in dependence on them is bound in cyclic existence. As soon as that person eliminates ignorance, she no longer creates polluted actions that propel cyclic existence. Her cyclic existence ceases, and that person—that mere I—attains liberation. Gradually, she can also remove the cognitive obscurations that prevent omniscience, and when this is done, that mere I attains buddhahood, the state of full awakening or nonabiding nirvāṇa, in which the person abides neither in cyclic existence nor in the personal peace of an arhat's nirvāṇa.

The four seals follow each other in a natural sequence. The existence of our body, mind, self, as well as the people and environment around us, is governed by causes and conditions. Thus their very nature is transient and momentary. The very causes and conditions that brought them into existence are the causes for their disintegration. In short, all conditioned phenomena are impermanent, the first of the four seals.

The external environment as well as factors internal to sentient beings—our bodies and minds—came about under the influence of our afflictions and polluted karma. Thus they are unsatisfactory by nature. As the second seal states, all polluted phenomena are duḥkha.

The story does not stop here, because there exists a powerful antidote—the wisdom realizing the emptiness of inherent existence—that is capable of totally eradicating ignorance, afflictions, and karma. All phenomena are empty and selfless, the third seal. When emptiness is realized directly and nonconceptually, and the mind becomes habituated with it through consistent meditation, all afflictions and karma causing rebirth are eradicated. In this way, cyclic existence is ceased and the fourth seal—nirvāṇa is peace—comes about.

The four seals are related to the four truths. The first two seals—all conditioned phenomena are transient and all polluted phenomena are unsatisfactory—describe the first two noble truths: the truths of duḥkha and its origins. But knowing this alone doesn't overcome our suffering. The last two seals—emptiness and selflessness, and nirvāṇa—speak of the third truth, true cessations, and imply the fourth truth, true paths, as the path that realizes them. By realizing the true path—the wisdom realizing emptiness—that knows all phenomena are empty and selfless, we uproot the ignorance that is the root cause of cyclic existence. Its cessation is the fourth seal, nirvāṇa is true peace.

Two Truths

From the perspective of subtle dependent arising, all phenomena are empty of inherent existence and exist by being merely designated by names and concepts. How, then, do we maintain a coherent notion of our everyday world? How can we accept causes producing results and maintain the distinctions among different objects if ultimately everything lacks inherent existence and exists by mere designation? The Buddha's teaching on the two truths—ultimate and conventional—helps us understand this.

Ultimate (*paramārtha*) truth—the emptiness of inherent existence of all phenomena—is the actual way phenomena exist. Ultimate truths are true in that they exist the way they appear to the nonconceptual wisdom of āryas. *Saṃvṛti*, the Sanskrit word translated as "convention," also means "veil," indicating that the actual truth of an object is obscured or veiled— the veil being ignorance, the mind grasping inherent existence. Due to ignorance, phenomena appear inherently existent, whereas they are not. Veiled truths are not true—they do not exist as they appear—they are true only for ignorance, and as such, are false. Our everyday world of people, things, and experiences are veiled truths.

To give another example, people gave me the title Dalai Lama. If you attend a public teaching that I give, you look at the person in the front of the room who is speaking and think, "This is the Dalai Lama," as if there were an objective person out there, a person that exists from his own side. But when you search for exactly what that person is, you can't pinpoint anything. You see the body of a Buddhist monk and hear a voice. Through my body language and speech, you have some idea of what is going on in my mind. But when you look in the body, speech, and mind, you can't find the Dalai Lama. He is not his body, speech, or mind. The appearance of the Dalai Lama as an inherently existent person is false. Actually he exists because on the basis of the collection of body and mind, your mind forms the conception of a person that you then designate the "Dalai Lama." The Dalai Lama exists by being merely designated by name and concept. That is his conventional nature. The deeper way he exists—his ultimate nature—is the emptiness of being an inherently existent Dalai Lama.

For each phenomenon, the two truths are present on that one base. For example, the mind has a veiled or conventional nature and a deeper reality or ultimate nature. Its conventional nature is its clarity and cognizance, the mind that perceives and experiences things. Its ultimate nature is its emptiness of inherent existence. These two truths exist inseparably with respect to the mind, although they are perceived by different cognizers. The conventional mind is perceived by a conventional reliable cognizer, while the ultimate nature of the mind is known by a wisdom mind that realizes emptiness. Although the two truths are different, they exist together and depend on each other. For that reason, the mind and its emptiness are said to be one nature but nominally different. The two truths are not two unrelated levels of being, with ultimate truth being some absolute independent reality separate from the world of interdependent things.

The very meaning of the term *dependent arising* enables us to gain insight into the union of the two truths. Everything exists *dependent* on or in relation to other factors that are not it. Flowers depend on seeds, a human being depends on his or her body and mind, space depends on the lack of obstruction. Being dependent, they are empty of inherent existence. But emptiness doesn't mean total nonexistence. Because flowers, humans, and space *arise*, these veiled truths exist.

Within the context of these appearances being dependent veiled truths, the Buddha taught the method aspect of the path to awakening. Because so many different kinds of forms and appearances exist, they are called "the vast" or "the varieties of phenomena."

Within the context of phenomena's ultimate nature being emptiness, the Buddha taught the wisdom aspect of the path. The emptiness of phenomena is called "the profound" because it is free from conceptual fabrications and is realized by a profound wisdom consciousness. Method and wisdom together are called "the stages of the vast and profound path."

By meditating on the two truths and their inseparability and by cultivating the method and wisdom aspects of the path, all faulty states of mind are gradually removed and the excellent attributes of a buddha's truth body and form body are developed. Buddhahood is attained through the unified cultivation of both method and wisdom. The chief wisdom is the wisdom realizing the emptiness of inherent existence, and in the Mahāyāna the chief method is the altruistic intention to become a buddha (*bodhicitta*), induced by great love and great compassion. Although practiced in tandem, method and wisdom each has its own principal result in buddhahood. The principal result of method is the form bodies of a buddha—the bodies in which a buddha manifests in order to teach sentient beings—and the principal result of wisdom is the truth body of a buddha—a buddha's omniscient mind and its ultimate nature.

Buddhadharma can also be spoken of in terms of basis, path, and result. The basis is the two truths—conventional and ultimate. The path is the two cultivations—method and wisdom. The result is the two bodies of a buddha—the form body and truth body. Here we see clearly the correlation of conventional truths, the method aspect of the path, and the form body of a buddha, and the correlation of ultimate truths, the wisdom aspect of the path, and the truth body of a buddha.

The topics introduced in this chapter are complex and important. Only when we understand the nature and relationship of the two truths according to the Madhyamaka viewpoint can we fully understand the meaning of the four truths and know the full meaning and purpose of taking refuge in the Three Jewels. This chapter gave you a glimpse of these, and the fuller explanations that follow will elaborate on them.

The four seals—impermanence, duḥkha, selflessness, and nirvāṇa (true cessation)—are among the most important objects for us to know on the path. For that reason, in the following chapter, we will explore the reliable cognizers that enable us to have correct knowledge.

2 | Gaining Nondeceptive Knowledge

A S HUMAN BEINGS, we act to accomplish certain goals and purposes. In the area of spirituality and religion, our aim is to attain a state of enduring fulfillment and peace. To determine if full awakening is possible, to know what to practice and abandon in order to attain awakening, and to discern the ultimate nature of all phenomena, we need to be able to test various claims and determine if they are accurate and nondeceptive. In a meditation session, we want to be aware of what type of cognizer is knowing impermanence and emptiness, because a correct assumption of emptiness is very different from a nonconceptual realization of emptiness. The disciplines of logic and epistemology contain the tools for doing so. The objects that we seek to ascertain with reliable cognizers include the two truths and those spoken of in the four seals—impermanence, duḥkha, selflessness, and nirvāṇa. When speaking of cognizers and perceivers, we are referring to minds that know objects. They are agents that perform the function of knowing their objects.

This chapter contains terminology and ideas that will be new to some readers. It takes time and further study to understand everything completely. You will understand some points now and can return to this chapter later as a resource in your future studies.

Three Kinds of Objects and Their Cognizers

As we learn the Buddhadharma, we are exposed to new concepts that may challenge our view of the world and of reality. We may wonder how to go about verifying or disproving them. Śāntarakṣita's *Compendium on*

Reality (Tattvasaṃgraha) quotes the Buddha as recommending an analytical approach:

> Do not accept my Dharma merely out of respect for me,
> but analyze and check it
> the way a goldsmith analyzes gold—
> by burning, cutting, and rubbing it.

First a goldsmith checks for external impurities, which can be detected by burning the gold. Then he looks for internal impurities by cutting the gold. Finally he searches for very subtle impurities using a special technique of filing the gold. Similarly, we must test the teachings thoroughly, looking for three types of "impurities": incorrect explanations regarding evident (*abhimukhī*) phenomena, slightly obscure (*parokṣa*) phenomena, and very obscure (*atyantaparokṣa*) phenomena. If there are none, we can accept the teachings with confidence. Each of the three types of phenomena is known by a specific kind of reliable cognizer.

Evident phenomena are those that ordinary beings can easily perceive. These include (1) external objects, such as colors, sounds, odors, tastes, and tangible objects, which are known by *direct reliable cognizers* that correspond to our five physical senses, and (2) internal objects, such as feelings of happiness, pain, hopes, and desires, which are known by the mental consciousness.

Slightly obscure phenomena cannot initially be directly perceived. Ordinary beings must initially know them by *factual inferential cognizers*—inferential reliable cognizers based on valid factual reasons. Examples of slightly obscure phenomena are subtle impermanence—the momentary arising and ceasing of conditioned things—and selflessness. The fact that the apple arises in dependence on causes and conditions is part of the conventional nature of the apple. Through understanding that its existence is a result of causes and conditions, we can know that the apple is impermanent.

The sun setting in the west is coarse change that is evident to our visual sense. But to understand the sun's subtle changeable nature, we must use reasoning. The sun rose in the east and in order to set in the west, it must move continuously, moment by moment, imperceptibly across the sky. This momentary change cannot be detected by our eyes; we need reasoning to know it.

To know a slightly obscure phenomenon such as selflessness—for example, the absence of a permanent, independent soul or self—we may use the reason of "dependence" and contemplate the syllogism *Consider a person, she does not exist as a permanent, partless, under-its-own-power soul or self because she depends on her body and mind.*

Very obscure phenomena are known by ordinary sentient beings by relying on *inferential reliable cognizers by authoritative testimony,* the attestation of someone who is authoritative in that field. We know our birthday by asking our mother, and we understand the subtle intricacies of karma by depending on the Buddha's teachings. While atoms and subatomic particles are slightly obscure phenomena that can be known by inference, most of us rely on the testimony of scientists to know their existence and characteristics.

According to Sautrāntikas, from the viewpoint of direct perceivers, all functioning things are evident phenomena because under the right conditions they can be perceived by our direct perceivers. From the viewpoint of conceptual consciousnesses, all knowable objects—both impermanent and permanent—are obscure phenomena because they can be known by a conceptual consciousness thinking about them. Conceptual consciousnesses are obscured because they know things by means of a conceptual appearance, which obstructs them from seeing functioning things directly.

Prāsaṅgikas describe evident and obscure phenomena differently, saying that evident objects are those that can be known through our own experience, without depending on inference; for example, sense objects. Obscure objects must initially be known by depending on a reason. They are objects of inference—for example, the subtle impermanence of the body and the selflessness of the person.

These categories are described in relation to ordinary sentient beings, not āryas. For an ārya, subtle impermanence and selflessness are evident phenomena, whereas for us they are slightly obscure. There are no obscure objects for buddhas because they are omniscient. Even in terms of ordinary sentient beings, these categories can vary according to our situation. When we are at a campfire, the fire is evident to us; we see it with our eyes and feel the heat on our skin. To people on the other side of a clump of trees, the campfire is slightly obscure; they must infer, "In the area behind those trees, there is fire because there is smoke." To our friends in another state, the campfire is very obscure. They know it because we call and tell them we are at a campfire.

Another example is devas—celestial beings such as the god Brahmā. For us human beings who live on Earth, Brahmā is very obscure; we know about him only through the testimony of a reliable authority. Our senses cannot see him and no amount of reasoning can prove his existence. To other living beings born in that realm, Brahmā is evident. Similarly, to people watching a spacecraft land on the moon, that event is evident, but to people who have no idea that such a thing is possible, it is very obscure. They must trust the testimony of those who witnessed it to know it happened.

An object becomes evident, slightly obscure, or very obscure in relation to an individual. For ordinary beings who haven't entered a path, subtle impermanence and emptiness are slightly obscure, while for āryas they are evident phenomena, known by yogic direct perceivers.

To our mother, our birthday is an evident phenomenon, but for us it is a very obscure phenomenon. Owing to the extremely long distance, the details of various stars and planets in the universe are very obscure to us. But they are evident to whatever life forms inhabit those places.

Various aspects of one thing may be different types of objects. Our friend's body is an evident phenomenon that we see with our eyes. His heart is a slightly obscure phenomenon that we infer because all human bodies have hearts. The karmic causes for our friend to be born into that body are very obscure phenomena known only by a buddha.

REFLECTION

1. Make examples of evident phenomena, slightly obscure phenomena, and very obscure phenomena that you already know. How did you come to understand them? Which type of reliable cognizer was involved?

2. Consider how we know things such as the existence of atoms, the Ice Age, or the qualities of other solar systems. Which of the three types of objects are they and how do we know them?

3. If you have never been to Antarctica, which of the three categories of phenomena is Antarctica in relation to you? Is it very obscure because

you have to depend on another person's testimony to know what it looks like? Is it slightly obscure because by seeing photographs or a 3D model you can infer what it looks like? Would it be evident because you could see it through live streaming on the Internet?

Seven Types of Awareness

Ancient Indian religious practitioners from many traditions discussed the topic of reliable cognizers at length. Dignāga (ca. 480–540 CE) and Dharmakīrti (ca. 600–660 CE) were the two foremost Buddhist sages in India involved in debating this topic with non-Buddhists and in establishing the systems of epistemology and logic studied by Tibetan Buddhists to this day. These topics of epistemology and logical reasoning are learned not for the sake of philosophical speculation or abstract theory, but for the purpose of actualizing human goals, in particular nirvāṇa. Dharmakīrti said in his *Drop of Reasoning* (*Nyāyabindu*), "Since correct [i.e., reliable] cognition is a prerequisite for achieving all human purposes, I shall explain it."

In monastic universities, students are first introduced to the topic of reliable cognizers in the context of the seven types of awareness (T. *blo rig bdun du dbye ba*), which is taught from the Sautrāntika point of view. As we will see, some of these seven are reliable cognizers, others are not.

1. A *direct perceiver* (*pratyakṣa*) is an awareness that knows its object directly, without a conceptual appearance of its observed object (*ālambana*). Direct perceivers do not involve thinking, imagining, or remembering.

2. An *inferential cognizer* (*anumāna*) is an awareness that correctly understands its observed object through a conceptual appearance—a mental image of the object—and by means of an inference. An inference must be a correct argument; arguments using spurious logic are not considered inference.

3. A *subsequent cognizer* is an awareness that realizes an existent object that has already been realized. It is the second moment onward following a conceptual or nonconceptual reliable cognizer. "Moment" has different meanings according to the context. When speaking of

cognizing objects, it refers to the period of time needed to ascertain the object; it does not refer to the smallest unit of time because to ascertain an object a series of smallest units of time is required. The second moment onward of a cognizer uninterruptedly follows the first moment; for example, the second moment onward of a sense direct reliable cognizer of blue or the second moment onward of an inferential reliable cognizer realizing the emptiness of the person.

4. A *correct assumption* is a conceptual awareness that correctly apprehends its object as a result of having read or heard an explanation of it, but does not fully or firmly grasp the meaning or conclusively ascertain its object. After learning a new topic, we have a correct general idea about it, but because we don't ascertain the meaning, our understanding is not firm and we could change our mind later.

5. An *inattentive awareness* is a direct perceiver to which its apprehended object clearly appears but is not ascertained. For example, while engrossed in watching a movie, our auditory consciousness hears the voices of people near us, but later we cannot say with certainty that people were speaking or what they were discussing.

6. *Deluded doubt* is an awareness that vacillates between two or more options and is inclined toward the wrong conclusion.

7. A *wrong awareness* (*viparyayajñāna*) is either a conceptual or nonconceptual consciousness that incorrectly apprehends its observed object. A hallucination hearing voices where there are none is a wrong sensory awareness. Holding the view that impermanent things are permanent or that what is foul is actually delightful are wrong conceptual awarenesses.

Reliable Cognizers and Unreliable Awarenesses

Dharmakīrti, who wrote from the Sautrāntika and Cittamātrin perspective, and Candrakīrti (ca. 600–650 CE), who taught from the Prāsaṅgika Mādhyamaka perspective, defined the Sanskrit term *pramāṇa* differently. According to Dharmakīrti, *pramāṇa* is a prime cognizer—a new and nondeceptive knower. "New" indicates that it is the first moment of a nondeceptive cognizer; the following moments in that continuity knowing the same object are subsequent cognizers and are not prime.

According to Candrakīrti, *pramāṇa* is a knower that is nondeceptive (*avidaṃvādi*) with regard to its principal or apprehended object (*muṣṭi-bandhaviṣata*). In his *Commentary on "The Four Hundred,"* he says, "Unde-ceived consciousness is seen in the world to be reliable cognizer (*pramāṇa*) itself."[4] "Nondeceptive" means incontrovertible; this knower is trustworthy and knows its object correctly. It does not have to be the first moment of a stream of moments of cognition. It is called a *reliable* cognizer because it can lead us to accomplish our purpose. Prāsaṅgikas say subsequent cognizers are reliable cognizers because they know the same apprehended object as the first moment that preceded it. Candrakīrti's *Clear Words* (*Prasanna-padā*) lists four types of reliable cognizers according to the objects to be comprehended:[5]

1. *Direct reliable cognizers* know their objects—evident phenomena—directly and nondeceptively, without depending on a reason or logical mark. With an unimpaired eye faculty, we see blue. This is a noncon-ceptual direct reliable cognizer. A subsequent cognizer can also be a direct reliable cognizer. A consciousness correctly remembering a conversation we had yesterday is a direct reliable cognizer even though it is a conceptual memory of the conversation. Similarly, many, but not all, scholars agree that the second moment onward of an infer-ential cognizer realizing impermanence is a direct reliable cognizer because unlike the first moment of that inferential cognizer, it does not depend on a reason. Although it is considered a direct reliable cognizer, it does not directly apprehend its object because it is a con-ceptual consciousness.

2. *Inferential reliable cognizers* know their objects—slightly obscure phenomena—nondeceptively purely in dependence on a reason (a logical mark). We know a car is impermanent because it is produced by causes.

3. *Reliable cognizers based on an example* are inferential cognizers that realize their object by understanding that it is similar to something else. Here an evident phenomenon such as an example, analogy, or model is used as the reason to understand the meaning, which is slightly obscure. For instance, the Potala is a slightly obscure phenom-enon for people who have never been to Lhasa. But if someone shows

them a model of the Potala and says, "It looks like this," they will understand what the Potala is.

4. *Reliable cognizers based on authoritative testimony* are inferential cognizers knowing very obscure phenomena that cannot be established through direct perceivers or other inferential reliable cognizers, but only by depending on the authoritative testimony of a trustworthy source, such as a credible person or scripture. For example, we understand the subtle workings of karma by relying on a credible scripture taught by the Buddha, who is a reliable person.[6]

The number of reliable cognizers differs according to context. In the above classification, reliable cognizers based on authoritative testimony and based on an example are forms of inferential reliable cognizers. They are listed separately due to their specific functions. In this case, an inferential reliable cognizer is one based on factual inference, a specific type of inference. Here the general name "inferential reliable cognizer" is given to a specific instance.

However, when we say the comprehended objects (*prameya*) of reliable cognizers are of two types—evident phenomena and obscure phenomena—then reliable cognizers are also two: direct reliable perceivers and inferential reliable cognizers.[7] In this case, reliable cognizers based on authoritative testimony and based on an example are included in inferential reliable cognizers, with that term now being used to refer to all inferential reliable cognizers. It is not uncommon that terms in a text have more than one meaning depending on their context, so we must take care not to get confused!

While reliable cognizers correctly ascertain their objects and give us reliable knowledge so we can accomplish our aims, other awarenesses—such as correct assumers, inattentive awarenesses, doubt, and wrong awarenesses—do not. These and other unreliable awarenesses cannot be trusted because we will not be able to achieve our purposes by relying on them. If we have bad eyesight and mistake an orange for a grapefruit, we will not purchase the fruit we want. Similarly, if we believe that the self is permanent or that phenomena exist as self-enclosed, independent entities, we will not be able to realize the emptiness of inherent existence or attain nirvāṇa.

Subsequent cognizers are minds that know what has already been known. The first moment of a visual consciousness knows red and the immediately subsequent moments of the visual consciousness also know red. Sautrān-tikas say subsequent cognizers are not prime cognizers because, unlike prime cognizers that know the object by their own power, subsequent cognizers know the object by the force of the prime cognizer inducing them. Prāsaṅgikas say subsequent cognizers are direct reliable cognizers. In the case of an inferential cognizer, this is because the second moment onward of an inferential cognizer remembers the object inferred directly—it doesn't rely on a reason or logical mark to know the object. It is a reliable cognizer because it incontrovertibly knows its object. For Sautrāntikas, "direct" in "direct perceiver" means without a conceptual appearance; for Prāsaṅgikas it means not relying on a reason.[8] However, in another context, such as speaking about a direct realization of emptiness, Prāsaṅgikas take "direct" to mean nonconceptual.

Our knowledge about an object may gradually evolve via these various cognizers. For example, a new science student hears about bacteria from his teacher and gains a rough idea of what they are; this is a correct assumption. His knowledge also involves inference by authoritative testimony, for he trusts his science teacher's knowledge even though he cannot yet verify the information for himself. He learns about the structure of bacteria by seeing a model or diagram, which is inference based on an example. If he then looks under a microscope and sees some bacteria, those bacteria become evident phenomena that he knows with a direct reliable cognizer. Through executing various experiments and gaining reliable data, he will be able to have an inferential reliable cognizer of other properties of bacteria that are slightly obscure phenomena.

However, he may be able to verify that his conclusion is an inferential reliable cognizer only later on. First he needs to make sure that the research data are valid and can be duplicated by others. Even if his data are reliable, they may not be complete, thus skewing a conclusion based on them. New data about other properties of bacteria may cause him to rethink his initial conclusions. For this reason, many scientists consider the initial knowledge from their research to be a correct assumption or even doubt.

In many areas of scientific research, human knowledge rests on assumptions. Even though scientists have supportive reasons for drawing certain conclusions, those conclusions are by no means hard and fast. They will be verified, denied, or revised later on as more data are collected. It may take a while for correct conclusions to be known by inference. Those of us who learn of new discoveries by listening to experts or reading scientific journals will have either a correct assumption or an inferential cognizer by authoritative testimony, depending on how well we understood the explanation.

REFLECTION

1. Consider why having reliable cognizers is important in your daily life and in your spiritual life.

2. Make examples of times when you have had an inattentive awareness or deluded doubt. How did they inhibit your full knowledge?

3. Make examples of wrong awarenesses, such as seeing things incorrectly or misunderstanding the meaning of what someone said. Have you ever had a wrong awareness but not known it was incorrect until sometime later?

4. Make an example of how your understanding of a topic began as a wrong consciousness or doubt and slowly evolved to a correct assumption and then to an inferential cognizer or direct perceiver.

CHART: RELIABLE COGNIZERS AND UNRELIABLE AWARENESSES ACCORDING TO CANDRAKĪRTI

RELIABLE COGNIZERS	UNRELIABLE AWARENESSES
1. Direct reliable cognizers[9] a. Sense direct reliable cognizers b. Mental direct reliable cognizers c. Yogic direct reliable cognizers	1. Wrong awareness
2. Inferential reliable cognizers	2. Deluded doubt
3. Reliable cognizers based on an example	3. Inattentive awareness
4. Reliable cognizers based on authoritative testimony	4. Correct assumption

Direct Reliable Cognizers

Reliable cognizers have specific characteristics, and not all our cognitions meet those standards. Learning the descriptions of the various types of reliable cognizers helps us to identify them in our own experience, and that lets us know whether to trust what we're seeing and thinking. Wrong awarenesses and correct assumptions are not reliable cognizers, even when we mistakenly think they are. Direct reliable cognizers are of three types: sense, mental, and yogic direct reliable cognizers.

Sense direct reliable cognizers know their objects—sights, sounds, smells, tastes, and tangible objects—directly by depending on a physical cognitive faculty. These reliable cognizers enable us to know our surroundings and the things within them.

Mental direct reliable cognizers correctly know their objects by depending on a mental cognitive faculty—that is, on another consciousness that induces it. Mental direct reliable cognizers include clairvoyance and consciousnesses that know our own feelings of happiness and pain. They also include conceptual subsequent cognizers induced by inferential valid cognizers, such as the second moment onward of an inferential cognizer of impermanence, and memory consciousnesses, such as the consciousness remembering a person we met last week.

Yogic direct reliable cognizers are mental consciousnesses that know their objects—the sixteen attributes of the four truths and subtle and gross selflessness—by depending on a union of serenity and insight. These direct perceivers are essential to overcome defilements.

An evident phenomenon, such as the sound of leaves rustling in the breeze, is known by a sense direct perceiver, in this case an auditory consciousness. By means of mental direct perceivers we know that we feel happy from hearing that sound, and we can remember the sound of rustling leaves the next day. A highly evolved consciousness, a yogic direct perceiver, realizes the subtle impermanence of both the sound of the leaves and the happy feeling.

Inferential Reliable Cognizers

To be able to benefit sentient beings most effectively, we must gain the direct, nonconceptual cognizers of a buddha so that we will clearly perceive all phenomena, both ultimate truths and conventional truths. Unlike buddhas, at present we ordinary beings are not capable of directly knowing slightly obscure and very obscure phenomena, but must rely on an inferential cognizer, a mind that nondeceptively realizes an obscure object in dependence on a reason.

Inferential cognizers must trace back to direct experiences and shared direct perceptions. Although our initial access to an object may be through reasoning, in time an inferential cognizer can lead to direct experience. We initially know emptiness through an inferential cognizer, but by continuously familiarizing our minds with it in meditation that is a union of serenity and insight, we will be able to dissolve the conceptual appearance and realize emptiness with a yogic direct reliable cognizer. An inferential cognizer not only depends on direct experience but also leads to it.

We use inferential cognizers often in our daily lives and at our jobs. According to classical Indian logic, an inference is generated by means of a syllogism (*prayoga*), a statement with four parts—a subject (*dharmin*), predicate (*sādhya dharma*), reason (*liṅga*), and example. To teach the parts of a syllogism, Buddhist monastics often use the syllogism *Consider sound, it is impermanent because it is produced by causes; for example, like the last moment of a flame.* Although this syllogism may not stir us, it was extremely important for Buddhists in ancient India. This is the argument they used to refute the assertion of brahmins who believed that the sound of the Vedas was permanent and unchanging.

In this syllogism, "sound" is the subject (A) about which something is to be proven. "Is impermanent" is the predicate (B), the attribute we want to establish about sound. "Because it is produced by causes" is the reason (C) we use to prove the thesis. "For example, like the last moment of a flame" is the example. The thesis (*pratijñā*) is what is to be proven—the combination of the subject and the predicate—in this case, "sound is impermanent."

To understand this, the person who hears the syllogism needs to understand three criteria of a correct inference: (1) The *reason applies to the subject* (*pakṣadharma*) corresponds to the major premise. This is the relationship between the subject and the reason, specifically that the reason is a property of the subject. Being produced by causes is a quality of sound. (2) The *pervasion or entailment* (*anvayavyāpti*) corresponds to the minor premise. This is the relationship between the reason and the predicate: If something is the reason, it is necessarily the predicate. If something is produced by causes, it is necessarily impermanent. (3) The *counterpervasion* (*vyatireka-vyāpti*) corresponds to the contrapositive of the minor premise. This is the relationship between the opposite of the predicate and the opposite of the reason: If something is not the predicate, it is necessarily not the reason. If something is not impermanent (i.e., if it is permanent), it is definitely not produced by causes.

The reason is the key to establish the three criteria. We must understand that the reason applies to the subject, is present in the predicate, and is not present in the opposite of the predicate. In simplified form:

C applies to A. The reason is a property of the subject.
If it's C, it must be B. There is pervasion.
If it's not B, it cannot be C. There is counterpervasion.

To gain an inferential cognizer, we must establish these three criteria in the syllogism. In general, the first criterion is something obvious; it can be established by means of a direct perceiver. We know that sound is produced by causes; we hear the sound after the bell is struck. Then through reasoning we try to establish something that is not obvious—that sound is impermanent and momentary.

If a syllogism is not formed correctly, it will not prove its thesis. That may mean that the thesis is wrong or that the person constructing the syllogism did not think well about the topic. *Consider sound, it is impermanent because it exists* is not a correct syllogism. Although the reason is established (sound exists), the pervasion doesn't hold (if something exists, it is not necessarily impermanent; permanent phenomena also exist).

In the syllogism *Consider this person, he will die because he was born,* "this person" is the subject, "will die" is the predicate, and "because he was born" is the reason. The reason applies to the subject because that person was born. The pervasion holds true because if someone is born, he will die. The counterpervasion is established: if there is no death, it is because birth did not precede it. When the full force of this syllogism dawns in our mind, it becomes a powerful motivator for us to practice the Dharma in order to cease the causes of rebirth in cyclic existence and thereby to cease death as well.

We do not necessarily realize the thesis of a correct syllogism immediately after hearing it. To realize the three criteria of a correct syllogism, we must have a certain level of knowledge and be mentally receptive. Three preliminary reliable cognizers are needed in order to ascertain the second criterion, the pervasion. In the syllogism *Consider sound, it is impermanent because it is produced by causes*, these are:

1. A *reliable cognizer ascertaining the reason.* "Being produced by causes" is a reason that can establish that sound is impermanent. It is suitable to be used as a reason in this syllogism.

2. A *reliable cognizer ascertaining that in the opposite of the predicate, the reason does not exist.* The opposite of the predicate is devoid of the reason. Among permanent phenomena, no products exist. Permanent phenomena are devoid of products.

3. A *reliable cognizer ascertaining that the predicate and its opposite are mutually exclusive.* Impermanent and permanent are mutually exclusive.

Sometimes ascertaining the three criteria requires a considerable amount of time and effort: a person may have to learn the meaning of terms or understand other syllogisms first. Many texts contain debates in which a syllogism is presented, followed by other syllogisms that help us understand important points so that we will be able to comprehend the first syllogism. When we encounter difficult topics, we must persevere and continue to contemplate the material. As with most other subjects, it may be difficult at the beginning, but through familiarization it becomes easier.

After presenting a syllogism to a person, three kinds of wisdom arise progressively over time: the wisdom arising from hearing or studying the Dharma; the wisdom arising from contemplating, thinking, and reflecting on it; and the wisdom arising from meditating. When we first learn about subtle impermanence by hearing a teaching or reading a Dharma book, our understanding is the wisdom arising from hearing. At best this is a correct assumption that is a general idea about subtle impermanence. It is not the incontrovertible knowledge of an inferential reliable cognizer. While correct assumptions and factual inferential cognizers both focus on subtle impermanence, the depth and stability of their understandings differ. A correct assumption can easily become vague if we don't repeatedly familiarize ourselves with the topic. Also, if we are presented with the opposite view, a correct assumption may degenerate into doubt.

By continuing to analyze, our correct assumption will become an inferential reliable cognizer that realizes subtle impermanence by means of a conceptual appearance. This is the wisdom arising from contemplation. This inferential understanding will not degenerate unless we allow the intensity of this cognition to deteriorate by ceasing to contemplate the topic. The deterioration of inferential reliable cognizers occurs because the seeds of wrong views haven't been eliminated completely from our mental continua and our familiarity with the correct view is not strong. For this reason, we must make effort to maintain the correct understandings we gain through repeatedly bringing them to mind.

To deepen our understanding, we continue to cultivate concentration and analytical wisdom so that we can attain the union of serenity and insight on subtle impermanence. This is the wisdom arising from meditation. Initially this wisdom is conceptual because the veil of the conceptual appearance of impermanence is present. With continuous meditation over time, that veil becomes thinner and thinner and will eventually disappear, and we will realize subtle impermanence directly and nonconceptually. This yogic direct perceiver of subtle impermanence is also the wisdom arising from meditation.

From the very beginning of their training in philosophy, when they are still young children, Tibetan monastics are taught that whatever is produced by causes necessarily has the quality of subtle impermanence. At the same time, their teachers caution them, "You have a highly learned mouth (you know all the words), but actual understanding will come through constant reflection after you have passed your geshe exam. Only then will there be the possibility of the actual realization dawning in your mind. Be realistic and patient and continue to work hard."

There is debate on whether a syllogism needs to be stated for someone to gain an inferential reliable cognizer. Prāsaṅgikas claim it is not necessary; they accept an inferential cognizer through example as a reliable cognizer. They also say that merely stating a consequence (*prasaṅga*)—that is, pointing out the internal contradictions in someone's argument—is sufficient for sharp-faculty people to gain an inferential reliable cognizer. For example, someone understands that the person is a dependent arising but also believes the person truly exists. By pointing out to him the unwanted consequence of his view by saying, "Consider the person, he isn't a dependent arising because of being truly existent," a sharp-faculty disciple will understand that the person is not truly existent. It isn't necessary to subsequently state the syllogism *Consider a person, she is not truly existent because of being a dependent arising.* For a person of more modest faculties, a follow-up syllogism is needed for him to understand.

To the contrary, the lower schools hold that an inferential reliable cognizer must come about through the power of reasoning, implying that it is always necessary to state a syllogism. In addition, they adhere to autonomous syllogisms in which the subject, predicate, and reason all truly exist, whereas Prāsaṅgikas establish the parts of a syllogism and all phenomena by convention.

REFLECTION

1. Identify the parts of the syllogism and the three criteria in the syllogism *Consider smoking, it is a health risk because it is directly responsible for approximately 80 to 90 percent of lung cancers.*

2. Behind our emotions we often find "syllogisms." Identify the parts of the following syllogisms and test them with the three criteria to see if they are correct.
   • *Consider me, I am an unlovable person because my friend is mad at me.*
   • *Consider my friend, he is untrustworthy because he didn't do what I wanted him to do.*
   • *Consider my ideas, they are always good because they are the ideas of a smart person.*

Reliable Cognizers Based on an Example

We often use analogies, models, and examples when learning something new. These evident phenomena—a map, picture, model, and so forth—illustrate a meaning that is obscure because the two have some similar characteristics.

In ancient India, a king was given a painting of the wheel of life, which illustrates the three realms (*tridhātu*) and six classes of saṃsāric beings (*ṣaṣgati*) and the process by which ordinary beings take rebirth. By contemplating the picture, the king understood the causal chain leading to rebirth in cyclic existence. This understanding of dependent arising, in turn, later led him to realize that there is no inherent existence.

A face in a mirror is an evident phenomenon, whereas emptiness is a slightly obscure phenomenon. When an intelligent disciple whose mind-stream is fully ripened is told that just as a face in a mirror lacks true existence, so does the person, by the power of this example she will understand the selflessness of persons.

Unlike the lower schools, Prāsaṅgikas accept inference by example as a means to generate a reliable cognizer. Whether someone generates an understanding through this means or through factual inference depends on the mindset and faculties of the individual. Although a few ripened disciples may be able to realize emptiness through inference by example, most people need to rely on factual inference.

Reliable Cognizers Based on Authoritative Testimony

A reliable cognizer based on authoritative testimony is used to gain knowledge about very obscure phenomena that we are unable to know through direct perceivers or other types of inferential cognizers. A reliable cognizer based on authoritative testimony uses as the reason to accept a statement as true the word of someone we have examined and determined to be a reliable authority on the subject. The validity of this inference hinges on the reliability of the person whose testimony we trust. Such a person should know the information, have no cognitive disability, and speak truthfully. For example, someone who wants to enroll in a school trusts the application instructions given by people working at the administrative office. Still it is our responsibility to examine their qualifications and not to believe things blindly.

In spiritual practice, this form of inference is also called "inference by belief" or "by scriptural authority." Important for spiritual progress, it involves accepting reliable scriptural passages in order to understand very obscure points that cannot be otherwise known. Such topics include the subtle workings of karma and its effects, the twelve sets of qualities bodhi-sattvas gain on the ten grounds, the causes of the Buddha's thirty-two signs, the inexpressible qualities of the resultant state of awakening, and the life spans of beings in realms imperceptible by our senses.

To correctly infer that a scriptural passage is accurate and free from fault, we must test it by means of a threefold analysis:

1. There is no reason to reject this statement or scripture in terms of its presentation of evident phenomena. To assess this, we examine if its presentation of evident phenomena can be refuted by direct perception.

2. There is no reason to reject this statement or scripture in terms of its presentation of slightly obscure phenomena. To assess this, we examine if its presentation of slightly obscure phenomena can be refuted by inference.

3. There is no reason to reject this scripture in terms of its presentation of very obscure phenomena. To assess this, we examine two factors: (a) The scripture's explicit and implicit meanings about very obscure phenomena are free from contradiction. The explicit meaning is the evident theme of the scripture; the implicit meaning is other topics that are the basis. The explicit meaning of the Prajñāpāramitā Sūtras is the doctrine of emptiness and the implicit meaning is the progressive stages of the paths that realize emptiness. (b) The former and latter passages of its presentation of very obscure phenomena are free from contradiction. What the scripture says in one place does not contradict what it says in another.

There is not a recommended number of pages to read in order to determine that a scripture is free from faults by the threefold analysis. Each person must read enough to be satisfied that his or her analysis is thorough. If a scripture meets these three criteria, accepting its statements as true gives us access to knowledge that is useful for our Dharma practice.

Dharmakīrti says that a scripture may also be considered trustworthy if its author is a reliable or credible person. A reliable person is one who is able to fulfill the desires of disciples in a nondeceptive manner. The Buddha is a reliable being because he has freed his mind from all defilements, developed all excellent qualities, and knows all phenomena directly with his omniscient mind. Motivated by compassion, he has the genuine wish to lead all sentient beings from duḥkha to the joy of liberation, and he has no reason to lie. Furthermore, what the Buddha said about the most essential aspects of the path—the four truths and emptiness based on dependent arising—can be validated by an inferential reliable cognizer. As we become convinced regarding these subjects, we begin to appreciate the possibility of attaining awakening and respect the Buddha as the one who taught such a wonderful path. Since the Buddha explained the essential aspects in a nondeceptive manner, we can infer that his statements on auxiliary topics that are very obscure phenomena are also trustworthy.[10] Āryadeva says (CŚ 280):

> Whoever doubts what the Buddha said
> about that which is very obscure
> should rely on emptiness
> and gain conviction in him alone.

Dharmakīrti makes a similar point (PV 1.217):

> Alternatively, since the true nature (*tattva*) of that which is to be avoided and that which is to be done along with the methods for doing so are well established, the statements of the credible person in question [the Buddha] are nondeceptive with regard to the most important issues [the four truths]. Hence, he is a source of inferential knowledge with regard to other objects.[11]

Tsongkhapa agrees that investigating one teaching of the Buddha—in this case dependent arising—and seeing its veracity gives us confidence in his other teachings. Tsongkhapa says (PDA 30):

> Through this very path of dependent arising,
> the rationale for your speech being peerless,
> convictions arise in me
> that your other words are valid too.

Inference by authoritative testimony is not the first choice for gaining knowledge. It cannot be used to prove evident phenomena that can be known by direct perceivers or to prove slightly obscure phenomena that must initially be known through inference. During debates, participants must use inference as much as possible. The quality of a debate deteriorates if students mistakenly believe that quoting a well-respected master is sufficient to prove a point that actually needs to be realized through inference. It is unsuitable to abandon our investigative abilities and blindly quote scripture to prove a point. However, scriptural statements on these topics are useful because they inspire our practice, reinforce our understanding, and suggest new perspectives.

An example of gaining knowledge about the subtle workings of karma by using scriptural inference is the syllogism *Consider the statement "Through generosity comes wealth; through ethical conduct comes upper rebirth." It is nondeceptive in its subject matter because it is a statement that is free from faults by the threefold analysis.* This statement is from Nāgārjuna's *Precious Garland* (RA 438), a text written by a great master; its content cannot be invalidated by the threefold analysis.

The sūtras of both the Pāli and Sanskrit traditions contain accounts of the Buddha and his disciples encountering living beings in very peculiar situations. The Buddha would often describe the karma that person had created in a previous life that brought about that situation. The *Connected Discourses with Lakkhaṇa* (*Lakkhaṇasaṃyutta*, SN 19) is dedicated to such accounts. It is helpful to read and think about these and use them as guidelines for our behavior. The *Sūtra of the Wise and the Foolish* (*Damamūrkha Sūtra*) also describes the subtle workings of karma and gives us much food for thought.

We ordinary people must use inference by authoritative testimony to understand the subtlest clear light mind. According to Nyingma and Kagyu presentations, the clear light mind is not only the subtlest mind that manifests after the dissolution of grosser conceptual levels of mind, but also the clear light mind that is present and pervades all mental states even when the grosser levels of mind are manifest. However, the *Guhyasamāja Tantra* says the clear light mind manifests only after the grosser winds and minds have dissolved. Highly realized practitioners with direct experience of this clear light do not need to prove its existence by inference because for them it is an evident phenomenon. For those of us who have not had this experience, it is very obscure, and neither direct perceivers nor factual inferential cognizers can prove its existence.

The minds of white appearance, red increase, and black near attainment that appear during the dissolution process are probably very obscure phenomena for us as well. We may get some inkling of these increasingly subtle states of mind culminating in the clear light by considering that the eighty indicative conceptions are classified into three levels according to their subtlety. Thus the combination of wind and mind that are their underlying foundation—the vivid white appearance, red increase, and black near attainment—should also be increasingly subtle and culminate in the clear light. For example, we may see three clouds moving at different speeds in the sky—one fast, another slower, and a third barely moving at all. Although we cannot see the winds moving the clouds, we can infer that those winds are moving at three different speeds.

Also, tantric texts that discuss the various levels of mind describe many things that we can verify through direct perceivers—we have experiences of the awake state, dream state, and state of deep sleep, which are increasingly subtle states of mind. This gives us confidence in the accuracy of other topics presented in these texts. Furthermore, we do not know of any evidence that contradicts the existence of the clear light mind. Therefore, based on the authoritative testimony of the Buddha and those meditators who have direct experience of the subtlest clear light mind, there seems to be more grounds for accepting its existence than disproving it

For us ordinary beings, the level of realizations of those who are more highly realized than we are is very obscure. In his commentary on the *Ornament* entitled *Golden Rosary* (*Legs bshad gser phreng*), Tsongkhapa said that no matter how many reasons ordinary beings apply or how much logic they use, they cannot infer the level of realizations of highly realized practitioners. However, for those with higher realizations, the level of realizations of people inferior to them are evident phenomena.

If we are speaking with our teacher in the classroom, and he says that there is a text on the table in another room, we can accept that as true by believing his words. While in general the book is an evident phenomenon, to us at that moment it is very obscure. We cannot see it with our eyes or know it by inference. At that time, the only way we have to know the book is by relying on the testimony of someone who does.

However, simply citing our teacher or a scripture that says, "All phenomena are empty because they are dependent" will not help us to understand emptiness initially. What is the difference between trusting our teacher's words to know the book and to understand emptiness? In general, a book is an evident phenomenon. We know what it is and have an image of a table with a book and a table without one. His words clarify for us which one it is. However, initially we do not have an idea of what emptiness is—or if we do, it's the emptiness of our stomach, which is not the kind of emptiness we're trying to realize! Quoting our spiritual mentor that phenomena are empty does not enhance our understanding of emptiness, even if we have tremendous devotion to our teacher. However, our trust in our teacher will inspire us to contemplate and meditate on emptiness according to the teachings, and through that we will understand the three criteria of the syllogism and in time will gain an inferential reliable cognizer of emptiness.

REFLECTION

1. Who do you trust as an authority and in what areas do you take them as authoritative? To what extent is that person fully reliable in terms of knowledge of that topic?

2. Those of us who are not scientists know the existence of atoms, the healthy range for human blood pressure, and so forth through accepting the word of scientists. Do we investigate their qualifications as authorities on the subject or do we blindly accept their word?

3. When politicians make various statements, to what extent do we check the reliability of their information and the reliability of their words before believing their statements?

4. In what other areas of life do you rely on the testimony of others to know something? Do you check the credibility of the person first or do you tend to believe something simply because someone said it or you read it somewhere?

Applying the Threefold Analysis

If direct reliable cognizers, inferential reliable cognizers, or other reliable scriptures contradict a particular scriptural passage, or if scientists can irrefutably prove that a scriptural statement is incorrect, we should not accept it. Vasubandhu's *Treasury of Knowledge* (*Abhidharmakośa*) describes the structure of the universe as a flat world with Mount Meru at the center, four surrounding continents, heavenly realms above, and hellish states below. The sun and moon are said to be the same distance from the Earth, and the sun is only slightly larger than the moon. I do not believe that we should accept this description as accurate. My reasons for this are based on the guidelines the Buddhist scriptures have set out for evaluating the veracity of a teaching.

In Vasubandhu's time the structure of our solar system was a very obscure phenomenon. Now, due to scientific advancement, some parts of its structure are evident while other parts can be known through factual inference. This new information affects our understanding of Vasubandhu's description. We must apply the threefold analysis necessary for inference by scriptural authority to determine whether to accept his statements regarding our solar system.

The first criterion, that the statement is not contradicted by direct perception of evident phenomena, is not fulfilled. One way of proving the nonexistence of something is to prove the existence of its opposite. Vasubandhu describes the sun and moon as being almost the same size—51 yojanas (20,400 km) and 50 yojanas (20,000 km) in diameter, respectively.[12] However, reliable scientific instruments have measured the sun's diameter as 1,392,000 km and the moon's diameter as 3,480 km. It is clear that the sizes of the sun and moon as written in the *Treasury of Knowledge* are inaccurate.

Furthermore, this treatise says that the sun and the moon are the same height above the ocean—40,000 yojanas (16,000,000 km)—and that they circle Mount Meru. Reliable scientific measurements have calculated that the sun is 150,000,000 km and the moon is 384,400 km from the Earth's oceans. Here too we see that the measurements in the *Treasury of Knowledge* are inaccurate. In addition, there is scientific evidence showing that the sun does not orbit the Earth.

Another criterion for inference by scriptural authority is that the scripture lacks internal contradictions. As a learned practitioner from Nālandā Monastery, Vasubandhu would have based what he wrote on material in Buddhist scriptures. We find various measurements and structures of the solar system presented in Buddhist scriptures. The presentation of the shapes of the worlds in the *Flower Ornament Sūtra (Avataṃsaka Sūtra)* differs from that in Vasubandhu's treatise. Because there are inconsistencies among Buddhist scriptures, a literal reading of their presentation of the world's structure is not reliable.

I consider myself a student of Vasubandhu and have full respect for his great learning and spiritual attainments. At the same time, the Buddha advised us not to accept teachings merely out of respect, but to investigate them. Having followed the Buddha's instructions and made a thorough investigation, I believe that if Vasubandhu were alive today, he would rewrite chapter 3 of the *Treasury of Knowledge* in light of current scientific knowledge.

The description of the world found in the *Kālacakra Tantra* and the scientific description also differ in several ways. It is possible that the description in the *Kālacakra Tantra* is designed to point out parallels between the external world and our internal human physiology, not as a description for space travel. In that case, it is valuable to use in meditation practice, although I find it difficult to accept literally.

Reflections on Scriptural Inference

Some people grow up in an environment where questioning a scripture's authority is unacceptable and disbelievers are shunned or threatened. These experiences may cause us to mistrust religious authority. In Buddhism no one asks us to have blind belief. Instead we are encouraged and even required to scrutinize a scripture's reliability by means of the threefold analysis and by examining the qualities of its author.

It is easier for serious, learned practitioners to examine a scripture's reliability. Such practitioners have studied Buddhist scriptures for a period of time and have gained an understanding of the four truths and emptiness based on dependent arising, which facilitates their ability to examine scriptural authority.

How do people who are new to Buddhism approach the issue of the reliability of Buddhist scriptures and of the Buddha as a teacher? When you hear a teaching that tallies with what you have experienced—a teaching that touches you deeply and that in your heart you know is true—you will naturally think, "The Buddha accurately described my experience in one area in a way that no one else has. He may have some special knowledge or spiritual realizations." In addition, when you put a teaching into practice and experience beneficial results, you will easily think, "I followed the Buddha's instructions on how to deal with this disturbing emotion and it worked. Other teachings he has given may be equally valuable." Like the Kālāmas, your trust in the Buddha and his teachings will increase due to your own experiences, as will your receptivity and interest.[13] In this case, it makes sense to continue learning and practicing the Dharma, using your intelligence to examine the teachings. If you don't find a particular point illogical or contradictory, you can accept it; this is not blind belief. The Buddha does not pressure anyone to follow his teachings and gives us full liberty to examine them. But if you don't fully understand a topic and doubts about it remain, leave it for the time being and focus on the parts that help you. You can come back to these more challenging topics later.

Dharmakīrti instructed that inference by authoritative testimony should be applied only to topics that are important to know in order to make spiritual progress. In general, cosmology, political issues, history, gender traits and roles, and so forth are not included. As Buddhist practitioners, we must scrutinize scriptural passages about such topics, weigh them against contemporary ideas of human rights, scientific knowledge, and historical analysis, and come to our own conclusions.

After recommending that the Kālāmas examine the various teachings they heard, the Buddha asked them a series of questions about what they observed to be the results of attachment, anger, and confusion. They replied that the results were consistently unpleasant. When questioned about the results of the absence of attachment, anger, and confusion, the Kālāmas replied that they were pleasant. After having them examine evident phenomena by means of their own experience, the Buddha taught them the meditation on the four immeasurables, and they practiced cultivating love, compassion, joy, and equanimity for all sentient beings. Again the Kālāmas experienced for themselves the beneficial results of following the Buddha's instructions. Having ascertained the reliability of some of the Buddha's teachings through their own experience, they came to trust the Buddha and his teachings and took refuge in the Three Jewels. Their confidence in the Buddha, in turn, made them more open to hear more complex teachings on topics that could be ascertained by factual inference and inference through authoritative testimony.

The Prāsaṅgikas' Unique View of Reliable Cognizers

The Prāsaṅgikas' presentation of reliable cognizers has several distinctive features that differentiate it from the presentations of the Svātantrikas and other lower tenet schools. These principally center on the Prāsaṅgikas' rejection of inherent or true existence. The lower tenet schools say that reliable cognizers and their comprehended objects exist inherently, whereas Prāsaṅgikas assert that they are established in dependence on each other. Candrakīrti states in *Clear Words*:

> When in that way it is posited that the aims of the world are realized by the four reliable cognizers, those also are established in mutual dependence. When reliable cognizers exist, there are comprehended objects, and when comprehended objects exist, there are reliable cognizers. The two—reliable cognizers and comprehended objects that are inherently established—do not exist.

The existence of reliable cognizers and reliable objects is established in dependence on each other. There are no objects out there, existing in their own right, waiting to be comprehended. Nor are there reliable cognizers existing from their own side without perceiving a comprehended object.

A second distinctive feature is the Prāsaṅgikas' assertion that a reliable cognizer can be mistaken. Veiled truths appear inherently existent to all consciousnesses of sentient beings except āryas' meditative equipoise on emptiness. When a sentient being looks at a table, that table appears to her eye consciousness as inherently existent even though it isn't. This consciousness is mistaken with respect to the appearance of the table. Still it is reliable with respect to the main object it cognizes—the table. It gives the person the information she needs to put her cup down. That visual consciousness is a reliable cognizer that is nondeceptive with respect to its apprehended object—its main object, in this case the table. At the same time, it is mistaken with respect to its appearing object (T. *snang yul*)—a table that appears to exist inherently although it does not.

Contrary to Sautrāntikas, Prāsaṅgikas assert that a yogic direct perceiver does not necessarily exist only in the mindstreams of āryas. Ordinary beings can have them as well, for example, the yogic direct perceiver apprehending subtle impermanence. This reliable cognizer is mistaken in that subtle impermanence appears truly existent to it, but nevertheless it correctly knows subtle impermanence.

Some people question whether Prāsaṅgikas can accept factual inference at all, saying that the Tibetan word for "fact," *dngos po*, implies inherent existence. Prāsaṅgikas do not agree that *dngos po* implies inherent existence in this context. They assert that phenomena do not have some "fact" or independent essence that inheres in them. They refute inherent existence on all phenomena and assert that everything exists by being merely designated, dependent on conventions.

Svātantrikas and below say that direct reliable cognizers must be nonconceptual and must be the first moment of knowing the object. Prāsaṅgikas define a reliable cognizer as a nondeceptive consciousness; it need not be the first moment of that cognizer. Glossing *direct* as meaning *not dependent on a reason*, they accept both conceptual and nonconceptual direct reliable cognizers. An example of a *conceptual direct reliable cognizer* is the second moment of an inferential cognizer realizing selflessness. This consciousness is conceptual and correct; it nondeceptively apprehends its main object selflessness that was ascertained in the first moment of that inferential cognizer. However, unlike the first moment, it apprehends selflessness without depending on a reason. Hence it is a conceptual consciousness that is a direct reliable cognizer. Another example of a conceptual direct reliable cognizer is a consciousness remembering the table after our visual consciousness saw it. It directly remembers the table that was seen without depending on a reason. For Prāsaṅgikas, subsequent cognizers are necessarily direct reliable cognizers.

Unlike Sautrāntikas, Prāsaṅgikas say that all consciousnesses, even erroneous ones, are direct reliable cognizers with respect to their appearing objects. For example, the erroneous conception of a turtle's moustache is a *reliable cognizer with respect to its appearing object*, the appearance of a turtle's moustache, because it knows the conceptual appearance of a turtle's moustache and can induce memory of it. However, it is not a *direct reliable cognizer* in general because it is erroneous; a turtle's moustache does not exist.

Knowing When We Have a Correct Reason and a Reliable Cognizer

We do not necessarily know that a particular reason is correct at the time we state it. This could happen for more than one reason. For example, weather forecasting involves factual inference. When a weatherperson predicts that it will be sunny in three days, he is doing so based on the data available to him at that moment. Since the causes and conditions influencing the weather can change quickly, it is unsure whether his conclusion will be correct and, even if it is, if his current reason will be the correct reason later on.

A similar process may occur with a Buddhist practitioner trying to realize emptiness. She may state many reasons to prove emptiness and reach a certain ascertainment or conclusion. But she is not totally confident in the validity of her reasons. Only later, when she has a profound realization, is she confident that her reasons were correct. This is not because the reasons were unsound, but because the initial understanding in her mind was not deep. It was a correct assumption because she did not incontrovertibly ascertain her conclusion at that time. With continued reflection, a correct assumption can become an inferential cognizer.

Although both of these examples involve factual inference in which the person may not be able to ascertain that the reason is correct when stating it, there is a difference between them. The reasons the weatherperson uses—barometric readings and so forth—could easily change as circumstances change. But the reason the Buddhist practitioner contemplates remains constant; it's just that at her current level she's not able to completely ascertain the reason as correct.

Knowing when we have a reliable cognizer is important. For example, when you drive a car and see an animal out of the corner of your eye, you need to find out if that is a direct reliable perception. If it is, you must brake to avoid hitting the animal. When medical researchers conduct trials for a new medication, they need to know that their interpretation of the data is a correct inference, because many people's lives depend on it. We may have certain experiences in our meditation practice, and we need to know if these are reliable cognizers or wrong awarenesses because that will determine whether we reinforce these minds or counteract them.

Tsongkhapa lays out three criteria for existent phenomena (LC 3:178): (1) The object is known to a conventional consciousness. (2) The existence of that object is not invalidated by another conventional reliable cognizer— another reliable cognizer that accurately knows conventional truths. (3) It is not invalidated by a mind analyzing suchness (emptiness).

While a consciousness is cognizing an object, it is unable to know if it knows the object correctly. For this reason, the second criterion is important: another reliable cognizer—which may be another person's reliable cognizer or a later reliable cognizer in our own mental continuum—does not disprove it. We may apprehend something protruding from a field and think it is a person. However, another person comes along and ascertains that it is a scarecrow. Third, a mind analyzing emptiness cannot disprove it. We may believe that inherently existent social castes exist, but a probing awareness analyzing emptiness can negate that.

Inferential Reliable Cognizers and Meditation

All Buddhist traditions share two forms of meditation: serenity, which is principally stabilizing meditation, and insight, which is principally analytical meditation. It is helpful to understand how inferential cognizers relate to these two types of meditation lest we mistakenly believe that inference is mere intellectualization unrelated to experience-based insight. In fact, factual inference can have a profound effect on our mind and totally change our outlook.

For us ordinary beings, deep states of concentration such as serenity are not evident phenomena that we have experienced, nor can we know their existence through factual inference. Rather, we depend on the authoritative testimony of the Buddha, arhats, and practitioners who have realized serenity to know that it exists. Based on their authoritative testimony, we develop faith in serenity, which leads us to aspire to actualize it. This, in turn, inspires us to listen to the instructions on the method to develop it and to apply effort to practice accordingly. Serenity is attained primarily through stabilizing meditation that trains the mind to focus on one object; doing this does not involve factual inference.

Factual inference is crucial for analytical meditation and the development of insight. By contemplating the reason of a syllogism, we come to understand it and to determine that it applies to the subject and is present in the predicate. This process occurs even when we do not consciously state a syllogism. When we establish mindfulness on the body, we do not necessarily verbally state the syllogism at the outset of a meditation session: "The body is unattractive because it is composed of unappealing parts." Rather, by examining the body and its components with strong mindfulness, we naturally come to see that it is unattractive because it is composed of bones, muscles, blood, internal organs, eyeballs, hair, tissue, and so forth. Such an inferential understanding has a strong effect on how we relate to our own and others' bodies and stimulates our determination to be free from cyclic existence.

We may not begin a meditation on mindfulness of feelings with the syllogism *Consider feelings, they are duḥkha (unsatisfactory) in nature because they are under the control of afflictions and karma.* However, this is the understanding we reach by mindfully exploring our pleasant, unpleasant, and neutral feelings. This, in turn, leads us to understand that there is no purpose in clinging to saṃsāric feelings of pleasure. Such knowledge is very freeing and profoundly affects our lives. Here again we see that deep meditation naturally leads us to understand the thesis of a syllogism, even though we do not consciously state a syllogism at the beginning of our meditation. A similar process occurs when establishing mindfulness on the mind, which brings the understanding that the mind is impermanent because it is produced by causes, and when establishing mindfulness on phenomena, through which we understand that all the various mental states are not I or mine because they are neither identical with nor totally unrelated to the I. In short, although we may not be aware that we are using reasoning to cultivate a correct assumption and then an inferential reliable cognizer, this is in fact what is happening.

It is also interesting to apply our knowledge of the three types of phenomena and the reliable cognizers that know them to the stages of the path. Some examples are helpful.

A human life is an evident phenomenon, but our precious human life is slightly obscure. We need to use the reason that we have the eight freedoms and ten fortunes to infer that we have such a wonderful life with all the conducive circumstances for practicing the path. We need to employ inference of authoritative testimony to know that our precious human life is a product of specific karmic causes.

In general, death and coarse impermanence are evident phenomena; we witness people dying and things breaking. But the fact that those of us who are presently alive will die is slightly obscure. We infer it by thinking that we will die because we were born. The exact time and circumstances of our death, however, are very obscure.

Regarding the meditation on unfortunate rebirths, animals are evident to us. Hell beings and hungry ghosts are very obscure; we know them through inference by authoritative testimony. Even if we have a correct assumption of the existence of these states, we may wonder, "How is it possible for a human being to take such a rebirth?" Here it is helpful to think about the continuity of mind that goes from one life to the next. Rebirth itself can be known through factual inference, but it may take us a while to gain the understandings preliminary to this. Sometimes contemplating passages in the sūtras where the Buddha directly speaks about rebirth boosts our understanding. For example, discussing the attainment of a vision of the truth, the Buddha says (DN 28.7):

He understands a human's unbroken stream of mind that is established in both this world and the next.

The Buddha also refers to a future life that follows death (SN 4.9):

This life span of human beings is short. One has to go on to the future life. One should do what is wholesome and lead the holy life; for one who has taken birth, there is no avoiding death.

To wholeheartedly take refuge in the Three Jewels, we must first establish their existence. The best way to do this is to transform our mind into the Dharma Jewel, which depends on having a yogic direct, nonconceptual perceiver of subtle selflessness. This is gained from first having an inferential reliable cognizer of selflessness, which is a slightly obscure phenomenon. In his *Commentary on Reliable Cognition*, Dharmakīrti set out the reasoning proving that it is possible to have a yogic direct perceiver of selflessness. The process begins by having a correct assumption, an understanding derived from hearing. This is deepened by means of the wisdom of reflecting—an inferential cognizer realizing selflessness—which is further enhanced by the wisdom of meditation until it becomes a yogic direct perceiver of self-lessness. This wisdom, which is a true path, is then used to progressively eradicate the afflictions from the mindstream and attain true cessations. The true paths and true cessations are the Dharma Jewel. From these we infer the existence of the Saṅgha Jewel, those beings who have attained these realizations. Following this, we can infer the existence of the Buddha Jewel, someone who has eradicated all obscurations.

At the present moment, our understanding of selflessness and of the process of actualizing true paths and true cessations may be a correct assumption. This is sufficient for us to understand that the Three Jewels have the ability to guide us from the dangers of cyclic existence in general and from unfortunate rebirths in particular. Understanding this has the power to impel us to turn to the Three Jewels for spiritual guidance, which is the purpose of the teaching on refuge.

Regarding the teaching on karma and its results, some of the results of our actions are evident, while others are slightly obscure or very obscure. An evident result is the reciprocal kindness we receive after treating someone else with care. A slightly obscure karmic result is a person's being compassionate from a young age. We can infer that this is due to her having cultivated compassion in previous lives. Barring any inhibiting factors, familiarity with compassion in previous lives will cause compassion to arise easily again in future lives.

A very obscure karmic result is the specific rebirth that is the maturation result of a complete karma we did today. Only an omniscient one, a buddha, can know this. Once an old man asked Śāriputra to ordain him as a monk. Even with his great clairvoyance, Śāriputra could not determine if this man had created the virtuous causes in the past to be able to ordain. It was only after he consulted the Buddha, who saw with his omniscience that indeed this man had created the virtuous karma, that he was able to become a monastic. Even for Śāriputra, the Buddha's disciple most renowned for his wisdom, the exact details of karma and its effects were very obscure.

The measure of understanding the meditation on karma is gaining an understanding of karma and its effects that is sufficient to make us increasingly conscientious of our physical, verbal, and mental actions so that we avoid engaging in harmful actions and are eager to create constructive ones. This is gained by understanding the causes of our experiences and results of our actions through direct perception, factual inference, and inference by authoritative testimony, as described above.

As we've seen in this chapter, reliable cognizers apply to many aspects of our lives and our Dharma practice. By learning about them, we will lay a foundation for the critical thinking necessary to correctly understand ever more profound subjects.

REFLECTION

1. What kind of reliable cognizers know the duḥkha of cyclic existence?

2. When you reflect on the kindness of others, what kind of reliable cognizers are at play?

3 | The Basis of the Self: The Body and Mind

THE BUDDHA'S TEACHINGS are studied and lived by those seeking to assuage misery and attain awakening. What is the nature of a person who does this? That person depends on a body and mind and lives in a universe filled with a plethora of other phenomena. In this chapter we will outline the phenomena that comprise the person and the universe as seen by Buddhist sages. The objects we endeavor to understand with reliable cognizers are these phenomena, their impermanence and unsatisfactory nature, the relationships among them, and their ultimate mode of existence.

Classifications of Phenomena

The classification of phenomena was one of the first topics I learned in my studies as a young boy. Although initially I just memorized definitions without understanding them, I later realized that since this terminology was used by the great sages and scholars, it was important in order to gain an understanding of their writings. This gave me impetus to study the terminology. The following presentation of phenomena is common to most Buddhist schools.

We begin with the selfless—that which does not exist inherently. This has two divisions: (1) The *existent* (*sat*) is that which is perceivable by mind, that which is suitable to be known by an awareness. Existent is synonymous with phenomena (*dharma*), object of knowledge, established base, and object. (2) The *nonexistent* (*asat*) is that which is not perceivable by mind.

If something exists, a consciousness must be able to perceive it. A table is existent; a rabbit's horn is not.

Existents are divided into: (1) permanent phenomena (*nitya*) and (2) things (*vastu/bhāva*) or impermanent phenomena (*anitya*). A permanent phenomenon does not change moment by moment, whereas an impermanent one—a functioning thing—does. *Permanent* does not mean eternal or existing forever without end. Something that is eternal may be impermanent or permanent. For example, the emptiness of a cup does not change moment by moment, but it ceases to exist when the cup breaks. This emptiness is permanent, but not eternal. The mind changes moment by moment and is eternal. It is impermanent, yet its continuity never ceases.

Permanent phenomena

Permanent phenomena are not produced by causes and conditions and are not products. They neither produce an effect nor change in the next moment. The number of permanent phenomena is limitless; some examples are unconditioned space—the absence of obstruction—and the emptiness of inherent existence. There are two types of permanent phenomena:

1. *Occasional permanents* may come into existence and go out of existence, although they do not arise or disintegrate momentarily under the influence of causes and conditions. The emptiness of inherent existence of this book is one example. This emptiness is the ultimate nature of the book; it came into existence simultaneous with the book and it will go out of existence when the book ceases. However, it does not change momentarily or disintegrate under the power of causes and conditions.

2. *Nonoccasional permanents* are eternal. Unconditioned space (*ākāśa*) is an example. This space exists everywhere, at all times, not just occasionally.

Analytical cessations (*pratisaṃkhyā-nirodha*) and nonanalytical cessations (*apratisaṃkhyā-nirodha*) are also permanent phenomena. The former are true cessations, the absence of obscurations through having applied the antidote—the direct realization of emptiness—so that those obscurations can never reappear. Nonanalytical cessations are temporary absences of afflictions because the conditions for the arising of those afflictions are not present. Our not being angry at this moment is not due to a true cessation by our having ceased the seeds of anger in our mindstream. It is due to not being in contact with a disagreeable object at this moment. Anger may arise later when the cooperative conditions—such as someone criticizing us—are present.

Things: impermanent phenomena
A thing is something that performs a function—it produces an effect. Things are impermanent; being conditioned phenomena produced by causes and conditions, they are products (*saṃskṛta*). Things are of three types: (1) form (*rūpa*), (2) consciousness (*jñāna*), and (3) abstract composites (*viprayukta-saṃskāra*). These three are mutually exclusive—something cannot be two or all three of them.

Form is defined in a general way as that which is suitable to be form. Forms include objects of the sense consciousnesses (colors and shapes, sounds, odors, tastes, and tangibles) as well as subtle forms such as the five cognitive faculties (the subtle material that enables us to see, hear, smell, taste, and touch objects). Tangibles include the four elements—earth (heaviness), water (cohesion), fire (heat), wind (movement)—and smoothness, lightness, cold, hunger, thirst, and so forth. Forms for mental consciousness—such as dream objects and special subtle forms that meditators create by the power of their meditative concentration—are also included among forms.

Gross forms—those apprehended by our senses—can be measured by scientific instruments. Other forms, as well as consciousness and many abstract phenomena, cannot be directly measured by scientific instruments because they are not atomic in nature.

Consciousness is defined as that which is clear and cognizant.[14] *Clear* indicates that it is not physical in nature and can reflect objects. *Cognizant* means that it can know and experience objects. It is of two types: mind (*citta*) and mental factors (*caitta*).

Mind is of six types: visual, auditory, olfactory, gustatory, tactile, and mental primary consciousnesses (*vijñāna*). These apprehend the presence or basic entity of an object: they know the type of object something is, for example, a sight, sound, a mental object, and so forth.

Mental factors fill out the cognition, apprehending particular attributes of the object or performing a specific function. Some mental factors, such as feeling, discrimination, intention, contact, and attention, accompany all consciousnesses. Other mental factors—such as love or anger—are manifest at some times and latent at other times. Some mental factors, such as the six root afflictions, are harmful; others, such as faith and compassion, are beneficial. Some mental factors—such as investigation and analysis—can be either virtuous or nonvirtuous, depending on what other mental factors accompany (are concomitant with) those consciousnesses.

Abstract composites are impermanent things that are neither form nor consciousness. Many of them—such as impermanence—enable the coming together of causes and conditions and the arising, abiding, and disintegration of things. To perceive abstract composites, we must perceive something else. For example, we know a person by perceiving his or her body, speech, or mind. We know impermanence by seeing an object change.

There are two types of abstract composites: persons and not persons. The term "person" (*pudgala*) has a wider meaning here than it does in general usage. Examples of a person are any living being: Joe, a woman, an accountant, a monastic, a Spaniard, an animal, and a god. A person is designated in dependence on his or her aggregates—the body and consciousness—but a person is neither of those. Abstract composites that are not persons (*apudgala-viprayukta-saṃskāra*) are such things as time, birth, aging, democracy, life force, area, number, absorption without discrimination, and absorption of cessation.[15]

Contemplating these categories enables us to see that not everything that exists is material in nature. In fact a wide variety of things that arise from causes and produce results exist, although we cannot apprehend them with our senses or measure them with scientific instruments. While we can measure the activities of the brain when a person is experiencing a particular emotion, the brain is form; it is not the emotion, which is consciousness.

Understanding these different types of phenomena is helpful when we explore the four truths, the thirty-seven harmonies with awakening, and emptiness. What may seem to be a dry list of categories comes alive when we ask questions. Is love brain activity or conscious experience? That is, is the brain consciousness? That is not possible because the brain is form and consciousness is clear and cognizant. Nevertheless, the brain and consciousness often influence each other. Is emptiness form, as the words in the *Heart Sūtra* literally say? Form is an impermanent thing and emptiness is permanent, and nothing can be both. However, emptiness is an inseparable quality of form.

If a truly existent person existed, we should be able to say what it is and we should be able to find it. When meditating on the selflessness of persons, we examine how the I exists: Is it the body, a primary consciousness, a mental factor, the collection of these, or something separate from them?

Five Aggregates

The five aggregates (*skandha*) is a schema for categorizing impermanent phenomena. In general, the five aggregates include all impermanent phenomena, but when they are spoken of in relation to a person, they are the basis of designation of that person. In his *Supplement* (*Madhyamakā-vatāra*), Candrakīrti defines the five aggregates:

> Form has the definition "suitable as form."
> Feeling has the nature of experience.
> Discrimination apprehends [entities and] characteristics.
> Miscellaneous factors contain [all the others].
> "Individually cognizing objects" is the specific definition
> of primary consciousness.

In general, the form aggregate consists of things that are material in nature. The other four aggregates are predominantly mental.

1. *Form* (*rūpa*) in general refers to objects apprehended by our sense consciousnesses—colors, shapes, sounds, odors, tastes, and tangibles. As noted above, it also includes forms for mental consciousness. When speaking of the five aggregates that constitute a person, the form aggregate refers to the body.
2. *Feeling* (*vedanā*) is the mental factor of the experience of pleasure, pain, or neutrality.
3. *Discrimination* (*saṃjñā*) is the mental factor that apprehends the distinctive characteristics of an object and can distinguish one thing from another.
4. *Miscellaneous factors* (*saṃskāra*) are mental factors other than feeling and discrimination, such as emotions, attitudes, and views, as well as abstract composites such as karmic seeds and latencies of afflictions.
5. *Primary consciousnesses* (*vijñāna*) consist of the visual, auditory,

olfactory, gustatory, tactile, and mental primary consciousnesses that apprehend the general type of object. Visual primary consciousness apprehends colors and shapes, auditory primary consciousness apprehends sounds, olfactory primary consciousness apprehends smells, gustatory primary consciousness apprehends tastes, tactile primary consciousness apprehends tangibles, and mental primary consciousnesses know mental phenomena.

Unlike other mental factors, feeling and discrimination are distinguished as their own aggregates. This is due to the special roles they play. Pleasant and unpleasant feelings evoke attachment and animosity, respectively. These emotions motivate sentient beings to create karma that ripens in birth in cyclic existence. Discrimination is the source of disputes because sentient beings discriminate one thing as attractive and another as repulsive, one idea as right and another as wrong. Becoming attached to their views, they quarrel with others who hold different views, thus creating karma that propels rebirth in cyclic existence.

REFLECTION

1. One by one, identify each of the five aggregates that constitute you as a person. Be aware of your body. Identify feelings of pleasure and happiness, discomfort and suffering, and neutral feelings that are neither. Notice the discriminations you make, the moods and emotions you have, and the types of primary consciousnesses that are present.

2. Identifying each aggregate in your own experience, contemplate their different functions and unique attributes.

3. Contemplate the characteristics common to all five aggregates: they change moment by moment (impermanent), they are under the influence of afflictions and karma (duḥkha by nature), they depend on other factors and are not a person (selfless).

Twelve Sources and Eighteen Constituents

An alternative method of classifying all phenomena is the twelve sources (*āyatana*), so-called because they are sources that give rise to consciousness. Six of the sources are external—the objects known by consciousness; and six are internal—the cognitive faculties of a person that enable an object to be cognized by a consciousness.

THE TWELVE SOURCES

INTERNAL SOURCE (COGNITIVE FACULTY)	EXTERNAL SOURCE (OBJECT THAT IS COGNIZED)
Eye source	Forms
Ear source	Sounds
Nose source	Odors
Tongue source	Tastes
Body or tactile source	Tangibles
Mental source	Phenomena

The eye source, ear source, and so forth are called internal sources because they belong to the person. The first five—the eye, ear, nose, tongue, and tactile sources—are not the gross organs such as the eyeball and the ear. They are subtle forms within the gross organ that are sensitive and receptive to their corresponding object. The mental source includes all six consciousnesses because they have the power to give rise to a mental consciousness that knows a phenomenon. For example, dependent on the visual consciousness seeing blue, the mental consciousness remembers blue.

The eighteen constituents (*dhātu*)—which consist of objects and their corresponding mental faculties and consciousnesses—are another way to categorize all phenomena, both permanent and impermanent. The phenomena source and the phenomena constituent include only objects known uniquely by the mental consciousness: permanent phenomena such as emptiness and permanent space, feelings, and forms for mental consciousness.

The latter consists of single particles, the appearance of clear space to the mental consciousness, imperceptible forms, dream objects, and forms generated in deep concentration. Although sense objects are also known by the mental consciousness, they are not included in the phenomena source or phenomena constituent.

When we think deeply about these diverse ways of classifying phenomena, we begin to see that the self we consider to be one unique item is actually a collection of diverse factors that function dependent on one another.

THE EIGHTEEN CONSTITUENTS

COGNITIVE FACULTY	OBSERVED OBJECT	APPREHENDING CONSCIOUSNESS
Eye faculty	Forms	Visual consciousness
Ear faculty	Sounds	Auditory consciousness
Nose faculty	Odors	Olfactory consciousness
Tongue faculty	Tastes	Gustatory consciousness
Body or tactile faculty	Tangibles	Tactile consciousness
Mental faculty	Phenomena	Mental consciousness

REFLECTION

1. In your own experience, identify each of the twelve sources. Observe the relationship between the internal source, the external source, and consciousness arisen from them for each sense.

2. Of the six senses, which ones prompt strong attachment in you? Which are the source of the greatest anger or aversion?

3. Identify the eighteen constituents, especially the ones that compose you as a person.

4. What is the relationship between you—the person—and the constituents that compose you? Are you one and the same as any of those constituents? Are you completely separate from them? Do you depend on them?

Consciousness: Mind and Mental Factors

There are many ways to speak about and classify types of consciousness: mind and mental factors, conceptual and nonconceptual consciousnesses, the seven types of awarenesses, and so forth. The Abhidharma makes the division of consciousness into mind and mental factors and describes the components of these categories. Later Indian sages such as Asaṅga and Vasubandhu elaborated on those descriptions in their *Compendium of Knowledge* (*Abhidharmasamuccaya*) and *Treasury of Knowledge*, respectively. When referred to together, these two texts are called the "Two Knowledges."

Learning about mind and mental factors enables us to better understand our mind. We will be able to identify in our own experience the mental factors that arise due to pleasant, unpleasant, and neutral feelings and that in turn create the causes of happiness and suffering by motivating the actions (karma) we do. Such introspective awareness of our own mental processes is essential in order to tame and transform our mind. We will also understand that Dharma practice entails subduing the destructive mental factors that lead to misery in cyclic existence and enhancing the constructive ones that lead to happiness in cyclic existence as well as to liberation and awakening. This in turn will positively affect our thoughts, words, and deeds.

The core of the meditation on emptiness is examining how the I or self exists. It appears to be very real and "solid," but can it be found in the aggregates individually or in their collection, or separate from the aggregates? It is not too difficult to understand that we are not the body, but the self strongly appears to be associated with the mind. Understanding the various types of mind and how they function will aid in understanding what the I is and is not, and its relationship to the aggregates.

As noted above, all cognizers consist of a primary consciousness and various mental factors that accompany it. Primary consciousnesses are of six types, as mentioned above: visual, auditory, olfactory, gustatory, tactile, and mental primary consciousnesses. Each of these apprehends the fundamental presence of its object. Although a primary consciousness and its accompanying mental factors are different, when they arise together as one mental state, they are the same nature. They are concomitant and share five similarities.

1. They have the same *basis* (*āśraya*): they depend on the same cognitive faculty.
2. They share the same *observed object* (*ālambana*): they apprehend the same object.
3. Both are generated in the same *aspect* (*ākāra*) of the object: they reflect a similar aspect of the object.
4. They occur at the same *time* (*kāla*): they arise, abide, and cease simultaneously.
5. They are the same *entity* (*dravya*): each mental state consists of only one primary consciousness and only one of each of its accompanying mental factors. Furthermore, the primary mind and all its accompanying mental factors are either conceptual or nonconceptual, either mistaken or nonmistaken.

The Pāli scripture *Milindapañha*[16] contains an excellent example of the relationship of a primary consciousness and its accompanying mental factors. King Milinda asked the monk Nāgasena Thera whether mental factors can be separated out such that we can see them as different parts of the puzzle: "This is contact, and this feeling, and this mentation, and this discrimination." Nāgasena Thera replied by asking if the king would be able to pick out each flavor, separate from all the others, when the royal cook made a syrup or a sauce with curds, salt, ginger, cumin seed, pepper, and other ingredients.

Clearly this would not be possible. All the various flavors together give the sauce its taste, even though each ingredient adds its own unique flavor. Similarly, the various mental factors accompanying a primary consciousness function together and cannot be separated out since they share the same basis, observed object, aspect, time, and entity. Nevertheless, the primary consciousness and each mental factor perform its unique function and contribute its own "flavor" to the cognizer.

To give another example, the primary consciousness is like the main light in a room, while its accompanying mental factors are like other lights in the same room. While each light is distinct, they blend together to illuminate the room. The fact that an auditory primary consciousness is present means that all its accompanying mental factors also perceive sound. If the mental factor of feeling experiences pleasure, the entire mental state is pleasurable.

The mental factors described below are not an exhaustive list; they are the principal ones that must be abandoned or cultivated in order to attain liberation. Their enumeration and precise definitions may differ according to the specific Abhidharma text. Here the prominent mental factors are counted as fifty-one and divided into six groups in accordance with the *Compendium of Knowledge*: (1) five omnipresent mental factors (*sarva-traga*), (2) five object-ascertaining mental factors (*viniyata*), (3) eleven virtuous mental factors (*kuśala-caitta*), (4) six root afflictions (*mūlakleśa*), (5) twenty secondary afflictions (*upakleśa*), and (6) four variable mental factors (*aniyata*).

Five Omnipresent Mental Factors

The five omnipresent mental factors accompany all minds. Without them complete cognition of an object cannot occur.

1. *Feeling* is an experience of pleasure, pain, or neutrality. Feeling experiences the results of our past actions and can lead to reactions of attachment, anger, confusion, and so forth.

2. *Discrimination* functions to distinguish "it is this and not that" and to apprehend the characteristics of an object. It differentiates and identifies objects.

3. *Intention* (*cetanā*) moves the primary consciousness and its accompanying mental factors to the object. It is the conscious and automatic motivating element that causes the mind to involve itself with and apprehend its object. It is action, karma. Although the mental factor of intention itself is not constructive, destructive, or neutral, it becomes so depending on what other mental factors—such as attachment or anger—accompany that mental state.

4. *Attention* (mental engagement, *manaskāra*) functions to direct the primary consciousness and its concomitant mental factors to the object and to actually apprehend the object. It focuses and holds the mind on an object without allowing it to move elsewhere.

5. *Contact* (*sparśa*) connects the object, cognitive faculty, and primary consciousness, thereby acting as a basis for feelings of pleasure, pain, and indifference. It is the cause of feeling.

The *Compendium of Knowledge* says that the five omnipresent mental factors accompany all primary consciousnesses. The Abhidharma system of the Pāli canon explains that each primary consciousness has seven omnipresent mental factors (P. *cetasika*): contact (P. *phassa*); feeling (P. *vedanā*); discrimination (P. *saññā*), which Pāli translators often render as "perception"; intention or volition (*cetanā*); one-pointedness (P. *ekaggatā*); life faculty or psychic life (P. *jīvitindriya*);[17] and attention (P. *manasikāra*).

Five Object-Ascertaining Mental Factors

The five object-ascertaining mental factors are so-called because they apprehend the individual features of an object. The *Treasury of Knowledge* says that these five accompany all mental states, whereas the *Compendium of Knowledge* asserts that they accompany only virtuous mental states. These five are not themselves virtuous, but become virtuous because of being associated with a virtuous mental state. In this case, the mindfulness accompanying a mental consciousness that apprehends and has aversion toward a repulsive object would not be the mindfulness of the five object-ascertaining mental factors, but would be another mental factor similar to it.

1. Aspiration (*chanda*) takes a strong interest in an intended object and is the basis for joyous effort.

2. Appreciation (belief, *adhimokṣa*) stabilizes the apprehension of a previously ascertained object and holds it such that it cannot be distracted by another view.

3. Mindfulness (*smṛti*) repeatedly brings to mind a phenomenon of previous acquaintance without forgetting it. It does not allow the mind to be distracted from the object and is the basis for concentration.[18]

4. Concentration (single-pointedness, *samādhi*) dwells one-pointedly for a sustained period of time on a single object. It is the basis for developing serenity and increasing wisdom.

5. Wisdom (understanding, intelligence, *prajñā*) functions to discriminate precisely with analysis the qualities, faults, or characteristics of an object held by mindfulness. It cuts through indecision and doubt with certainty and maintains the root of all constructive qualities in this and future lives. There are various types of intelligence:

a. Inborn intelligence is the natural acuity of mind that comes as a result of karma from previous lives.

b. Acquired understanding or wisdom is cultivated in this life. A person may generate it with respect to various topics of the stages of the path. It is of three types:

   i. The understanding or wisdom arising when hearing, learning, or studying a topic. It brings initial knowledge of the topic and lays the foundation for the other two types of understanding.

   ii. The understanding or wisdom arising from critical reflection or contemplation is generated by thinking about a topic on our own or debating and discussing it with others. Through it, we gain a correct conceptual (inferential) understanding of the topic.

   iii. The understanding or wisdom arising from meditation is derived from deeper personal experience when understanding of the topic arises automatically in our minds because we are very familiar with it.[19]

Our current mental factors of concentration and wisdom are the uncultivated bases for the actual concentration and wisdom that arise due to sustained Dharma practice. The wisdom referred to in the expression "method and wisdom" and the concentration referred to in the phrase "concentration found in the fourth jhāna" are very different in strength, acuity, and effectiveness from the mental factors we have now that bear the same names. Nonetheless, our present mental factors of concentration and wisdom can be nourished and transformed into serenity and insight.

Eleven Virtuous Mental Factors

The eleven virtuous mental factors cause the omnipresent, object-ascertaining, and variable mental factors to take on a virtuous aspect and bring peace to oneself and others. Each of the eleven is an antidote to particular afflictions.

1. *Faith* (confidence, trust, *śraddhā*) is confidence in such things as the law of karma and its effects and the Three Jewels. It produces a joyous state of mind free from the turmoil of the root and auxiliary afflictions and is the basis for generating the aspiration to develop new constructive qualities and enhancing virtuous aspirations already generated. It is of three kinds: *Inspired faith* knows the qualities of the object and rejoices in them. *Aspiring faith* knows the qualities of the object and aspires to attain them. *Convictional faith* (believing faith) knows the qualities of the object and thereby has confidence in it.

2. *Integrity* (*hrī*) avoids negativity for reasons of personal conscience and self-respect. It enables us to restrain from harmful physical, verbal, and mental actions and is the basis for ethical conduct.

3. *Consideration for others* (*apatrāpya*) cares about the effect of our actions on others and avoids negativity for their sake. It enables us to restrain from harmful physical, verbal, and mental actions, acts as the basis for maintaining pure ethical conduct, prevents others from losing faith in us, and causes joy to arise in the minds of others.

4. *Nonattachment* (*alobha*) is not the mere absence of attachment, but the opposite of attachment and the direct antidote to it. Referring to an object in cyclic existence, nonattachment prevents and counteracts attachment and subdues obsession with attractive objects and people.

5. *Nonhatred* (*adveṣa*) is the opposite of animosity—it is love and benevolence, not just the absence of anger and ill will. When referring to someone who harms us, the harm itself, or the cause of the harm, it has the characteristic of love and directly overcomes anger and hatred. It is the basis for the prevention of hostility and the increase of love, benevolence, forgiveness, and fortitude.

6. *Nonconfusion* (*amoha*) is the opposite of confusion. Arising from an inborn disposition and nurtured by study, reflection, and meditation,

it acts as a remedy for confusion and ignorance and accompanies the firm wisdom that thoroughly analyzes the nature and specific characteristics of an object. It prevents confusion, increases the four types of wisdom, and helps to actualize constructive qualities.

7. *Joyous effort* (*vīrya*) counteracts laziness and joyfully engages in constructive actions. It acts to generate constructive qualities that have not been generated and to bring those that have to completion.

8. *Pliancy* (flexibility, *praśrabdhi*) enables the mind to apply itself to a constructive object in whatever manner it wishes and dissipates any mental or physical tightness or rigidity.

9. *Conscientiousness* (*apramāda*) values the accumulation of virtue and guards the mind against that which gives rise to afflictions. It brings to fulfillment and maintains all that is good, protects the mind from pollution, and is the root for attaining all grounds and paths.

10. *Nonharmfulness* (noncruelty, *ahiṃsā*) is compassion. Lacking any intention to cause harm, it wishes all sentient beings to be free from suffering. It prevents disrespecting or harming others and increases the wish to benefit and bring them happiness.

11. *Equanimity* (*upekṣā*) does not allow the mind to be greatly affected by restlessness and laxity without having to exert great effort to prevent them. Important for the development of serenity, it enables the mind to settle and remain on a virtuous object. This equanimity differs from the equanimity of the four immeasurables and the equanimity that is a neutral feeling.

Six Root Afflictions

These six are called root afflictions because they are primary causes of cyclic existence and are the root or cause of the auxiliary afflictions. They are the basis for all distorted conceptions and emotional conflict. Sometimes the last root affliction, afflictive views, is subdivided to make ten afflictions.

1. *Attachment* (*rāga*) arises based on projecting or exaggerating the attractiveness of an object within cyclic existence (people, things, ideas, places, and so forth). It wishes for, takes a strong interest in, and clings to that object.

2. *Anger* (*pratigha*) arises based on projecting or exaggerating the

unattractive qualities of an object or person. It agitates the mind through being unable to bear or through wanting to harm that object or person. It arises in reference to someone who harms us, the suffering itself, or the cause of the harm.

3. *Arrogance* (*māna*) is based on the view of a personal identity that apprehends an inherently existent I or mine. It strongly grasps an inflated or superior image of ourselves.

4. *Ignorance* (*avidyā*) is a state of unknowing brought about by the mind being unclear about the nature of things such as the four truths of the āryas, karma and its results, and the Three Jewels. This definition is held in common by all Buddhist tenet systems, although each system has its own unique way of defining ignorance. This will be discussed in depth later.

5. *Deluded doubt* (*vicikitsā*) is indecisive wavering that tends toward an incorrect conclusion about important points such as karma and its results, the four truths, and the Three Jewels.

6. *Afflictive views* (*dṛṣṭi*) are either an afflictive intelligence (corrupt understanding) that regards the aggregates as being inherently I or mine or, in direct dependence on such a view, an afflictive intelligence that develops further mistaken conceptions.

   a. The view of a personal identity (*satkāyadṛṣṭi*) is an afflictive intelligence that, when referring to the conventional I or mine, grasps it to be either inherently I or mine. It is called "intelligence" in the sense that it analyzes something.[20] It is the root of saṃsāra and acts as the basis for all afflictions.

   b. The view of extremes (*antagrāhadṛṣṭi*) is an afflictive intelligence that, when referring to the I or mine grasped by the view of a personal identity, regards them in an absolutist or nihilistic fashion. It prevents us from finding the view of the middle way free from extremes.

   c. The view holding wrong views as supreme (*dṛṣṭiparāmarśa*) is an afflictive intelligence that regards other afflictive views as the best views. It increases our attachment to other afflictive views.

   d. The view of rules and practices (*śīlavrataparāmarśa*) is an afflictive intelligence that believes purification of mental defilements occurs by engaging in ascetic practices, inferior codes of ethical conduct, and mistaken practices that are inspired by wrong views.[21] It is the basis for wasting time on incorrect modes of practice that do not lead to our spiritual goals.

e. Wrong views (*mithyādṛṣṭi*) is an afflictive intelligence that denies the existence of something that in fact exists—for example, karma and its effects, past and future lives, and the Three Jewels—or that believes a divine creator or primal substance to be the cause of sentient beings. It functions to prevent us from engaging in virtue and to lead us to create nonvirtue.

Twenty Auxiliary Afflictions

The twenty auxiliary afflictions are branches of the root afflictions and similarly disturb the mind. These will be explained in more depth in the next volume of the Library of Wisdom and Compassion. For now, suffice it to list them: wrath, resentment, spite, jealousy, cruelty, miserliness, haughtiness, restlessness, concealment, lethargy, laziness, lack of faith, forgetfulness, nonintrospective awareness, pretension, deceit, lack of integrity, inconsideration for others, heedlessness, and distraction.

Four Variable Mental Factors

In themselves, the four variable factors are neither virtuous nor nonvirtuous, but become so in dependence on our motivation and the other mental factors that accompany the same mental state.

1. Sleep (*middha*) makes the mind unclear, gathers the sense consciousnesses inward, and renders the mind incapable of apprehending the body. Sleeping out of attachment and laziness is destructive, sleeping because the body is tired is neutral, sleeping with the intention to resume our compassionate activities after resting is virtuous.

2. Regret (*kaukṛtya*) regards an appropriate or inappropriate action that we have performed of our own accord or under pressure as something we do not wish to repeat. Regretting negativities is virtuous, but regretting our constructive actions is nonvirtuous.

3. Investigation (coarse engagement, *vitarka*) arises depending on intention or wisdom and examines an object in general. Investigating the meaning of impermanence is virtuous, whereas investigating someone's faults with the intention to criticize is nonvirtuous.

4. Analysis (subtle engagement, *vicāra*) arises in dependence on intention or wisdom and analyzes the object in detail. Analyzing the nature of reality with the motivation of bodhicitta is virtuous, but analyzing how to make more efficient weapons with the intention to kill is destructive.

While there is much that can be said about each of these mental factors, the brief descriptions above give an idea of how our mind operates and the various kinds of thoughts, attitudes, and emotions that arise in it at different times. Such a list of views, emotions, and attitudes provides a structure that helps us to get to know ourselves. We become more aware of our mental states by naming our thoughts and emotions. While meditating or going about our daily activities, it is helpful to practice identifying various mental factors and discerning whether they are conducive to happiness and constructive action or detrimental to them. When an affliction manifests in our mind, we must identify the mental factors that are opposed to it and then activate them.

REFLECTION

1. Read the description of each mental factor, contemplate its meaning, and try to identify it in your own experience.

2. Look especially at the eleven virtuous mental factors and the six root afflictions. Give examples of when you have experienced each of these mental states.

3. Outline both the external events and internal causes (thoughts, moods, and so forth) that make each of these virtuous and nonvirtuous mental factors arise.

4. What effects does each mental factor have on your life, your spiritual practice, and your progress on the path to awakening?

Conceptual and Nonconceptual Consciousnesses

Another way to classify consciousness is into nonconceptual and conceptual consciousnesses. A nonconceptual consciousness knows its object directly, without the medium of a conceptual appearance (*artha-sāmānya*)[22] appearing to the mind. Sense consciousnesses are always nonconceptual—they are direct perceivers—whereas mental consciousnesses may be either conceptual or nonconceptual. Examples of nonconceptual mental consciousness are clairvoyance or a yogic direct perceiver of emptiness.

Reliable sense consciousnesses correctly and directly perceive their object; they see color and shape, hear sounds, and so forth. Based on these direct perceivers, we then think about and remember objects. These are conceptual consciousnesses.[23] Thought is conceptual; it does not know its object clearly but only via a conceptual appearance of the object appearing to the mind. Dharmakīrti says (PV), "Whatsoever consciousness has clear appearance is asserted to be nonconceptual."[24] A direct perceiver sees the building; conceptual consciousnesses plan its construction.

In the *Collected Topics* (*bsdus grwa*), a conceptual appearance of a pot is defined as "that factor of superimposition that is the appearance to the conceptual cognizer [of a pot] as a pot despite its not being a pot." The appearing object of this conceptual consciousness is the conceptual appearance of the pot, not the actual pot.

A conceptual appearance is a representation of the object; it is the appearing object of a conceptual consciousness. It is not the actual object, but it allows us to think about various qualities and aspects of the object. Memories, thoughts, views, plans, imaginings, and afflictions are all conceptual consciousnesses. Conceptuality covers a wide range: from the thought "this is a pot," to the conception grasping inherent existence, to a correct assumption of the meaning of emptiness, to an inferential cognizer of emptiness on the path of preparation that will soon transform into a nonconceptual, direct perceiver of emptiness on the path of seeing.

Sense consciousnesses directly perceive their objects, while thought apprehends its object in an indirect way by means of negation. When we think about yellow, the opposite of nonyellow appears to our mind. This is the conceptual appearance of yellow.

A conceptual consciousness does not know its object directly, but knows it through a negative process. Its appearing object is a conceptual appearance—an image of the object that comes about by negating everything that is not that object. In other words, what appears to a thought that knows a flower is the elimination of everything that is not a flower. This image expresses the general meaning of flower by combining the characteristics of many flowers with different characteristics that sense consciousnesses perceived at different times.

Because a conceptual appearance comes about through a process of elimination and negation, it is generally considered a permanent phenomenon, although the mind to which it appears is impermanent. There is debate about this, however.[25]

The *appearing object* to the conception of a flower—the primary object that appears to that conceptual consciousness—is the conceptual appearance of the flower. The *apprehended object* of that mind—what that consciousness apprehends—is the flower. Conflating the actual flower with the appearance of the flower to a conceptual consciousness enables us to think about the flower. Conceptual consciousnesses are useful because through them we understand the broader properties and potentials of things and the relationships among them. Conceptual consciousnesses enable us to learn about things that we cannot perceive directly through sense perceivers. Scientific theories, planning a benefit event to help a charity, and considering measures that will stop global warming all depend on our ability to conceptualize objects, their causes, results, relationships, abilities, and so forth. In fact, most of our education entails learning terms and concepts.

Direct perceivers are immediate: they know objects that exist in the present. Nonconceptual direct perceivers apprehend the color, shape, texture, temperature, taste, and smell of an apple. Thought is able to apprehend objects that do not exist in the present moment, thus giving us the ability to remember our previous experiences and to plan for the future.

A visual direct perceiver sees many things in its field of perception, whereas conceptual consciousnesses are selective and focus on only a few aspects of the object. A thought picks out certain attributes and constructs a conceptual appearance of the object. Our memory of something consists of a few details that we happened to pay attention to when directly perceiving the object.

In forming conceptual appearances, conceptual consciousnesses conflate the time, place, or characteristics of several objects. We think, "This is the same table I saw yesterday," when in fact yesterday's table no longer exists and we are seeing today's table. Here the tables of two different times—yesterday and today—have been conflated to form the conceptual appearance of that table. The conceptual appearance of the table appearing to our mind is neither yesterday's table nor today's table. It is simply the general meaning of that table.

When shopping for a table, we may think, "This is the same table I saw at my friend's house." In fact they are different tables, but thought conflates the two tables that are in different places. There are over seven billion human beings on our planet. Each one is different, yet when someone says, "Think about a human being," the general meaning of a human being appears to our mind. This conceptual appearance obscures all the variations among human beings and emphasizes a few common characteristics.

REFLECTION

1. When eating a meal, pause before each bite and be aware of what you expect the taste and texture of the next bite to be. What appears to your mind is a conceptual appearance based on having eaten similar kinds of food in the past.

2. Take the next bite and be aware of the taste and texture of the food. This is a direct perceiver of the food.

3. Was your expectation of the taste and texture accurate? What was the difference between conceptual imagination of the taste of the food and your direct perception of it?

Both nonconceptual and conceptual consciousnesses have their advantages and disadvantages in daily life and in Dharma practice. Perceiving objects directly gives us information about the immediate environment around us. However, these direct perceivers cannot remember these objects, nor can they relate one object to another to invent new items, plan how to use the things, or remember our previous experience with them so that we can apply what we learned to what we will do now. Thought enables us to do all this. However, the price we pay with thought is that the conceptual appearance is a conflation of objects at different times, in different places, or with different characteristics. Conceptual consciousnesses lack the vividness and clarity of direct perceivers.

Hearing the sounds of Dharma teachings on impermanence or seeing the black squiggles in a book about this topic involve nonconceptual, direct perception with our auditory and visual consciousnesses. Understanding and contemplating the meanings of these sounds and squiggles are done by conceptual consciousnesses. After we realize impermanence through inference with a conceptual consciousness, we continue meditating until we break through the conceptual appearance and perceive impermanence directly and nonconceptually. This realization is much more profound.

In my conversations with scientists I asked if they differentiate conceptual and nonconceptual consciousnesses. It seems that at this moment they do not. I wonder if there is a difference in brain activity between these two ways of cognizing objects. This is a new and interesting area to research.

Since a conceptual appearance of a table appears to be a table but isn't, conceptual consciousnesses are mistaken (*bhrānti*) in that they confuse the conceptual appearance with the actual object. However, not all conceptual consciousnesses are erroneous (*viparīta*). Confusion about an object can occur on two levels: the level of appearance and the level of apprehension. Conceptual consciousnesses that misapprehend their object—for example, thinking a scarecrow is a human being or believing that the person is truly existent—are erroneous and are not reliable cognizers. However, conceptions may also know their objects correctly even though they are mistaken. When we think about cooking food in a pot, the conceptual appearance of the pot mistakenly appears to be a pot. The conceptual cognizer of the pot correctly knows the pot and is useful in cooking a meal. It does not *apprehend* the pot and the conceptual appearance of the pot to be one—it does not think the conceptual appearance of the pot *is* this pot. Thus it is not an erroneous mind. However, on the level of appearance, the pot and its conceptual appearance *appear* to be mixed and this mind is mistaken with respect to its appearing object, the conceptual appearance of a pot, although it is not erroneous with respect to its apprehended object, the pot.

Language and thought are related. When we conceive an object, we give it a name, and when someone says that name, a conceptual appearance of the object appears in our mind. If someone says, "monkey," we think of a monkey. Can someone who does not know language—such as a baby or an animal—still have conceptions and thoughts? In the *Essence of Eloquence* Tsongkhapa says that although animals such as cows do not know words and terms, they do have thoughts, and these thoughts enable them to identify their calves.

By observing babies and animals, we can see that they identify things by means of conception, even though they don't know language. Although a baby does not know the word "mother," after some time he or she is able to identify a certain person and know this person is helpful. This is due to the conceptual appearance conflating the characteristics of his mother on many different days. He also understands she is very kind, even though he cannot express this understanding in words. A mother dog may smell another animal in the area near her puppies. Although she lacks language, she knows that danger is nearby and responds by protecting her puppies.

Learning to differentiate the way conceptual and nonconceptual consciousnesses apprehend their objects gives us a new and valuable tool to understand how our minds work. It enables us to be more aware of when we are conceptualizing and forming a myriad of opinions and judgments about someone, versus when we are actually experiencing and directly knowing the person. Seeing a person directly is very different from fabricating an image of him and daydreaming about him with our conceptual consciousness. Direct perceivers see the color and shape of food and smell its odor. This is different from imagining its taste and wondering if we will like it. If we think the food will be delicious, attachment will arise. But if the food isn't as good as we had anticipated, we will be discontent. So many emotions can arise in us based on these thoughts.

Differentiating conceptual and nonconceptual consciousnesses brings into vivid relief how we superimpose our past experiences onto the present and develop false expectations. If a child was bitten by a dog and experienced pain, his memory of that unpleasant experience is a conceptual consciousness. Later, when he sees a similar-looking dog, he remembers the previous experience and the conceptual consciousness conflates the present dog with the previous dog, causing him to become afraid of the dog in front of him even if the present dog is friendly. When he brings his attention to the present dog, he stops conflating the past and present dogs and stops projecting his memory of the previous dog onto his interaction with the present one.

REFLECTION

1. To identify conceptual and nonconceptual consciousnesses in your own experience, look at a color and listen to a sound. Minds that know these things are nonconceptual, sense direct perceivers.

2. Close your eyes. Remember the color, then the sound. These remembering consciousnesses are conceptual mental consciousnesses to which a conceptual appearance appears.

3. Which way of knowing the color and sound is more vivid and immediate, seeing or hearing it directly or remembering it?

4. Which is more useful for understanding how a muscle works—a direct perceiver of the color of the muscle or a conceptual consciousness thinking about the way to strengthen the muscle through correct exercise?

It can be challenging to greet situations and people freshly, without our conceptual consciousnesses superimposing previous pleasant or unpleasant memories or associations on them. Although in some cases our memories may have some truth that gives us useful information, at other times they are overlain with attachment, aversion, and confusion. The Zen expression "beginner's mind" refers to clearly seeing what is presently in front of us without projecting biased conceptions from the past onto present objects and people.

When we meditate, some of our distractions may be sparked by sense direct perceivers, for example, hearing a sound. If we just notice the sound and return to our object of meditation, the meditation session continues. However, sometimes we start thinking about the sound, "What a loud sound! Who made it? Doesn't she know I'm trying to meditate?" All these thoughts about the sound and the person making it are conceptual consciousnesses that become a major distraction.

We may think about someone, and an image of her appears to our mental consciousness. This conceptual appearance is not her; it is created by our mind having selected and pieced together a few of her characteristics. Ruminating on this image and on memories of past interactions with her, we generate judgments and opinions. Pretty soon, we find ourselves angry, even though the other person may be across the country. We may spend an entire meditation session being furious and planning what we're going to say to get revenge, when in fact nothing has happened. All this is due to faulty conceptualization.

REFLECTION

1. In the morning when thinking about who you will meet that day, notice your expectation of how an interaction will go with a person with whom you have had difficulty in the past.

2. Be aware that that person is not here now and today's interaction has not yet occurred.

3. To what extent will your expectation—which is just a conceptual appearance to your mind—become a self-fulfilling prophesy?

4. Try to release that expectation and approach the person with a relaxed and open mind. How does the interaction differ from your expectation?

Conceptions are involved in cultivating wisdom. The process of studying, reflecting, and meditating on the Buddha's teachings requires conceptual consciousnesses that give meaning to sounds and squiggles. Remembering what we have learned, reflecting on it, discussing and debating its meaning with others also involve conceptual consciousnesses. When we meditate, our initial understanding of topics such as emptiness is conceptual and our first realization is by means of an inferential cognizer, a conceptual consciousness. Although conceptual realizations cannot substitute for direct perceivers of emptiness, they are a useful and necessary stepping stone to gain a direct perceiver of this slightly obscure phenomena. By meditating on emptiness further, the veil of the conceptual appearance is gradually removed and emptiness appears directly and vividly to the mental consciousness, which is now a yogic direct perceiver.

In this chapter we have explored the varieties of phenomena that make up persons and our world. These include permanent and impermanent phenomena; among impermanent phenomena there are forms, consciousnesses, and abstract phenomena. We explored various way of looking at consciousness including differentiating primary consciousnesses and mental factors and discerning nonconceptual and conceptual consciousnesses. Being able to identify these phenomena and being mindful of their functions and relationships is the gist of understanding the external world of form as well as our internal world of mind. When we later investigate the question of what is the self, we will examine all these phenomena to determine if any of them is the person.

4 | Choosing Spiritual Mentors and Becoming a Qualified Disciple

THE DHARMA IS the key to having a meaningful and happy life now and in the future. To practice it seriously, two conditions must be present: The external condition is relying on the guidance of a qualified spiritual mentor. The internal condition is a precious human life with the freedom and fortune to practice the Dharma. The stages of the path begin with these two essential topics. This and the next chapter address the relationship between a qualified spiritual mentor and a qualified disciple, as well as the importance of those qualities and the method to cultivate them.

Importance of Relying on Spiritual Mentors

When we are seriously interested in following the path, forming a healthy relationship with a qualified spiritual teacher is essential. If we need teachers for ordinary skills such as driving or typing, we certainly need them for more complex and delicate endeavors such as transforming our mind into that of a buddha. Tsongkhapa tells us (LC 1:70):

> Thus the excellent teacher is the source of all temporary happiness and highest goodness, beginning with the production of a single good quality and the reduction of a single fault in a student's mind and eventually encompassing all the knowledge beyond that.

Spiritual teachers play a unique and important role in our lives. Qualified spiritual mentors guide us along the path by giving us teachings,

Dharma advice, precepts, oral transmissions, and empowerments. When we experience blocks in our practice, they teach us the antidotes to overcome them. When we have spiritual experiences, they help us determine if the experiences were authentic or deceptive. When our practice is progressing well, our spiritual mentors encourage us to continue. The *Sutta on Half (of the Holy Life)* (*Upaḍḍha Sutta*, SN 45.2) relates a conversation between the Buddha and his disciple Ānanda about the importance of a spiritual teacher. Thinking that a successful Dharma practice is half due to spiritual teachers and half to one's own effort, Ānanda says to the Buddha, "Venerable Sir, this is half of the holy life, that is, spiritual friendship, spiritual companionship, spiritual comradeship." While our own effort is undoubtedly essential, to emphasize that the spiritual path cannot be actualized without a spiritual mentor, the Buddha replies:

> Not so, Ānanda! Not so Ānanda! This is the entire holy life, Ānanda, that is, spiritual friendship, spiritual companionship, spiritual comradeship. When a monastic has a spiritual friend, a spiritual companion, a spiritual comrade, it is to be expected that he will develop and cultivate the noble eightfold path... By the following method, too, Ānanda, it may be understood how the entire holy life is spiritual friendship, spiritual companionship, spiritual comradeship: By relying on me as a spiritual friend, Ānanda, beings subject to birth are freed from birth; beings subject to aging are feed from aging; beings subject to death are freed from death; beings subject to sorrow, lamentation, pain, displeasure, and despair are freed from sorrow, lamentation, pain, displeasure, and despair. By this method, Ānanda, it may be understood how the entire holy life is spiritual friendship, spiritual companionship, spiritual comradeship.

This passage has sometimes been taken out of context and interpreted to mean that having ordinary friends who practice the Dharma is the entire spiritual life. While having such friends is a boost to our practice, it is clear in the sūtra that the Buddha is referring to himself as the spiritual teacher whose spiritual friendship is crucial and must not be neglected. By extension, our spiritual mentors become the virtuous friends that guide us when the Buddha is no longer physically present.

In the context of training in samādhi and meditation, Buddhaghosa emphasizes the importance of relying on a spiritual teacher (Vism 3.126):

> When he dedicates himself to a teacher, he should say, "I relinquish this, my person, to you, Venerable." For one who has not dedicated his person thus becomes unresponsive to correction, hard to speak to, and not amenable to advice, or he goes where he likes without asking the teacher. Consequently, the teacher does not help him with either material needs or the Dhamma, and does not train him in the scriptures. Failing to get these two kinds of help, he finds no footing in the doctrine, and he soon descends to inappropriate behavior or to the lay state. But if he has dedicated his person, he is not unresponsive to correction, does not go about as he likes, is easy to speak to, and lives in dependence on the teacher. He receives the twofold help from the teacher and attains growth, increase, and fulfillment in the doctrine.

Spiritual Mentors

The Sanskrit name for a spiritual teacher is *guru*—*lama* in Tibetan. Both of these terms have the connotation of someone heavy with good qualities and superior in spiritual qualities. These terms do not have the connotation of someone being a living buddha, for not all gurus are awakened. If we said that all gurus are buddhas, there would be some gurus who became buddhas without working very hard on the path! Mistakenly thinking that all teachers are buddhas and later discovering that a certain person lacks all the qualities of an awakened one not only leaves us disappointed but also puts the lama in a difficult situation. The only thing the lama can do then is just shake his head because he lacks all of a buddha's qualities. Therefore it makes more sense to follow the real connotation of the terms "lama" and "guru" because genuine spiritual teachers have superior qualities in comparison to their followers.

Being a Dharma teacher depends on other people wanting to take that person as their teacher. In Tibet in the past, a person did not become a teacher by being appointed by some authority. Rather, through diligent training a person became a good practitioner. A small group who saw that person's qualities asked him to teach. As those students practiced and developed good qualities, others gained respect for the teacher, and gradually that person became known as a great teacher.

Similarly, nowadays in monasteries the process of becoming a teacher occurs within the monastic structure. Monastics study for their geshe or khenpo degree. Students in the lower classes then ask the new geshes and khenpos who are respected for their learning, understanding, and memorization to teach. When students benefit from the explanations and guidance of the new geshes and khenpos, they become known as good teachers and other monastics are eager to attend their classes.

In the contemporary secular world, "teacher" connotes someone in an academic field who, after completing certain requirements, is certified as a teacher by an organization, whether or not that person has any students. Perhaps in the West that model would be better. That is for Westerners to determine. In that case, Buddhists could form an organization that certifies people as teachers after examining their Dharma understanding as well as their personal conduct. However, an organization cannot certify someone's spiritual attainments, so issuing certificates attesting to attainment of spiritual realization or level of the path does not make sense. In any case, it is not necessary to be a realized master to teach at a Dharma center. A good education in Buddhism, personal integrity, and genuine care for the students' well-being are sufficient.

Although we are the ones who choose our spiritual mentors, there are certain conditions under which someone becomes one of our teachers—for example, if they give us refuge and the five precepts, monastic ordination, bodhisattva ethical restraints, or tantric initiation. For this reason, it is necessary that we check the person's qualifications before attending these ceremonies and not rush blindly into things.

Buddhism is spreading to countries where it has not existed before, and there it encounters different cultural values and ways of doing things. The model of a spiritual mentor-disciple relationship that has existed for centuries in Asia does not easily transplant into a secular modern society.

Traditional spiritual mentors and contemporary students raised in secular societies both enter into a teacher-student relationship with expectations that they may not be aware of.

In traditional Tibetan Buddhist monasteries, there are many types of teachers: Some are like parents who look after the physical well-being of the young monastics, teach them the alphabet, and guide them in appropriate behavior in the monastery. More advanced students teach the lower-level debate and philosophy classes. Geshes teach the more advanced classes, while rinpoches—both ordained and lay—and some geshes give initiations and tantric teachings. Tibetan monastics and lay followers relate to these people differently, according to their role in that individual's practice, their standing in the monastery, and their reputation in Tibetan society. When Tibetans go to other countries, people in the Dharma centers do not necessarily know what kind of teacher is coming, and out of respect they treat everyone as though he were a highly esteemed lama. This can create misunderstandings.

The expectations for a secular teacher and a Dharma teacher differ greatly. In a secular educational facility, students trust that the school hires competent teachers. They often do not choose their teachers; if they need to attend a required class, students take it from whoever is teaching it. The teacher's job is to impart information and knowledge; they seldom get involved in a student's personal development as a human being. Students who are experiencing difficulties are usually referred to a school counselor. Students in colleges and universities pay to attend, and they fill out evaluation forms of the classes and teachers at the end of the semester. Teachers are hired employees in a paid position who can be fired if their work or behavior is not up to standard. Teachers and students do not live together, and after the semester is done they go their separate ways.

In the past, children in secular schools were taught to respect their teachers, but depending on the country, that is often not the case nowadays. The advent of online classes has changed the teacher-student relationship even more, so that teachers and students may never meet in person. The teacher's job is to plan the curriculum and assess the student's assimilation of knowledge; the student's job is to learn the material. There is little sense of personal connection to each other, the other person simply being a name or face on the computer screen.

A relationship with a Dharma teacher—here meaning a qualified spiritual mentor who teaches the sūtras and commentaries—is different. The focus of this relationship is not only the conveyance of knowledge but also character building. The teacher is responsible for guiding students spiritually over time so that they become ethical, kind, and wise human beings with the correct understanding of the Buddha's teachings and the ability to meditate on them.

In the context of the Dharma, disciples and students are expected to investigate a prospective teacher's qualities before taking him or her as one of their spiritual mentors, because a mentor-disciple relationship is expected to be lifelong. This is not the case when studying with a secular teacher in school.

In addition, Dharma teachers traditionally do not charge for teachings and students do not pay their teachers; they support them by making offerings and volunteering their services. Here the motivation is one of gratitude, and the offering is given to create merit; it is not payment due, as in a business relationship. As part of their spiritual development, Dharma students are taught to appreciate and respect their teachers. This helps to reduce the students' arrogance and increases their receptivity to learning the Dharma. There is a natural hierarchy in the spiritual mentor-disciple relationship that is useful for subduing students' self-centered attitude. Students do not seek equal status with their teachers.

In traditional monastic settings, teachers and students may live in the same building, with students caring for some of the teacher's personal needs, such as preparing meals, cleaning, making appointments, running errands, and organizing events.

In entering a relationship with a spiritual mentor, having appropriate expectations is important. Although we may have emotional needs, the role of Dharma teachers is not to fulfill these. Complications arise if we have conscious or unconscious expectations that our spiritual mentors will meet our emotional needs, be our psychotherapist, tell us whom to marry, or choose our career. The role of spiritual mentors is to guide us in learning the Dharma, critically reflecting on its meaning, and correctly meditating on it. This is why it is so important to be under their guidance. However, spiritual mentors do not do the work of gaining realizations for us. We must practice the Dharma ourselves.

In brief, the differences in roles and expectations between a traditional Dharma teacher-disciple relationship and a contemporary, secular teacher-student relationship are great. It is important for everyone to be aware of these as we navigate the uncharted waters of the Dharma as it flows into new countries and cultures.

REFLECTION

1. Why is it important to have spiritual mentors?

2. How does the relationship with a spiritual mentor differ from one with a schoolteacher or professor?

Three Types of Practice, Three Types of Spiritual Mentors

Tibetan Buddhism includes three types of practice, each with its own emphasis, method of practice, and ethical restraints: Fundamental Vehicle, Perfection Vehicle, and Vajra Vehicle. In the Fundamental Vehicle, students learn the four truths of āryas and come to seek liberation from cyclic existence. To bring this about, they take refuge in the Three Jewels and practice the three higher trainings. In terms of ethical restraints, they avoid the ten nonvirtues and take prātimokṣa precepts as a lay or monastic follower of the Buddha. The lay precepts consist of the five precepts—to abandon killing, stealing, unwise or unkind sexual behavior, lying, and taking intoxicants. The monastic precepts include those of novice and fully ordained monastics.

On this basis, we go on to practice the Perfection Vehicle, which is one branch of Mahāyāna.[26] Here students learn and meditate on the methods to cultivate bodhicitta and come to seek full awakening in order to benefit others most effectively. To actualize this, they take the bodhisattva precepts and engage in practicing the six perfections of generosity, ethical conduct, fortitude, joyous effort, meditative stability, and wisdom.

The Vajra Vehicle is also a branch of the Mahāyāna, and thus the motivation to practice it is the same. Practitioners enter the Vajra Vehicle because their compassion is exceptionally strong. They want to attain awakening quickly because they cannot endure sentient beings' suffering. To accomplish this, they receive empowerment into the practice of a tantric deity and engage in the practice of deity yoga. All tantric practitioners adopt the bodhisattva ethical code, and those initiated into the yoga tantra and highest yoga tantra also adopt the tantric ethical code.

These three types of practice have three types of teachers. Many similarities exist in the qualifications of each type of teacher and the way students relate to them, but differences also exist. Fundamental Vehicle, Perfection Vehicle, and Vajra Vehicle texts reveal a progression in the way of regarding and relating to teachers. Our Fundamental Vehicle teacher instructs us in the four truths, gives us refuge and lay or monastic precepts, and teaches us the Vinaya, the monastic discipline. As such, he or she acts as a representative of the Buddha. We see our teacher as a teacher, our preceptor as a preceptor, and relate to him or her on a human level. We regard him as a wise elder, a sincere practitioner from whom we can learn.

For monastics, three Vinaya teachers are important for their training. The first is their preceptor or abbot/abbess (*upādhyāya, upādhyāyā*), the person heading the saṅgha of monastics that ordains them. Second is the activity instructor (*karma ācārya*), who gives guidance and instruction during the ordination ceremony. Third is the interview instructor (*raho 'nuśāsaka ācārya*), who privately interviews the candidate to see if obstacles to ordination exist. Another important teacher is the resident teacher (T. *gnas kyi bla ma*), the principal teacher of the monastery in which the monastic resides. Vinaya puts great importance on the resident teacher because that is the person who trains the junior monastics on a daily basis.

Perfection Vehicle texts speak of buddhas and bodhisattvas emanating in many forms to benefit others. Since our Perfection Vehicle teacher leads us on the bodhisattva path and gives us the bodhisattva ethical restraints, we view that person as an emanation of the Buddha or a high bodhisattva. Here the teacher is seen as equal to, or like, a buddha in the sense that the karma accumulated in relation to our teacher is similar to that accumulated in relation to the Buddha. By making offerings to or harming our Perfection Vehicle teacher, we accumulate karma equal to acting in a similar way toward the Buddha himself.

When we have trained in the Fundamental Vehicle and Perfection Vehicle practices and are sufficiently mature in the Dharma, we may request empowerment into practices of various tantric meditational deities. Students imagine the guru giving the empowerment to be the meditational deity and the environment to be the deity's abode or maṇḍala. When doing tantric practice following empowerment, we imagine ourselves and all sentient beings as buddhas and the environment as a pure land. In this case not seeing our tantric master as a buddha would be strange.

Only in tantric practice is it essential to regard the tantric master as a buddha. This view should not be taught to beginners who are not mature in the Dharma, because it is open to misinterpretation and confusion.

I recommend going about the stages of practice in a gradual way. First form a relationship with a Fundamental Vehicle teacher, learn the four truths, and take refuge and some level of prātimokṣa precepts. Later, as your practice progresses, seek out a spiritual mentor who can teach you the bodhisattva path, practice the six perfections, and undertake the bodhisattva ethical restraints. After some time, when you are properly prepared, seek a qualified tantric master, receive empowerment into that practice, and meditate on deity yoga.

Shabkar Tsokdruk Rangdrol, the great Tibetan yogi who did extensive retreat and was a prolific writer, speaks of these three kinds of teachers:

> From the teacher who showed the path of deliverance,
> I received the sacred teachings of individual liberation.
> My practice was to shun wrongdoing and cultivate virtue.
>
> From the bodhisattva teacher,
> I received the sacred Mahāyāna teachings on generating
>   bodhicitta.
> My practice was to cherish others more than myself.
>
> From the Vajradhara teacher,
> I received the sacred teachings, empowerments, and
>   instructions of the secret Mantrayāna.
> My practice was to meditate upon the generation and
>   completion states, and Dzogchen.[27]

Investigate a Person's Qualities

If, like a spiritual mentor, the pilot of a plane is not well trained, traveling with him or her is risky. To help disciples assess the training of a potential spiritual mentor, the Buddha explained the qualities of the various types of spiritual teachers. Students are responsible for evaluating the qualifications of prospective teachers and choosing with whom they wish to form a mentor-disciple relationship. Sakya Paṇḍita commented that people are very careful and diligently test the purity of jewels before purchasing them. Examining spiritual mentors and teachings is even more important than checking the quality of jewels, since we are seeking the truth that will lead us to lasting happiness. We should not run after spiritual mentors like dogs gobbling up meat. Instead of being impressed by titles and elaborate thrones, we must seek spiritual mentors who are learned and practice well.

Some people are naive and easily misled by charismatic teachers who claim to be spiritually realized. In the West this may happen because Buddhism is new and people do not yet know the qualities to look for in good teachers. Difficulties arise in Asia too. Some years ago, a person from mainland China came to see me and said that a false lama from Tibet had gone to China and claimed to be a Dharma king, but was actually seeking money and sex. Blind to his true motivation, some Chinese were devoted to him. Similar things have happened in Mongolia as well.

The Buddha would not have described in detail the qualifications for choosing suitable spiritual guides if simply having great faith in anyone called a "teacher" or "lama" were sufficient. Although we may be attracted to a person who is charismatic, entertaining, or makes us feel good, these are not signs of having Dharma knowledge or spiritual attainments. Our spiritual teachers should be people we can rely on and trust and who have correct knowledge of the Dharma and its practice.

We must investigate and examine a teacher thoroughly before deciding that he or she will be one of our teachers. Immediately accepting someone as our teacher without proper investigation is unwise. I recommend that people attend Dharma teachings and get to know the person first. At this time, do not regard him or her as your teacher, let alone as a buddha. Consider the person as a Dharma friend who shares information with you. Observe his or her conduct in daily life, and assess his understanding of the teachings as best as you can. Ask other students about the teacher's qualities, and look at the qualities of those students to see if you want to become like them by following the same teacher. Check if the teacher has a good relationship with his or her teachers. In addition, read Dharma books so that you have a general knowledge of Buddhist tenets and can assess if this person's teachings are correct. After some time, if you see that this person teaches in accord with the Buddhadharma, is reliable, knowledgeable, ethical, kind, and a good practitioner, then form a mentor-disciple relationship with him or her.

The Buddha recommends that prospective disciples examine even the Buddha himself (MN 47). But how is an unawakened, ordinary being who "does not know the mind of another as it really is" to investigate this? The Buddha instructs us to first use empirical observation, watching the person's behavior and listening to his or her speech to see if defilements are present or if his speech and deeds are pure. Then examine how he or she handles the role of a teacher: Is he attracted to gaining respect and offerings or does he have genuine compassion for his disciples and a sincere wish to guide them on the path? Third, directly ask the teacher if he has eliminated observable faults and if he is accomplished in the Vinaya and the Dharma. Doing this assumes the person is neither deluded regarding his own practice nor lying. It is rather bold to ask a teacher this question, and most accomplished teachers will be hesitant to discuss their level of attainment. However, if we are satisfied so far by our investigation of the teacher, we then practice what he teaches and see the results for ourselves. If, through diligent and correct practice, we realize the result the teacher described, then we know with certainty through our own experience that he is a reliable spiritual mentor.

Having a hundred or even a thousand qualified spiritual mentors is fine. But if teachers are not qualified, it is better not to have any and to rely on Dharma texts until we meet qualified mentors. However, to receive monastic ordination or tantric empowerment, we must rely on a living person. We cannot receive these from a text or by ourselves. Since this is the case, in these areas you must wait until you meet a qualified teacher.

Qualities of a Spiritual Mentor

According to the three types of spiritual teachers, there are three sets of qualities to look for. Śākyaprabha's *Three Hundred Verses on the Novice* (*Śrāmaṇeratriśatakakārikā*) describes the qualities of a suitable Vinaya teacher:

1. Keeping pure ethical conduct.
2. Having knowledge of what to practice and abandon on the path as well as of Vinaya rituals and procedures.
3. Having compassion for the sick.
4. Having disciples who are gentle, kind, and wise.
5. Providing their monastic disciples with requisites for living and Dharma teachings.
6. Being able to teach a Dharma topic at the right time to a disciple capable of benefiting from it.

In short, a Fundamental Vehicle teacher should have the following three qualities:

1. This person is worthy of respect because he or she is self-disciplined and has refined behavior as a result of keeping the precepts purely and serious Dharma practice. Also, this person is willing to help the disciple whenever required.
2. He or she has stable ethical conduct. For monastics, this means the person has been fully ordained for at least ten years.
3. He or she is learned and wise, having profound knowledge of the three baskets of scriptures (Tripiṭaka).

Fundamental Vehicle teachers should also be disillusioned with cyclic existence and not seek worldly success or many possessions for themselves. They should also have strength to endure the difficulties involved in teaching and guiding disciples.

In *Ornament of Mahāyāna Sūtras* (*Mahāyānasūtrālaṃkāra*), Maitreya described the ten qualities of a fully qualified Perfection Vehicle mentor (17.10):

> Rely on a friend who is subdued, calm, and quiet;
> has more virtue, is energetic, learned in scripture;
> has realized suchness, is endowed with eloquence, has
>   a compassionate nature, and ignores weariness.

To present these qualities in an expanded way, a fully qualified Perfection Vehicle teacher:

1. Is disciplined and subdued in his or her behavior (higher training in ethical conduct).
2. Has serenity and meditative experience (higher training in concentration).
3. Is pacified through developing wisdom (higher training in wisdom).
4. Has more qualities than the student.
5. Is enthusiastic to practice Dharma and benefit others.
6. Is learned in the scriptures.
7. Has realized the emptiness of all phenomena, not just the emptiness of the person. This refers to having the correct view of selflessness.[28]
8. Is skillful in giving teachings, articulate, and able to explain the Dharma clearly.
9. Is compassionate, always wishing to benefit others.
10. Does not easily become tired or discouraged by expounding the Dharma to others.

It is important for a Mahāyāna spiritual mentor to possess the first three qualities—the three higher trainings—because without having disciplined and subdued one's own body, speech, and mind, subduing those of others will be difficult.

Someone may be able to discipline her own mind, but without other qualities she will not be able to adequately guide others in the methods for transforming their minds. Thus wide knowledge and understanding of the Mahāyāna teachings as expressed in the fourth, sixth, and seventh qualities are necessary. Such a teacher has discerned the exact meaning of the Buddha's teachings by employing reasoning and scriptural quotations. She also has a broad knowledge and understanding of the path, which is necessary to lead sentient beings with a variety of dispositions and capabilities to awakening.

The remaining qualities—the fifth, eighth, ninth, and tenth—demonstrate that a spiritual teacher wishes to benefit others and has the ability to endure the hardships of guiding them.

The ten qualities of an excellent spiritual mentor may be abbreviated in three: he or she should be learned and wise, disciplined, and have a kind heart. His discipline should not prevent learnedness, and his learnedness should not lead to the neglect of discipline. Even if he has both learning and discipline, if he lacks a kind heart, he will not be able to help others on a vast scale. If he has a kind heart, but lacks learning and discipline, he will likewise be unable to lead others on the path. Thus all three qualities are necessary.

Although finding teachers with all ten qualities fully developed may be difficult, try to find teachers with as many of those qualities as possible. Follow teachers who have at least more good qualities than negative ones, are more interested in future lives than in this life, and consider others more important than themselves.

The qualities of a suitable tantric master are explained in all four classes of tantra. This person should have the qualities of a Perfection Vehicle spiritual mentor and have received empowerment into Vajrayāna. In addition to keeping the tantric precepts and commitments purely, he or she should have studied the practices well, completed the appropriate retreats and concluding fire pūjā, and experienced some deep insight through this path. In the case of a highest yoga tantra guru, the person should optimally have some stability in, if not realization of, the completion stage. Otherwise seek a person who has stability in the generation stage practice; however, if they do not have the correct understanding of emptiness, their practice is lacking. For a tantric guru, the determination to be free from saṃsāra and an understanding of emptiness that is complemented by bodhicitta is presupposed. Clearly not everyone who recites tantric sādhanas is qualified to give empowerments and tantric instructions! In *Fifty Verses of Relying on a Spiritual Master* (*Gurupañcāśikā*), Aśvaghoṣa describes the qualities of a vajra master in detail. These will be explained in a later volume on tantra.

Do not be too quick to regard a person as your spiritual mentor. Rather, for however long it takes—two years, five years, or longer—regard this person as a spiritual friend. In the meantime, examine his or her behavior, attitudes, and ways of teaching until you are confident of his or her integrity and ability to guide you.

In certain situations a Dharma connection is automatically formed, and after that you should regard that person as one of your spiritual mentors. A person who gives you refuge, the five lay precepts, or monastic precepts becomes one of your Vinaya teachers. Those from whom you receive the bodhisattva ethical restraints become your Perfection Vehicle teachers.

Someone who gives you an empowerment, tantric transmission, or tantric commentary becomes one of your Vajrayāna masters.

REFLECTION

1. One by one, contemplate qualities for a Fundamental Vehicle, Perfection Vehicle, and Vajrayāna spiritual mentor.

2. Reflect on the purpose of the three sets of qualities and how each applies to the respective stage of development of the disciple.

3. Make a determination to examine the qualities of prospective spiritual mentors and to choose wisely.

Seek Internal Qualities, Not Titles or External Appearance

Some people may believe that the titles a person has indicates whether he or she is a qualified spiritual mentor. However, this is not necessarily the case. Each Buddhist tradition employs an array of titles that can be confusing to newcomers and that are not necessarily used in a systematic fashion.

Nowadays the title *lama* is used in a variety of ways—in some cases it indicates a Dharma teacher, in others it indicates someone who has completed a three-year retreat. Some people are qualified teachers, but out of humility do not want to be called lama, while some people who have not done extensive study and practice are eager to assume that title.

Geshe is a degree awarded by the large monasteries after the completion of many years of serious scriptural study and debate. In general, geshes have vast learning in the scriptures and some also have meditative experience and realizations. However, after completing their studies, some geshes are eager to go abroad not just to teach but to receive offerings.

Khenpo indicates an abbot of a monastery and *khensur* a former abbot, although in some Tibetan traditions, khenpo is an educational degree similar to geshe. *Gen-la* is used to address adult monks, our own Dharma teacher, or teachers of secular subjects as well. *Choe-la* is the respectful way to address a nun.

Tulku is a title given to someone recognized as the reincarnation of a previous master. *Tulku* literally means an emanation body of a buddha, but not everyone with this title is an emanation of the Buddha or even a bodhisattva. There are different levels of tulkus according to the respect and renown of the previous master.

Rinpoche, which means "precious one," is often used to address tulkus. Some students call their teachers who are not recognized incarnations "Gen Rinpoche" (precious teacher) to indicate their respect. Having the title *rinpoche* does not indicate that one has spiritual realizations. Some may be manifestations of buddhas or of ārya bodhisattvas—those who have directly perceived emptiness and compassionately manifest to benefit sentient beings. Others may be lower-level bodhisattvas who have not yet eradicated afflictions and are not able to control the rebirth process. Still other people are identified as incarnations of great masters due to their accumulation of merit in the past, even though they have not entered even the first of the five bodhisattva paths. We should not assume that everyone who uses the title rinpoche is a realized being.

The system of recognizing incarnations of previous spiritual masters is a Tibetan cultural tradition. It is not a practice taught by the Buddha. In the 1960s I discussed limiting the number of tulkus, but one adviser told me that would be difficult because it is the Tibetans' custom. Nowadays being recognized as a rinpoche has become a position of social status, not one of religious import, and this is not healthy.

We should seek teachers who are well-educated in the Dharma, practice it sincerely, and have compassion for others. In looking at Tibetan society, I often see people ignoring learned geshes and khenpos but showing great respect to rinpoches who are not learned. I tell the young rinpoches that they should not rely on the reputation of their previous lives but should study diligently, practice sincerely, and be humble in this life. If they do, they will be an honor to their predecessor's name. If they do not and merely use their social status to manipulate or deceive others, they are a disgrace, not only to their predecessor but also to the Buddhadharma.

Nowadays, many people look for the incarnations of their deceased teachers, but letting a child speak for him- or herself is better. A child may display obvious characteristics, such as clearly remembering a previous life or reciting texts not memorized in this life. In such cases, we cannot fail to recognize that the child is unusual. Only then could recognition as a tulku possibly be beneficial.

I favor allowing children to grow up naturally and to develop their qualities in this life. Those who have gained spiritual realizations in the past will naturally progress in their own practice and benefit others in this life whether or not they are identified and given a title.

Some people who are unknown in Tibetan society go to the West or Taiwan and suddenly have many titles and are publicized as great teachers. This is completely inappropriate. One lama from Amdo commented to me that in the past lamas' names were short but the list of their realizations was long. But now they have very long and lofty titles, and the list of their realizations is short.

Teachers who are monastics must wear monastic robes, and those who are not monastics should not wear monastic robes or even maroon clothing that resembles monastic robes. The general public as well as Buddhists become very confused when they see a teacher, whom they believe to be a monastic, with a spouse and children. Lay teachers should wear lay clothes, or if they wear a long robe, it should be white and their upper shawl should be predominantly white but with some maroon stripes. For many years I have recommended this and am happy to see at least some lay teachers follow my advice.

Although the Buddhadharma flourished in Tibet, the general public's level of understanding of the Buddhadharma was low. Many people would look at the height of a teacher's throne or the number of horses in his procession to determine who to respect. They didn't consider that a famous bandit would also have many horses in his caravan!

In Tibet, and now in exile, some people placed great emphasis on external appearance—brocade robes, colorful costumes, and the shape and size of hats. But our Teacher, Śākyamuni Buddha, did not have a hat; nor did he wear special robes. His robes were the same as those of other monastics. Even though some of the Indian masters, such as Asaṅga and Candrakīrti, are depicted with big hats, it is questionable whether such hats were worn in the great Indian monastic universities such as Nālandā.

In Tibet there was perhaps some reason for wearing a hat because the weather was cold. Bald teachers especially found hats helpful! However, Tibetans went to an extreme and made hats in elaborate shapes, sizes, and designs, so much so that some foreigners came to distinguish the different schools of Tibetan Buddhism by the color of their hats. This is very unfortunate. In addition to the yellow, red, and black hats that are so famous, perhaps monastics nowadays could wear green hats, indicating that they care for the environment!

We must try to understand the essence of the Buddha's teachings and the commentaries of the great Indian masters. By doing so, we will see that the true gauge for evaluating the quality of a teacher is his or her understanding and behavior. Faith in spiritual teachers should be well earned. Some great teachers, such as Milarepa, looked like poverty-stricken beggars. The Kadam master Dromtonpa was a humble nomad. The twentieth-century Dzogchen master Dza Patrul Rinpoche looked like an ordinary wanderer. These truly great spiritual masters had no external appearance of grandeur. Our priority should be understanding the meaning of the Dharma, not wearing elegant robes, donning colorful costumes and hats, sitting on expensive seats, or riding in luxurious vehicles. Nowadays we have to add sporting expensive watches and displaying a range of costly technological gadgets to this list. Of course, every lama says this when teaching, but in their own lives some do not follow it.

Recently the emphasis on elaborate rituals—complete with drums, cymbals, dances, and colorful masks—has increased in the Tibetan tradition, and the emphasis on teaching has diminished. The time has come to change this and to return to the Nālandā tradition of ancient India. Practitioners' philosophical views and conduct must be grounded in the teachings of the Buddha and the great Indian masters. We must simplify ceremonies and rituals, strengthen our philosophical understanding, and implement the teachings in daily life. If we do this, Buddhism will play an important and meaningful role in the upcoming centuries. If we do not, it could degenerate into mere show.

It is important for all of us who consider ourselves to be followers of the Buddha to constantly check our motivation. In my own case, whenever I sit on a high throne to teach, self-importance and pride seldom arise. Even so, I notice that occasionally my thoughts become defiled by the eight worldly concerns. I think how nice it would be if people complimented me on my

Dharma talk and how disappointed I would be if they criticized it. Our vulnerability to worldly concerns is real, so we must be extremely careful. To ensure that we are engaging in genuine Dharma practice, we must check that our motivation is not defiled by the eight worldly concerns. Otherwise, self-importance will lead us to have other faults. It then becomes easy to abuse power, greedily seek offerings from the faithful, or manipulate others. We may even envy other teachers and compete with them. All of these corruptions arise once we become proud. However, when we honor the responsibility that comes with sharing the Dharma with others, we will constantly monitor our motivation and repeatedly turn our mind to benefiting others.

REFLECTION

1. Why is following the guidance of a spiritual mentor important?

2. What kind of qualities do you want to look for in selecting a spiritual mentor?

3. Are you easily influenced by titles, external appearances, and charisma? If so, what ideas do you have for redirecting your focus to important qualities?

Becoming a Qualified Disciple

In addition to seeking qualified teachers, we must make ourselves into receptive vessels so that we can benefit from our mentors' instructions. We may receive profound teachings from excellent mentors, but without attempting to develop the qualities of a good disciple, the benefit will be minimal. Āryadeva describes the qualities of a disciple who will realize the meaning of selflessness (CŚ 276):

> An unprejudiced, intelligent, and interested
> listener is called a vessel.

The first quality for suitable Mahāyāna students is being *impartial and open-minded*. We should try to be free from preconceptions and not close-mindedly cling to our own views. If we are biased, we will follow only the teachings that please our ego and accord with our own ideas. Dismissing valuable teachings that challenge our opinions hampers our spiritual progress.

Intelligence is the second quality of a disciple. This does not refer to intelligence in academic subjects, but to having the discriminative intelligence that can discern correct and incorrect views as well as what to practice and what to abandon. Without intelligence, our actions, meditation practice, and view will be skewed.

Intelligent and discerning disciples also examine the source of a teaching and are not satisfied unless they know it originated with the Buddha. They investigate if that teaching has been studied and explained by sages, actualized by yogis, and translated by excellent translators. Using reasoning and scriptural citations, they establish a teaching's validity.

Even if students are open-minded and intelligent, if they do not practice, they will not progress. Therefore, *interest*, diligence, eagerness, and commitment to engage in the practice are essential for spiritual transformation.

Two more qualities of a suitable disciple are often added to these three. The first, *respect and veneration* toward the teacher and teaching, makes us a receptive vessel to receive the Dharma, whereas arrogance and apathy prevent spiritual growth. Appreciating our teachers' wisdom and kindness and respecting the excellent qualities of the teachings moistens our minds, making it receptive to the Buddhadharma.

Attentively taking the teacher's advice and instructions to heart by putting them into practice enables us to plumb the depth of the teachings and integrate them into our very being. Do not think that these instructions must be given one-on-one. Even when we are in an audience of a thousand people, our mentor's spiritual instructions remain the key to actualizing the path.

People who sincerely wish to attain liberation or full awakening will cultivate these qualities in order to become receptive disciples and increase the benefit they receive from listening to teachings. In doing so, they become more self-confident and responsible in their Dharma practice. With clear understanding, they will be capable of receiving teachings and empowerments from various spiritual mentors and lineages without becoming either confused or sectarian. Not falling into mistaken ideas of "surrendering everything to the guru," they will not be led astray by teachers with impure motivations. Instead they will derive great benefit from relationships with qualified spiritual mentors. Their clarity of mind and good qualities will increase, and they will become good examples for newcomers on the path.

This book began with an explanation of the two truths, the four truths of the āryas, and the noncontradictory nature of dependent arising and emptiness. These instructions guide a practitioner of middle capacity on the path to liberation and enable a sharp-faculty advanced disciple to ascertain the possibility of attaining full awakening. When you understand these instructions well, you will know the kind of qualities a spiritual mentor must have to guide a disciple on the path to liberation and full awakening. You will also understand the qualities a disciple must have to be a receptive vessel, and the way the disciple should rely on the spiritual mentor.

To illustrate the importance of being an intelligent disciple, the Buddha gives the example of misguided people and intelligent ones who want to get the poison from a water snake in order to use it as medicine. A misguided person grasps the snake's coils or its tail, enabling the snake to turn its head around and bite him. The poison that this person sought to make into medicine now makes him suffer. Similarly, a person may hear or read the Dharma but not think about it clearly. He thereby injects his own preconceptions into the teaching, twisting the meaning to conform to his ideas, which are based on attachment and animosity. Or, due to ignorance, he misunderstands the actual meaning of the teachings and practices that. This person may also have the wrong motivation, learning the Dharma for the sake of criticizing others or winning a debate. Sadly, a person who incorrectly grasps the teachings often does not realize he is doing so and instead proceeds to share his distorted understanding with others, harming not only himself but others as well. This damage may affect many future lifetimes.

On the other hand, intelligent people grasp the snake's head, and by pressing it in a certain way, extract the poison and make it into medicine. Similarly, wise disciples learn the Dharma and examine the meaning with wisdom. Through wise investigation, they will come to correct conclusions and accept the teachings. Their motivation is to derive spiritual benefit, and they succeed in doing this, thus bringing happiness to themselves and others for a long time to come. The Buddha concludes the simile with this advice (MN 22.12):

> When you understand the meaning of my statements, remember it accordingly; and when you do not understand the meaning of my statements, then ask either me or those monastics who are wise about it.

We, too, should ask our teachers and other senior Dharma students when we do not understand a teaching. Even when we think we understand a teaching properly, it is always good to check our understanding with those who are more knowledgeable and skilled in practice than we are. In that way, the Dharma will be wonderful medicine that cures our own and others' suffering.

In case someone misunderstands the simile of the snake and thinks that Dharma is something to grasp onto and identify with, the Buddha continues the sūtra using the simile of the raft. This simile illustrates that, having understood the teachings correctly, we should use them to cross the ocean of saṃsāra and reach the shore of nirvāṇa, without clinging to the teachings unnecessarily.

A traveler comes across a large body of water. The bank where he stands is dangerous, but the far side is safe. Since there is no ferry, he binds branches together to make a raft and, holding onto the raft correctly, paddles to the other shore. Feeling relieved upon safely reaching the other shore, the traveler should not hoist the raft on his shoulder and carry it around because of attachment to the raft. The sensible thing to do is to set the raft down and go on his way.

Similarly, we are on the frightful, dangerous bank of the ocean of saṃsāra, the other side is nirvāṇa, and the raft to carry us there is the Dharma. When learning the Dharma, we must make sure we hold it correctly. However, once we attain liberation, we will not be attached to the Dharma, cling to an identity of being a Dharma practitioner, or boast of our attainment to others. Just as the purpose of the raft is to cross dangerous water, not to have something to carry around with us, the purpose of the Dharma is to liberate us from cyclic existence, not to give us an identity to grasp with attachment. The Buddha says (MN 22.14):

> When you know the Dhamma to be similar to a raft, you should abandon even the Dhamma; how much more so what is contrary to the Dhamma.

The Pāli commentary indicates that here *Dhamma* refers to serenity and insight. Practitioners should not get attached to even the peace of serenity and the sublimity of insight, let alone cling to wrong views such as thinking attachment to sensual pleasure is not an obstruction on the path. While exerting effort to cultivate serenity and insight is essential, we should not cling to the peacefulness that these states bring, but continue to practice until we gain complete liberation.

The Buddha makes a similar point in the *Greater Discourse on the Destruction of Craving (Mahātaṇhāsankhaya Sutta)*, where he questions the monastics regarding their understanding of how the four nutriments perpetuate the five aggregates of saṃsāra. The monastics assure him that they have understood with proper wisdom not only how the aggregates arise because of the four nutriments but also how they cease when their respective nutriments cease. The Buddha replies (MN 38.14):

> Monastics, purified and bright as this view is, if you adhere to it, cherish it, treasure it, and treat it as a possession, would you then understand that the Dhamma has been taught as being similar to a raft, to be used for the purpose of crossing over, not for the purpose of grasping?—"No, venerable sir," [replied the monastics].

A view may be correct and sublime, but if we treat it as a personal possession, create an identity out of it, or adhere to it with attachment, we have missed the boat. However, going to the other extreme and thinking we can cross the water without a raft is unwise, as is casting the raft aside before we have reached the other side. Open-minded and intelligent disciples will discern the correct view and then contemplate and meditate on it without clinging to it with attachment.

Leaving the raft behind after reaching the other shore does not mean that those who are liberated give up the Buddha's teachings and do whatever they like. They show their incredible gratitude and reverence for the Dharma by teaching others and guiding them on the path.

By means of the similes of the snake and the raft, we see the importance of making ourselves into suitable vessels to receive and hold the Dharma. While having a fully qualified spiritual master is necessary to progress on the path, it is not sufficient. The more that we put effort into developing correct understanding and good qualities, the more our spiritual mentor will be able to lead us on the path to awakening.

REFLECTION

1. What are the five qualities of an excellent disciple? How will developing each one help you on the path?

2. What ideas do you have to increase the five qualities of a suitable disciple in yourself?

3. What have you learned from the simile of the snake and the simile of the raft?

5 | Relying on Spiritual Mentors

AT PRESENT we have a precious human life complete with access to Dharma teachers and teachings. This fortunate situation came about due to great merit that we created in previous lives. Not wanting to waste the efforts of our previous lives, we should take advantage of this rare opportunity by learning and practicing the Dharma. If we are too busy to attend Dharma teachings while both we and our teachers are alive, we may later regret having lost the chance.

In a Pāli sūtra there is the story of a spirit who had full confidence in Bhikkhunī Sukkā and lamented that the people of Rājagaha did not take advantage of the teachings she gave. Even though a large assembly was present at a teaching, he was eager for more beings to benefit, and so went around the town of Rājagaha chanting (SN 10.9):

> What has happened to these people in Rājagaha?
> They sleep as if they've been drinking mead.
> Why don't they attend on Sukkā
> as she teaches the deathless state?
>
> But the wise, as it were, drink it up—
> that [Dhamma] irresistible,
> ambrosial, nutritious—
> as travelers do a cloud.

Dharma teachings are more life sustaining than ordinary food and drink. The more we imbibe the Dharma, the more joy fills our minds and hearts. With this in mind, we now turn our attention to how to cultivate a good relationship with our spiritual mentors, the ones who kindly instruct us on the path.

The Benefits of Relying on Spiritual Mentors

Some people translate the term *bshes gnyen bsten pa* as "guru devotion." This English term may be misleading, evoking the image of blindly surrendering to a holy authority figure, which is certainly not the intended meaning. *Bshes gnyen* means spiritual friend or spiritual mentor. *Bsten pa* means to rely or depend on. For our Dharma practice to be successful, we must properly rely on a wise and compassionate spiritual mentor and guide.

Before engaging in any activity, it's helpful to know the advantages of doing so and the disadvantages of not doing so or doing it improperly. Many benefits accrue from properly relying on a spiritual mentor or mentors.

- Our thoughts and words will become virtuous because we will follow our spiritual mentor's wise advice.
- For the same reason, we won't bring suffering on ourselves or others.
- We will complete the two collections of merit and wisdom and attain full awakening by following reliable teachings.
- We will be able to work for the benefit of sentient beings, including those who have entered wrong paths.
- Because our spiritual mentor teaches us how to purify our negativities, we will exhaust destructive karma that would have ripened in lengthy, unfortunate rebirths. It may instead ripen in this life as comparatively mild discomfort or harm.
- Due to the important role our spiritual mentors play in our lives, we will create great merit, more than is created by making offerings to limitless buddhas.
- By properly relying on our spiritual mentors in this life, we will meet qualified spiritual mentors in future lives.
- Our good qualities will increase, and we will accomplish the welfare of ourselves and others.
- Under our teachers' compassionate guidance, we will feel supported and inspired in our practice.

All of the benefits come about because we listen with an open mind to teachings from a qualified spiritual mentor and put them into practice. However, if we despise, disdain, or reproach our spiritual mentors, many disadvantages accrue. We will have to endure unfortunate rebirths because of the destructive karma we create from insulting or getting angry at them. We will experience harm and illness in this life. Our good qualities will degenerate and no new good qualities will arise because we won't practice the Dharma. In short, none of the advantages will accrue to us, while their opposites will.

REFLECTION

1. Imagine your spiritual mentors appearing in the space in front of you and looking at you with kindness.

2. Contemplate each advantage of properly relying on a spiritual mentor.

3. Contemplate the disadvantages of not relying on a spiritual mentor or of improperly relying on one.

4. Conclude with a determination to rely on a spiritual mentor with a pure heart and to follow his or her instructions in a systematic way.

Cultivate Trust by Seeing Their Qualities

We rely on our spiritual mentors in two ways: through our thoughts and our actions. Relying on them through our thoughts entails cultivating two attitudes: trust and faith in our mentors, which are developed by reflecting on their good qualities, and appreciation and respect for them, which arise from reflecting on their kindness to us.

Faith moistens our minds and makes it receptive. It also energizes us to accomplish our goals. The *Ten Teaching Sūtra* (*Daśadharmaka Sūtra*) says (LC 1:80):

> Faith is the best of vehicles,
> definitely delivering you into buddhahood.

Therefore, persons of intelligence
rely on the guidance of faith.

Virtues will not arise
in those who have no faith,
just as green sprouts do not grow
from seeds scorched by fire.

Common faith is faith we have in a particular teacher, although we may
not be his or her student at this time. It is called common because it is
shared by those who are his disciples and those who are not. Uncommon
faith is the faith held by a teacher's students. With such trust and faith, we
feel close to our teachers, which enables them to influence us in constructive ways.

Trust is generated by reflecting on our teachers' qualities and the role
they play in our lives, which is similar to the role the Buddha would play if
he were alive today. Our spiritual teachers play a singular role in our lives,
for they are the ones who teach, guide, and encourage us along the path.
Through their actions they evince the conduct of realized beings. Without
their compassionate assistance, it would be extremely difficult for us to cultivate wisdom and to progress toward awakening. The more we practice, the
closer we become to our mentors' minds and the Buddha's mind, strengthening and increasing our faith in the teachings and, by extension, in those
who teach and guide us.

An example of this is the young spiritual seeker Sudhana, the main character of the *Array of Stalks Sūtra* (*Gaṇḍavyūha Sūtra*). Sudhana earnestly
sought to learn the bodhisattvas' practices. Each spiritual mentor he went
to taught him a portion and then referred him to another spiritual mentor
to continue his learning. As Sudhana learned and practiced the bodhisattva
deeds, his regard for his spiritual mentors increased. Here is the scene in
which Sudhana approaches Avalokiteśvara, the twenty-seventh of his fifty-
three mentors:

> Transported with joy on seeing Avalokiteśvara, his eyes fixed on
> him, his mind undistracted, full of the energy of faith in the
> spiritual mentor, thinking of seeing spiritual mentors as at once

seeing buddhas, thinking of the reception of the multitudes of all truths as originating in spiritual mentors, thinking of the attainment of all virtues as deriving from spiritual mentors, thinking of how hard it is to meet spiritual mentors, thinking of spiritual mentors as the source from which the jewels of knowledge of the ten powers are obtained, thinking of spiritual mentors as the source of vision of inexhaustible knowledge, thinking that the growth of the sprouts of goodness depends on spiritual mentors, thinking that the door of omniscience is revealed by spiritual mentors, thinking that the way to enter the ocean of great knowledge is pointed out by spiritual mentors, thinking that the accumulation of the store of omniscience is fostered by spiritual mentors, Sudhana approached Avalokiteśvara.[29]

By reflecting on our teachers' qualities, ethical conduct, kindness, meditative abilities, and so on, we will have a positive view of them. Our trust and inspiration will increase and our minds will be receptive to their teachings. This is not blind faith, because there are reasons to hold this person in high regard and to have confidence in his or her ability to guide us on the path.

However, if we don't use our capacity for critical thinking to contemplate the reasonings proving emptiness and instead employ it to analyze the faults of our spiritual mentor, we put ourselves in the precarious position of possibly angrily cutting off the relationship with our mentor and abandoning Dharma practice. We are the ones who suffer the most, should this happen. The benefit or loss that accrues to us in our relationship with our spiritual mentor depends on which qualities we choose to focus.

We may have more than one spiritual mentor; it is up to us. Atiśa had over 140 mentors, while Dromtonpa had less than five. Since it is important to have a positive regard for our teachers, if we have an extremely critical and judgmental mind, it may be better to have fewer teachers.

Having faith and respect for teachers sitting on high thrones, whom we seldom see, is easy. It is much more challenging to appreciate the teacher who gives us daily or weekly Dharma teachings and to whom we offer service. We tend to treat that mentor like an old friend and cease to appreciate his or her qualities and kindness. Because we may easily start to criticize his habits or stop listening to his advice, we must take special care in our relationships with the teachers we see often to ensure that our attitude and behavior do not sabotage this most precious relationship.

Since we learn by observing the example of others, reflecting on our teachers' positive qualities will inspire us to make an effort to develop them ourselves. If we have the opportunity to live near our teachers and help them with various projects, we will witness Dharma lived in daily life by observing how our teachers treat people and manage a variety of situations judiciously and compassionately. Learning by observing a wise practitioner is a precious opportunity, one that cannot be gained by reading a book.

Whether or not our teachers are highly realized, we benefit by seeing them in a positive light. If we think someone is an ordinary person, even if he or she teaches us a profound topic, we will not listen or take their words seriously. But if we think an awakened being is teaching us, we will listen carefully and put the teachings into practice. In this way trust and faith in our spiritual mentors supports us in our practice and uplifts us when we feel discouraged.

Cultivate Appreciation and Respect by Seeing Their Kindness

Countless buddhas have appeared in the past, and of these, Śākyamuni Buddha is the kindest to us because he expounded the teachings in our world. Although we did not have the fortune to receive teachings directly from him or from the lineage of sages in India and Tibet that carried his word to the present day, our spiritual mentors act as messengers delivering these priceless teachings to us. Through their kindness we have access to the vast and profound teachings that show us the path to awakening.

Due to our teachers' kindness, we now have the opportunity to gain some Dharma understanding, leave positive imprints on our mindstream, and gain realizations. Although our parents and close friends love us and wish us well, they do not have the ability to lead us out of the morass of saṃsāra. The kindness of our spiritual mentors—who alone have the knowledge and skill to guide us—is incomparable. The *Ten Teaching Sūtra* says (LC 1:83):

> Develop the following ideas with respect to your teachers: I have wandered for a long time through cyclic existence, and they search for me. I have been asleep, having been obscured by con-

fusion for a long time, and they wake me...I have entered a bad path, and they reveal the good path to me. They release me from being bound in the prison of saṃsāra... They are the rain clouds that put out my blazing fire of attachment.

Thinking of the kindness of our teachers in this way, heartfelt gratitude, appreciation, and veneration will naturally arise for them. This joyful attitude removes obstacles and facilitates our practice. The *Array of Stalks Sūtra* expresses the immense kindness of our spiritual mentors (LC 1:83–84):

> The teachers are those who protect me from all miserable rebirths; they cause me to know the equality of phenomena; they show me the paths that lead to happiness and those that lead to unhappiness; they instruct me in deeds always auspicious; they reveal to me the path to the city of omniscience . . . they cause me to enter the ocean of the sphere of reality; they show me the sea of past, present, and future phenomena; and they reveal to me the circle of the āryas' assembly. The teachers increase all my virtues. Remembering this, you will weep.

Sudhana reflects:

> I, Sudhana, have come here
> thinking one-pointedly, "These are my teachers, instructors
>   in the teachings,
> the ones who totally reveal the good qualities of all things
> and then fully teach the bodhisattva way of life . . .
>
> "These bodhisattvas have caused my mind to develop,
> they have produced my awakening as a bodhisattva,
> therefore, these, my teachers, are praised by the buddhas."
> With such virtuous thoughts, I have come here.
>
> "As they protect the world, they are like heroes;
> they are captains, protectors, and refuge.
> They are an eye providing me with happiness."
> With such thoughts, I respect and serve my teachers.

REFLECTION

1. Had you not met your spiritual mentors, what might your life be like now? What would you be doing? What might the state of your mind be?

2. Among all those whom you hold dear and who love you, do any of them have the ability to guide you on the path to full awakening?

3. What do the Dharma teachings mean to you? How valuable are they? Allow yourself to feel gratitude and respect for those who have taught you.

Seeing Spiritual Mentors as Buddhas

Because of the influence of Vajrayāna in all four Tibetan Buddhist traditions, disciples are instructed to cultivate the perception of their gurus as buddhas. It is important to understand this correctly in order to avoid confusion. In the context of tantra, seeing the guru as the Buddha is important. A guru who is able to give all four empowerments of highest yoga tantra based on his or her own experience is definitely a buddha, and seeing him or her as a buddha is reasonable. Some gurus who give empowerments do not have that experience, but if we see them as buddhas, it increases our concentration and enhances our meditative experience.

When we view our spiritual mentors as the Buddha, buddhahood does not seem so distant. We come to feel close to the Buddha and begin to think that awakening is possible and awakened beings actually exist. Although not all spiritual mentors are buddhas—some of our mentors are ordinary beings—our practice will progress well from maintaining a positive view of them. For example, in the past the presidents of a country were fully qualified—they were honest, responsible, and cared for the citizens. Later on the quality of the presidents declined. Nevertheless, we see these people as presidents because they have that title, perform that function, and represent our country. We respect them but do not blindly follow them.

The teaching to see the spiritual mentor as the Buddha is borrowed from highest yoga tantra and is often taught earlier on the path to prepare disciples to receive tantric empowerments. However, this teaching is not appropriate for beginners because it is open to misunderstanding. As noted above, the Fundamental Vehicle and Perfection Vehicle do not instruct us to view our teacher as a buddha, although we may personally choose to do so.

We Tibetans say that it's best not to bring the topic of seeing the spiritual mentor as the Buddha to the debate ground because the argument cannot be sustained. In a debate, one monk once asked another, "Some texts say that our spiritual mentors are buddhas. Do you agree?" The second monk replied affirmatively. Then the first monk asked, "You have disciples here in the monastery. Are you also a buddha?" at which point the second monk was chagrined because he knew he was not.

Tsongkhapa's presentation of relying on a spiritual master in the *Lamrim Chenmo* is well balanced, and if we follow that, less confusion will arise. He says (LC l: 81–82):

> Moreover, pay attention to the good qualities that the guru does have—such as ethical conduct, learnedness, and faith—and reflect on these qualities. Once you have become conditioned to this, you may notice that your guru has a small number of faults. However, this does not impede your faith because you are focusing on the good qualities.

Tsongkhapa does not say to see our teacher's faults as good qualities or to see all his actions as perfect. In the *Lamrim Chenmo* he expounds very little on seeing the guru as the Buddha,[30] and when he does, his purpose is to prevent us from damaging our relationship with our guru. He encourages us to see their good qualities so that we will benefit from their teachings and guidance.

We should avoid fanciful ideas, such as thinking, "Since my mentor is a buddha, he doesn't get sick," and not call the doctor when he is ill. We live in the conventional world and must act appropriately. If our teacher makes a mistake while reading a text or explaining its meaning, it is fine to respectfully point it out. We should avoid thinking that since he is an omniscient buddha he should know the way to a distant place, and then become disillusioned when he asks us directions.

Also to be avoided is idealizing our spiritual mentors. There is a Tibetan saying, "A student who is too devoted makes the lama into a hypocrite." The lama cannot possibly live up to the glowing acclaim the disciple has spread about him or her in the community. Having an idealistic attitude sets us up for disappointment. It is impossible for anyone to continually fulfill our unrealistic expectations.

The measure of gaining proper reliance on the spiritual masters is whole-heartedly appreciating their good qualities and not focusing on their weak-nesses. In general, seeing the spiritual mentor as a buddha is a form of useful and constructive imagination; in most cases it is not a reliable cognizer. Even though there are definitely ordinary beings and bodhisattvas among those who teach the Dharma, regarding our teachers as buddhas, listen-ing to their teachings, practicing accordingly, and respectfully serving our mentors enables us to be more receptive to teachings and wise advice and to experience many other positive results.

The meditation to see our spiritual mentors as buddhas is similar to the meditation to imagine the entire Earth covered with skeletons: both involve imagination that is consciously cultivated and will have a beneficial effect on our minds. Ignorance is not the cause of imagining bones covering the ground, so this is not a wrong consciousness. We intentionally meditate in this way to derive benefit; in this case, the reduction of attachment to our body and to saṃsāric existence. Similarly, while our spiritual mentors may or may not be buddhas, we benefit from thinking of them as such because it makes us listen attentively to their teachings and take their Dharma instructions seriously.

If our mind seizes every opportunity to find imperfections in our spiri-tual mentors, it is helpful to reflect, "Why am I here? It is not to notice my teachers' shortcomings but to learn from their good qualities." This brings us back to the reason we are practicing the Dharma.

Should we see flaws in our teachers we can transform them into a learn-ing experience. If our teacher behaves rudely, we think, "This is how I look when I am rude." This way we will learn from the situation. If we can't give our spiritual mentors—who have more good qualities than faults—space to be human, it will be difficult to develop tolerance and forgiveness toward sentient beings who have many faults.

Sometimes the "faults" we find in our mentors are actually differences in personal preference. Our teacher likes to wake up early; we like to sleep late. Our mentor loves butter tea; we think it's unhealthy. Our teacher likes to have a long teaching session with no breaks; we prefer shorter ones with a lot of breaks. None of these are ethical faults on the part of the teacher. Observing how we make differences into faults gives us insight into our habitual way of thinking that needs to be corrected.

We should not force ourselves to see our spiritual mentor as the Buddha out of fear of creating destructive karma or "doing it wrong." Past masters recommend this practice because they benefited from it. If we try following their advice, we may see a favorable effect. But if this feels uncomfortable, we can turn our minds to topics that inspire us.

The Role of Devotion

The spiritual mentor is often said to be the root of the path, in that this relationship nourishes and stabilizes our practice. But just as a plant also depends on a seed, water, fertilizer, and warmth, we need additional conditions to grow in the Dharma, such as purification and accumulating merit; listening to teachings; cultivating renunciation, bodhicitta, and the correct view; and practicing the three higher trainings and the six perfections. If only respecting and serving our spiritual mentors were adequate for attaining awakening, the Buddha would not have taught a myriad of other practices.

The above is a general explanation applicable to the great majority of people. There are a few cases in which a specific individual, because of his or her very strong devotion and singular karmic connection with a special teacher, is liberated by means of an encounter with that spiritual mentor. Such a situation depends on a highly qualified disciple encountering a highly realized spiritual mentor. In such a case, if the disciple has deep devotion for the spiritual master, it is possible that the grosser levels of mind are neutralized and the subtlest mind becomes active. With this comes the understanding and experience of emptiness. Genuine compassion arises toward sentient beings who are totally immersed in duḥkha and ignorant of that fact. Here compassion arises automatically as a byproduct of the subtle mind experiencing emptiness.

There are stories of a few exceptional disciples, and I have met a few individuals who have had profound experiences or have gained realizations through an encounter with their teacher. Their faith in their spiritual mentor was so strong that it was as if they had fallen unconscious. But when they revived from this unconscious state, it was apparent that they had had a deep experience of clear light.

Someone may ask, "Is such a thing possible if the teacher is not highly realized but the disciple has tremendous faith?" Both the spiritual mentor and disciple must be fully qualified for this to occur. If the teacher is not, how could that person spark in a disciple's mind a realization that is not present in his or her own mind?

Most of the exceptional cases of gaining realizations primarily through faith are found in the Kagyu and Dzogchen lineages, where devotion is emphasized. A quotation from a Kagyu text says there is no doubt about the possibility of being liberated through devotion and veneration. This refers to those few individual cases in whom all the causes and conditions have come together for this to happen. Applying this notion to the general Buddhist population would be a mistake. If everyone could be awakened only through intense devotion, there would be little difference between Buddhism and theistic religions. Furthermore, the Buddha would not have given teachings that constitute more than one hundred volumes in the Tibetan canon. Here we again see that the teachings and modes of practice relevant to specific individuals differ from those given in the general system of Buddhist teachings and practice. It is important not to confuse these. The teachings of the Nālandā tradition are given from the perspective of the general structure of the path and pertain to practitioners in general, whereas these exceptional cases apply primarily to mahāsiddhas.

Relying on Spiritual Mentors in Our Actions

Having contemplated how to rely on spiritual mentors through our thoughts, we now turn to relying on them through our actions. There are three principal practices.

First, we make material offerings to our spiritual mentors. Because of their qualities, kindness, and the important role they play in our lives, our mentors are potent objects with which we create karma. By making offerings we create great merit, which we dedicate for the awakening of all sentient beings. From the side of spiritual mentors, the quality or quantity of offerings must not influence the diligence with which they guide disciples. Geshe Sharawa, one of the twelfth-century Kadam geshes, said that a spiritual mentor who pays attention to the offerings he or she receives is not a suitable teacher for a disciple aspiring to full awakening.

Second, we respect and serve our mentors, offering our time and energy to assist in their various projects to benefit others. Offering service also includes tending to their personal needs, such as cooking, cleaning, running errands, and caring for them when they are ill.

Third, we offer our practice, meaning that we practice according to our mentors' instructions. This is the best offering, far excelling the first two, because it involves taming our minds by putting the Dharma instructions into practice. Doing this is the offering that most pleases our spiritual mentors.

The Pāli scriptures say that the seven trainees—approachers and abiders who are stream-enterers, once-returners, and nonreturners, and approachers to arhat who have realized impermanence, duḥkha, and selflessness and have some realization of nirvāṇa—serve the Teacher, the Buddha, with acts of love. Arhats, who have eliminated all afflictions and causes for cyclic existence, completely serve the Teacher with acts of love.

When addressing a group of self-indulgent and lax monastics who did not keep the precepts well or make effort in the practice, the Buddha said (MN 70.26):

> Even with a [non-Buddhist] teacher who is concerned with material things, an heir to material things, attached to material things, such haggling [by his disciples] would not be proper: "If we get this, we will do it; if we don't get this, we won't do it." So what [should be said when the teacher is] the Tathāgata who is utterly detached from material things?

Even in the case of a non-Buddhist teacher who seeks material gain with attachment, it is not suitable for students to be demanding or rebellious, following the teacher's instructions only if it pleases their self-centeredness and not following when they don't feel like it. Needless to say, this should not be the behavior of disciples who have an actual tathāgata as their teacher. We must recall that our teachers instruct us for our benefit, not theirs. Wanting to progress on the path, we should listen well to the teachings and put them into practice so as not to waste either our teachers' efforts or our own time. The Buddha continues (MN 70.27):

> For a faithful disciple who is intent on fathoming the Teacher's dispensation, it is proper that he conduct himself thus: "The Blessed One is the Teacher, I am a disciple; the Blessed One knows, I do not know." For a faithful disciple who is intent on fathoming the Teacher's dispensation, that dispensation is nourishing and refreshing. For a faithful disciple who is intent on fathoming the Teacher's dispensation, it is proper that he conduct himself thus: "Willingly, let only my skin, sinews, and bones remain, and let the flesh and blood dry up on my body, but my energy shall not be relaxed so long as I have not attained what can be attained by human strength, human energy, and human persistence." For a faithful disciple who is intent on fathoming the Teacher's dispensation, one of two fruits may be expected: either final knowledge here and now or, if there is a trace of clinging left, [the state of a] nonreturner.

Our spiritual mentors' kindness in teaching us and caring for us is like that of the Buddha toward his disciples. To benefit from our mentors' guidance, we should abandon all arrogance and competitiveness and be humble and receptive. With sincere aspiration to gain realizations, we should let go of all worldly distractions and focus intently on Dharma study and practice. In that way, we will gain realizations and become bodhisattvas and eventually buddhas.

Behavior toward Spiritual Mentors

Generating faith by reflecting on our teachers' qualities and generating gratitude and respect by reflecting on their kindness are the method to rely on our teachers mentally. As we become habituated to these attitudes, they will be reflected in our actions. When we admire and trust someone, we automatically want to live in a way that pleases him or her. In the Dharma this means training our mind through the systematic approach of the three higher trainings, the six perfections, and tantra.

Some sādhanas—meditation or ritual texts—especially those of guru yoga, say, "May I do only what pleases you [the spiritual mentor]." This phrase improperly understood can generate misconceptions. In some cultures, pleasing someone may be a way to curry a powerful person's favor or to avoid their punishment. A student with such a preconception may seek to please his teacher by offering goods or service with the wish to create merit, but also with the hope to receive recognition or appreciation. If the teacher doesn't reciprocate with sufficient appreciation, the disciple feels offended. It is important that we understand that *pleasing our guru* means to transform our mind into the path.

Some people appear to be devoted, humble disciples in their teachers' presence, but in other situations are obnoxious and rude. Others seek to please the teacher because he is holy, but are inconsiderate to other disciples and sentient beings in general. These behaviors are inappropriate. Assisting sentient beings and treating them well is one aspect of pleasing our guru because it fulfills his or her purpose of benefiting others.

We should avoid being possessive of our teachers or jealously competing with other disciples for their attention. Nor should we use them to increase our sense of self-importance. Geshe Potowa reflected (LC 1:87):

> We present-day followers do not value the teachings at all, but only value the guru's assigning status to us as demonstrated by each cup of tea that the guru gives us. This is a sign of our deep corruption.

Following our teachers' instructions is a skill we must develop. Sometimes we are resistant to advice that does not please our self-centered thought. Other times we take the advice out of context, thinking that an instruction to an individual student should be generalized to everyone. It is important to differentiate general advice that is applicable to everyone and advice meant for a specific individual. If someone walking on a narrow path between two precipices is too close to the left side, we call out, "Go right!" But if the person is too near the right side, we shout, "Go left!" Taken out of context these instructions seem contradictory, although they are not. To avoid confusion, we should inquire about the context in which an instruction was given and to whom it was given.

It is important to respect and to follow the advice of the resident teacher in the place where we live, even though that teacher may not be our principal mentor. The resident teacher heads the community, and for the sake of community harmony as well as for our own spiritual benefit, we should follow her guidance.

When we begin to give Dharma talks, we must avoid competing with our teachers, thinking, "More students come to my Dharma talks" or "I'm a more eloquent speaker than my teacher." Also to be avoided is trying to prove to our spiritual mentors how learned and articulate we are. In all ways, we should be genuinely humble and fully aware that any Dharma we know is due to their kindness and fortitude in teaching unruly disciples like us. Sometimes we may become frustrated or angry and blame our spiritual mentor for our unhappiness. At these times it is especially important to remember that our unhappiness is due to our previous destructive behavior that left karmic latencies on our consciousness, and our anger is due to the seed of anger within ourselves. We are responsible for our emotions, so rather than blame our mentor, it is wise to look inside ourselves and apply Dharma antidotes to our afflictions.

Usually after we calm down, we will feel regret for any harsh words we spoke to our mentors or misleading statements we may have made to cover up our faults. It is wise to go to our teacher and apologize so we can start afresh.

If we have difficulties in our relationships with our spiritual mentors, it could be due to relating to them in an improper way in previous lives. Engaging in purification practices with a strong determination to restrain from such actions in the future will help us clear these obstacles.

REFLECTION

1. How would you benefit from having an open and honest relationship with your spiritual mentor?

2. Contemplate and make examples of specific ways to make offerings to your spiritual mentors of material goods, service, and your practice.

3. What are appropriate ways to behave with your mentors?

4. What are inappropriate ways? How can you protect against engaging in them?

We may encounter situations in which we hold different opinions from our teachers. We may be a vegetarian, but our teacher is not; we may think one political policy would be effective, while our teacher favors another. These are issues of personal preference. Respecting our mentor does not mean we have to agree on every issue. We must remember that we came to our spiritual mentor to learn the path to awakening, not to learn cosmology or debate human rights.

Even the Buddha's disciples didn't always agree with him. For example, one day the Buddha said to his close disciple, "Kassapa, you are getting old now. You've been wearing coarse and uncomfortable robes made of rags. Wear nicer robes offered by lay followers. Instead of eating food gathered only on alms rounds (*piṇḍapāta*), accept lay followers' invitations to eat at their homes. Also, dwell in a simple residence, not in the forest." Kassapa replied that he wished to continue these ascetic practices not only because they were conducive for his own practice but also because future generations would follow his example and derive benefit from them. The Buddha affirmed that this was Kassapa's way of caring for the welfare and happiness of others, his way of demonstrating compassion for the world (SN 16.5). Kassapa respectfully explained to his spiritual master, the Buddha, the reasons for not following his instructions. Seeing the virtue in Kassapa's explanation, the Buddha approved of his actions. There was no contention or resentment, only love between them.

Even advanced disciples may have differing views from their teachers on important issues, such as the correct view of emptiness. Atiśa's respect for his spiritual mentor Serlingpa was incomparable, but he did not follow him in every respect. Serlingpa espoused Cittamātrin tenets, while Atiśa held the Madhyamaka view. This difference did not impinge on the closeness of their mentor-disciple relationship.

Mipham Rinpoche composed a Dharma text and one of his disciples from Amdo wrote a critique of it. Someone questioned the disciple, "How can you critique your guru's work?" to which the disciple responded, "If something unacceptable is said, someone has to counter it." Similarly, even though the *Sūtra Unraveling the Thought* is the Buddha's teaching, Nāgārjuna and other sages critiqued it, saying its meaning is interpretable, not definitive.

In my own case, I had a difference of opinion with my junior tutor, Trijang Rinpoche, concerning the practice of Shugden. I explained to him my reasons for not doing this practice and for discouraging others from doing it. Trijang Rinpoche understood, and there was no damage in our relationship. I still hold him in the highest regard, and my faith in him has not decreased at all.

Preventing Difficulties

All Buddhist traditions have faced difficulties with teachers who do not behave properly or abuse their status to gain offerings, respect, or sex. This is totally against the Dharma and harms not only the other person(s) involved but also the teacher and the existence of the Dharma. Some unfortunate situations have occurred in the West and Taiwan regarding a few teachers in the Tibetan tradition. This has caused great confusion and feelings of hurt and betrayal in students' minds.

Many of these problems have arisen because the transmission of Tibetan Buddhism abroad is in its early stages. There is no central organization that affirms people's suitability to teach, so it is possible for unqualified people to go abroad and set up a Dharma center. Some people who would never be in a position to give teachings or initiations in the Tibetan community suddenly become "great lamas" in other countries. This is admirable if it is someone who remained humble and did not have the opportunity to show their great qualities in the Tibetan community. But if someone is merely taking advantage of being in another place to promote themselves, it is sad.

Once in another country, these people are separated from the support—and watchful eyes—of their peers and teachers. Isolated and perhaps lonely, they are flattered by the attention and offerings showered on them by devotees. This is no excuse for their poor behavior; everyone is responsible for their own actions. However, having two or three Tibetans of the same sex—or Westerners in the case of Western teachers—living at a Dharma center could help prevent temptation.

Because Buddhism is new in the West, students do not know how to evaluate a teacher's qualities and may rush into a guru-disciple relationship without adequate knowledge. Some students see Tibetans as exotic and mysterious—akin to the Western fascination with Shangri-La. Such an attitude is akin to blind faith and is not conducive for establishing a healthy mentor-disciple relationship. Monastics studying at the monastic universities in India have a much more realistic attitude about their teachers.

Because students are new to Buddhism, they may have blind devotion and obedience to spiritual mentors. Hearing about the great merit gained from making offerings to spiritual mentors, they may give them many donations and gifts—things that someone living in India would not have. The teacher becomes spoiled by the gifts and esteem of the students, and if he is not careful, this could lead to his taking advantage of well-meaning students.

I have received many letters from people in other countries asking me to do something about this, but it is not in my control. Tibetan Buddhism is not organized like the Catholic Church with a pope and Vatican administration. I cannot make someone return to India or force him to stop wearing robes. When I teach, I give clear instructions about suitable behavior for teachers, both monastic and lay. If people do not listen to me then, it is doubtful that they will heed instructions from my office or the Department of Religious and Cultural Affairs.

As Buddhism becomes rooted in other cultures and people understand it better, they will know the criteria for qualified teachers and will examine potential teachers with care; they will enter into guru-disciple relationships with greater understanding and clarity. In addition, more teachers will live and travel abroad, and people will be able to choose among them.

When looking at damaging situations that have arisen in previous years, I believe both sides have responsibility to prevent such happenings in the future. A spiritual mentor is responsible for his or her behavior. A student is responsible for not going along with any improper behavior on the teacher's part. So education is needed on both sides. Until now, no special training is given to people who become spiritual mentors; their spiritual training is seen as sufficient. Compassion and altruism are the very nature of Buddhist practice. If teachers have cultivated these, they will not abuse their influence on others. I hope Tibetan monasteries will speak more directly to their members about the challenges of living in the West and in Taiwan. Lay Tibetan teachers should seek out ways to prepare themselves to teach in different cultures.

Unusual Behavior

Some past Buddhist siddhas behaved in unconventional ways—they drank alcohol and had consorts. These siddhas were fully realized lay practitioners who could discern what was of long-term benefit to self and others, and their actions were in accord with training on the completion stage of highest yoga tantra. They could demonstrate miraculous abilities, which allayed the public's concerns about their level of realization. For example, they could cause an apple to fall from a tree a distance away and then make the apple go up and reattach to the tree, and Bhikṣuṇī Lakṣmī is said to have cut off her head and then reattached it.

Nowadays there are very few people who are qualified to practice in this way, and because of the difference in society, such conduct is harmful to the Dharma. Nevertheless, some people act in an unconventional manner and proclaim realizations, but do not have any demonstrable exceptional qualities to display in order to confirm their spiritual attainments. Even if they did, I wonder if it would be wise in today's society to show them. The siddhas of old generally displayed their miraculous powers to small, select groups of people who had the karma to benefit from seeing them. Today such an event would be flashed around the world by modern telecommunications. Reporters would want to interview the siddhas and companies would ask them to promote their products. I doubt such attention would be beneficial to either the Buddhadharma, the siddha, or society. Even if our realizations are equal to those of divine beings, our behavior should conform to convention.

Padmasambhava said that as we perfect our realization of emptiness, our respect for karma and its effects and for ethical conduct correspondingly increases. Gaining the correct view is not easy; many misunderstandings about emptiness exist. A prominent one is to claim that since everything is empty, there is no good or bad, and that someone who realizes emptiness is beyond ethical precepts. Some people state this on the basis of faulty reasoning; others because they have had some sort of experience in meditation that is a "wrong realization." They then use this as a rationalization to take advantage of others or to justify enjoying sense pleasures.

Although conventional phenomena do not appear to someone who is in nondual meditative equipoise on emptiness, that does not mean they are nonexistent. Conventionalities exist and the law of cause and effect functions, no matter what our level of realization. If the people who say there is no good and no bad really believe that in their hearts, why do they gravitate toward sense pleasures and self-indulgent behavior? They would not discriminate between attractive and unattractive things at all. If they had genuinely realized nonduality, they would eat poor-quality food, live in the streets and help the poor, do relief work in war zones, and serve others who are suffering. All these situations would be the same to them.

The Buddha was always humble, and he is our Teacher. He worked hard on the path—he lived simply, mixed with everyone, and practiced continuously. Many people nowadays think they are more privileged than the Buddha and do not need to live and practice as he did. In fact no one is above the Buddha; we should follow his example.

Everyone is accountable for his or her behavior, and the practice of tantra is never an excuse for unethical behavior. The *Six-Session Guru Yoga* says, "I shall abandon the four roots, liquor, and unsuitable activities." The *Kālacakra Tantra* states that the ideal lay tantric practitioner should follow the monastic discipline, except for wearing robes and participating in monastic ceremonies. That means that an ideal lay tantric practitioner would be celibate and abstain from intoxicants.

Although a small amount of alcohol is placed on the altar during some tantric rituals, only a few drops should be consumed after doing the meditation dissolving it into emptiness and transforming it into pure nectar. Recreational drinking by teachers or students at Dharma centers is inappropriate and should be abandoned.

In our present situation of cyclic existence, we are constantly deceived by the false appearances of objects that seem to exist inherently. Our afflictions arise on the basis of these false appearances. Dharma practice is designed to stop false appearances and the grasping at them. What, then, is the purpose of deliberately cultivating more false appearances through taking intoxicants?

Although some highly realized yogis and yoginīs in the past drank and sometimes took on the appearance of being drunk, they were exceptional practitioners with direct nonconceptual realization of emptiness. For them, ingesting feces, urine, and alcohol were all the same. However, I do not think most practitioners nowadays would drink urine or eat feces with the same enthusiasm they have when drinking alcohol!

On a very advanced level of highest yoga tantra, the joining of the male and female organs is a technique for making the subtlest mind manifest and using it to realize emptiness. Here the physical body is used as a mechanical device for furthering insight. Ordinary lust and uncontrolled emission or orgasm are absent. This union is a method for overcoming ordinary desire. It is not free license to indulge in sexual intercourse with everyone. In the past, in Tibet a practitioner had to demonstrate supernatural powers, such as flying through the sky, to qualify to train in such practice. If the person was a monastic, he or she would disrobe first and then do this practice in a circumspect manner.

Tantric precepts govern this practice and practitioners must adhere to them. Tantra is a higher practice, which implies that a person who takes tantric ethical restraints has sufficient control over his or her body, speech, and mind to keep the Vinaya and bodhisattva ethical restraints, which are comparatively easier to keep. People who find it difficult to observe the five lay precepts are not suitable vessels for tantric practice because they lack the restraint needed to fulfill the tantric precepts and pledges.

It may happen that an unmarried teacher meets an unmarried student. If the relationship develops in a normal way, with mutual agreement and respect, and they decide to marry, it is fine. These two people treat each other equally, so there is no difference in power or status when deciding to have sexual relations. The teacher is not on a throne then! However, if the teacher is with one student one month and another the next, that is not right. Coercing or forcing sexual contact is wrong. Teachers should not manipulate a student into having a sexual relationship by saying she has the signs of being a ḍākinī or has great Dharma potential, or that having sex with him is a special blessing. Some people who have been sexually abused by Buddhist teachers give up their faith and respect for the Buddha. This makes me very sad.

Some texts make statements such as, "See all actions of your spiritual mentor as perfect" and "Follow your mentors' instructions exactly with complete devotion." These statements are made in the context of highest yoga tantra and apply to exceptional cases in which both the spiritual master and the disciple are highly qualified—for example, Tilopa and his disciple Nāropa, and Marpa and his disciple Milarepa. If we are not the caliber of Nāropa and our mentor does not have the qualities of Tilopa, these statements can be greatly misleading. Hearing stories of Tilopa's seemingly abusive treatment of Nāropa—instructing him to jump off a cliff and so forth—and Marpa instructing Milarepa to build stone buildings and then tear them down, some people think that following their teachers' instructions includes allowing themselves to be abused. This is not the case at all! Marpa told Milarepa, "Do not treat your students like I treated you or the way the great Nāropa treated me. Such practice should not be continued in the future." This is because it is very rare to find both a teacher and a disciple who have realizations comparable to those great masters.

I have had many teachers whom I value greatly, but I cannot accept seeing all their actions as perfect. When I was in my teens, my two regents fought with each other in a power struggle that involved the Tibetan army. When I sat on my meditation seat, I felt both teachers were extremely kind and had profound respect for them; their disagreements did not matter. But when I had to deal with the difficulties caused by their dissension, I said to them, "What you are doing is wrong!" I did not speak out of hatred or disrespect, but because I love the Buddhadharma, and their actions went against it. I felt no conflict in loyalty by acting in this way. In our practice we may view the guru's behavior as that of a mahāsiddha, but in the conventional world we follow the general Buddhist approach, and if a certain behavior is harmful, we should say so.

The advice to see all the guru's actions as perfect is not meant for general practitioners. Because it is open to misunderstanding, it can easily become poison for both mentors and students. Students naively whitewashing a teacher's bad behavior by thinking anything the guru does must be good gives some teachers a free hand to misbehave. On the teacher's part, poor behavior is tantamount to drinking the hot molten iron of the hellish states, and it contributes to the degeneration of the Dharma in the world. Only in particular situations and to particular practitioners should it be taught that all the guru's actions are perfect. Buddhism is based on reasoning and wisdom and must remain so.

Because I frequently give Dharma teachings, many people place great faith in me. But for many years I was also their secular leader. If they saw every action I did as perfect, it would adversely affect the administration. It was important for them to share information and ideas with me and not simply acquiesce to everything I said out of respect.

If you have taken someone as your spiritual mentor and discover he is engaged in some questionable behavior, you may stop attending his teachings. Avoid disrespect or antipathy; anger will only make you miserable. The *Kālacakra Tantra* advises maintaining a neutral attitude and not pursuing the relationship any further. Keep your distance and cultivate relationships with other teachers, but do not angrily denounce this person. He benefited you in the past, and it is appropriate to acknowledge and appreciate that even though you do not follow him now.

Resolving Problems

Just as there are these three types of spiritual mentors and three ways of relating to them, there are three ways of responding if our mentor asks us to do something outside the general framework of the Buddhadharma—any action that contradicts the Dharma or reasoning. According to Vinaya, we should not follow that advice and should express our reason to our teacher. According to general Mahāyāna, if an instruction conforms to the Buddhist path, follow it; otherwise, do not. According to Vajrayāna, if your guru gives an instruction that does not accord with the Dharma, that is illogical, or that you are incapable of doing, do not follow it. Explain your reasons and discuss the situation with your teacher. This advice comes directly from the Buddha and is found in the scriptures. Tsongkhapa explains (LC 1:86):

> *Question*: We must practice in accordance with the gurus' words. Then what if we rely on the gurus and they lead us to an incor-

rect path or employ us in activities that are contrary to the three ethical restraints? Should we do what they say?

Reply: In this regard, Guṇaprabha's *Vinayasūtra* states, "If the abbot instructs you to do what is not in accord with the teachings, refuse." Also the *Cloud of Jewels Sūtra* (*Ratnamegha Sūtra*) says, "With respect to virtue, act in accord with the gurus' words, but do not act in accord with the gurus' words with respect to nonvirtue." Therefore you must not listen to nonvirtuous instructions.

Nevertheless it is improper to take a guru's wrong actions as a reason to misbehave yourself, such as disrespecting or despising your guru. Rather, excuse yourself politely and do not engage in what you were instructed to do. The *Fifty Verses of Relying on a Spiritual Master* says:

If you cannot reasonably do as the guru has instructed,
excuse yourself with soothing words.

A story in the *Jātaka Tales* tells of Śākyamuni Buddha's previous life as a bodhisattva-disciple of a teacher who told his students that stealing was virtuous. While the other students nodded in agreement and prepared to fulfill their teacher's instruction to rob others, the bodhisattva sat quietly. Asked to explain his silence and lack of enthusiasm, he said that stealing was unethical and contradicted the general conduct explained in the teachings. The teacher, who had been testing the students, then praised him.

If you think the advice of your teacher is unskillful or unwise even though it may be ethical, explain your way of thinking and discuss the issue with the teacher. It is appropriate to ask questions in order to clear your doubts. This leads to better communication, fewer misunderstandings, and may increase your respect for your teachers.

In 1993 at a conference with Western Buddhist teachers in Dharamsala, Western teachers told me of a few Buddhist spiritual mentors whose behavior regarding finances, sexual relationships, and so on deeply disturbed people and gave the wrong impression of Buddhism. I told them that these "teachers" do not follow the Buddha's teachings. I encouraged them to speak frankly with these teachers, and if they do not listen, then they should make their behavior public. Although these teachers do not care about the Buddha's teaching, perhaps they will care about their reputation and change their ways. Some people ask me to speak to these teachers, but that has little effect. If they do not listen when I give teachings and if they do not respect the Buddha's teachings, they will not listen if I give them personal advice.

You may wonder what to do if a friend is a student of a teacher whose ethical conduct is questionable. Tantric teachings speak of the destructive karma created by separating a mentor and student, yet you want to prevent your friend from harm. If you see that your friend's relationship with a teacher is definitely harmful, it is suitable to warn him or her, simply stating facts in a nonjudgmental manner. But if that relationship is not harmful, it is best to leave things alone. The key to whether you create the negative karma of separating a disciple and teacher lies in the motivation. Actions motivated by an angry, judgmental attitude are to be avoided, whereas those based on compassion and tolerance are encouraged.

When Tibetan teachers ask you to raise money or give donations to their monasteries, use your discriminating wisdom. In some cases a legitimate need exists and the funds will benefit people. In that case, it is good to help support worthwhile projects if you can. But when such funds will be used for other purposes, such as buying unnecessary consumer goods for the teacher's family or sending them on a holiday, there is no need for you to give.

As with most problems, the best approach is to take steps to prevent them. I recommend preparing Tibetan teachers to teach in other countries, establishing support systems so that they are not cut off from their peers while teaching abroad, and ensuring that they have enough time for their own Dharma practice.

Also, I suggest educating Westerners on the qualities of good spiritual mentors, the meaning and purpose of the mentor-disciple relationship, and constructive modes of dealing with uncomfortable requests. Of course, both parties need to learn, reflect, and meditate on the Buddhadharma and to adhere to the basic Buddhist tenets and guidelines for ethical behavior. When they do, spiritual mentors and disciples alike benefit, as will many other living beings.

When Our Spiritual Mentors Pass Away

Because our spiritual mentors are valuable in our lives and dear to us, when a spiritual mentor passes away we will probably feel a great loss. When Dromtonpa was dying, he lay his head in the lap of one of his close disciples, the great scholar Potowa. Saddened by the fact that his teacher was leaving, Potowa was crying, and a tear fell on Dromtonpa. Drom looked up and asked, "Why are you crying?" Potowa responded, "Up to now, I've had you as my guru, so there was always someone I could ask questions and seek counsel and guidance from. But now you are leaving, and I will have no one to clarify points of doubt and guide me on how to practice."

Dromtonpa counseled Potowa, "You do not need many gurus. From now on, seek your guru in the Tripiṭaka, the three baskets of scriptures. The sūtras, tantras, treatises, and commentaries by the great sages will be your teacher and spiritual guide. Rely on them, because I would give you no advice different from that of the Buddha and the great masters." This advice is important for us to bear in mind.

It is beneficial to repeatedly make aspirational prayers to meet qualified Mahāyāna spiritual mentors in the future and to accumulate merit and wisdom, which are the causes to be cared for by such mentors, until we reach full awakening.

Advice to Spiritual Mentors and Disciples

Years ago I heard about an abbot in Kham, Tibet. Some visitors came to see him. He was not there and his attendant told the visitors, "He has gone to scare the people in the nearby town." It seems that this lama told people they would go to hell if they didn't heed his instructions. This is not the Buddhist way.

I would like to speak frankly to both spiritual mentors and Dharma students. From 2012 to 2015 I taught the eighteen lamrim texts. Some of these texts emphasize that the guru is Vajradhara, and if you don't listen to your guru's instructions, you will be born as a hell being. What is all this about? The Buddha never said if you don't listen to his teachings and don't do as he says you will be reborn in hell! The Buddha said we should not accept teachings with blind faith but through having investigated and analyzed them. This is the true way to follow the Buddha's teachings.

If something doesn't hold up to reasoning, we should not accept it unless it can legitimately be interpreted to mean otherwise. For this reason even some Nālandā masters rejected statements in the sūtras. After examination I eschewed the traditional cosmology with Mount Meru at the center. When I said this during teachings in South India, some monks were initially uncomfortable. How can the Dalai Lama reject Mount Meru? But no one could say I was no longer a good Buddhist because I disagreed with Vasubandhu on that topic. Our having freedom to examine the teachings is wonderful; this is a special quality of Buddhism that the Buddha himself encouraged.

Nowadays we need to introduce people to the Dharma by teaching the two truths and the four truths of āryas so that people will understand the real teachings of the Buddha. Contemplating those topics gives people confidence; they will understand the Dharma and appreciate their precious human lives. With faith based on reasoning and understanding, they can later learn the ten powers of a buddha based on understanding the *tathāgatagarbha*, the potential to become a buddha. Otherwise it seems that the teacher is imposing beliefs on disciples and threatening them with a hellish rebirth should they have doubts. It also appears that some teachers impose the notion that the guru is the Buddha on disciples who do not understand the true Dharma, and in this way manipulate disciples.

If you study well, you will gain confidence in the Dharma based on understanding. A teacher who encourages you to think about the teachings is a good teacher. People who want to teach the Dharma must have knowledge and experience and act with integrity. The more respect a spiritual mentor receives, the humbler he or she should become. Mentors must discipline their body, speech, and mind by practicing the three higher trainings and should not be content with a partial understanding of the Dharma. Since there are false gurus, students must check carefully.

In short, we need to be twenty-first century Buddhists. Following tradition and believing with blind faith is the old way. To be Buddhists now, we must have a fuller knowledge of Buddhism, especially the Nālandā tradition, which presents the Dharma in a systematic fashion. Nālandā masters refute wrong views, establish their own views, and then clarify any remaining questions. We must read, study, and hear teachings on the texts by these great Indian masters and then use our human intelligence to the maximum to investigate their meanings.

For forty years now, I have urged monasteries that principally perform rituals to do more study. I've made sure that the nuns have access to higher studies and have encouraged lay Buddhists to study as well. When you learn the Dharma, don't limit yourself to what is said in the textbooks of your own monastery. Study broadly.

6 | How to Structure a Meditation Session

Types of Meditation

OUR HAPPINESS AND SUFFERING is directly related to the objects our mind focuses on and our thoughts and interpretations of them. A mind habituated to focusing on our own or others' faults, exaggerating them, and angrily complaining about them is an unhappy mind. A mind steeped in seeing others' kindness, appreciating it, and wishing them happiness is a peaceful mind. Mental purification is needed to release destructive mental habits and cultivate beneficial ones. Transformation occurs through familiarizing ourselves with wholesome objects and beneficial perspectives.

Familiarization occurs in both formal meditation sessions and in the time between sessions when we go about our daily life activities. Because our unsatisfactory experiences in cyclic existence have no break, neither should our efforts to transform our mind and free it from afflictions. As long as we are under the influence of ignorance and karma, it is necessary to make continuous effort on the path and to discipline and transform our mind in both meditation sessions and break times.

There are several ways of speaking about the various types of meditation. One way is in terms of stabilizing and analytical meditation. *Stabilizing meditation* (T. *'jog sgom*) channels the energy of the mind and generates single-pointedness. It enables the mind to remain on a virtuous object, such as the Buddha, or a neutral object, such as the breath, for as long as we wish without distraction or laxity, and it enhances our concentration (*samādhi*). Concentration brings many benefits: it enables us to investigate objects such as impermanence and emptiness intensely and to familiarize ourselves with virtuous emotions such as love and compassion without distraction.

Analytical meditation (T. *dpyad sgom*) enables us to penetrate and understand an object. Meditation on emptiness cannot be done unless we understand what emptiness is and can identify it correctly. Reasoning is necessary before we can progress to direct nonconceptual perception. Analytical meditation is also used with other lamrim topics—precious human life, death, the qualities of the Three Jewels, and so forth. Here we contemplate the various points the Buddha and great masters have employed to explain these topics. Reflecting on the points one by one can bring deep, transformative understanding.

Both stabilizing and analytical meditation can be done in one meditation session. For example, we reflect on the qualities of our precious human life with analytical meditation. Understanding the purpose and rarity of our precious human life, we automatically feel extremely fortunate, like a beggar who has found a jewel. We then concentrate on that feeling with stabilizing meditation to integrate the experience with our mind. This enables us to remember the preciousness of our life in the break times and influences the choices we make in life. Similarly, analytical meditation is employed to refute inherent existence and leads to a correct understanding of emptiness. We then focus on this absence of inherent existence with stabilizing meditation to accustom our mind to it.

Another way of discussing meditation is meditation on an object and meditation to transform our subjective experience. In *meditation on an object*,[31] we work to apprehend a particular object—impermanence or emptiness, for example—that we haven't previously apprehended. Investigating that object with wisdom, we cultivate a correct ascertainment of it and then familiarize ourselves with that. The mind meditating on impermanence first focuses on a particular thing, such as the body, and then develops an understanding of its attribute of impermanence—the body's momentarily changing nature—which we haven't previously realized. The meditating mind realizes the body's impermanence, and impermanence becomes that mind's apprehended object.

The meditation on emptiness is similar. Emptiness is an object we haven't perceived previously, and the meditating mind endeavors to understand and then see it more clearly. First we obtain a rough idea of the lack of inherent existence, then we apprehend it with a correct inferential cognizer. Finally, we remove the veil of the conceptual appearance and cognize emptiness directly.

In *meditation to transform our subjective experience*,[32] we mold the mind into a particular subjective experience. Compassion is not a separate object that we try to ascertain, as in meditation on an object. Rather, we want to transform our mind into the subjective experience of compassion. To do this, we contemplate sentient beings' kindness and their duḥkha. A wish for them to be free from duḥkha and its causes arises in us, whereby our subjective mental experience becomes compassion. Through familiarization with this experience over time, our compassion gains in strength, until eventually it arises naturally whenever we see a sentient being. To cultivate faith, fortitude, and love, we similarly meditate to transform our subjective experience.

When meditating on compassion, the observed object of our meditation is sentient beings who experience any of the three types of duḥkha. The aspect is the wish to free them from this duḥkha. Compassion does not apprehend freedom from suffering. It is an aspiration and a heart-transforming experience.

Another type of meditation involves visualization, for example, imaging a Buddhist deity and its maṇḍala (environment). Imagining being and acting like a buddha encourages us to create the causes to become one.

Meditation sessions enable you to deepen your understanding and intensify your concentration on the meditation object. In the break times when eating, walking, or engaging in daily life activities, do not forget the meditation topics. With a corner of your mind recall what you have meditated on. You may wish to choose one lamrim topic each day, meditate on it in the morning, and view your experiences that day through the lens of that topic. One day dwell on precious human life—investigate it during meditation sessions and be aware of your fortune and the opportunity it provides during the day. The next day focus on death and impermanence, and as you go about your daily activities, recall that you and the people and environment around you are transient. In this way, avoid becoming attached to anything. The following day, focus on refuge, and so on, cycling through the lamrim topics. In this way, integrate the meaning of each lamrim topic into your life day by day.

You may prefer to focus on one lamrim topic for a week or even a month before going on to the next. This enables you to go more deeply into each one. Alternatively, focus on the topic that seems most appropriate to help subdue the afflictions likely to arise that day, tailoring your practice to your needs each day.

Regularly reading texts about your meditation topic and discussing it with Dharma friends are also helpful. This is like keeping a fire's embers glowing overnight so that the fire is easy to start the next morning. Similarly, cultivating mindfulness of a lamrim topic during break times invigorates and intensifies our meditation sessions and aids our mental development.

In this way, gradually develop your mind. I often advise my friends, including those doing long retreats, not to expect spiritual development to occur in only a few years. The key is to make effort daily so that over time gradual change occurs. We progress toward our long-term goal of buddhahood day by day.

REFLECTION

1. Review the meaning of meditation on an object and meditation to transform our subjective experience. Make examples of each.

2. Review the meaning of stabilizing and analytical meditation. Make examples of how you could employ those in your practice.

Meditation on the Lamrim

Having a consistent and continuous meditation practice produces stable changes in our mind. I would now like to outline how to do a regular daily meditation practice based on the lamrim—stages of the path—in the hopes that you will implement this for your own and others' benefit. With a strong foundation gained through meditation on the lamrim, your natural perspective on life will be the Buddhist worldview, and your character will be shaped by the aspirations for liberation, bodhicitta, and wisdom.

Some people prefer to read a Dharma book, review notes taken during oral teachings, listen to recordings, or watch videos of Dharma talks before meditating so they can meditate on the meaning of what they just studied. Other people prefer to meditate first and study later. Such time for study, reflection, and meditation is important for your emotional, physical, and spiritual health. Make a place for this quiet time in your life and let it become a habit. You'll experience the benefits.

The best time for meditation is in the early morning as the mind is clearer and sharper then and not yet distracted by the day's activities. Familiarizing yourself with wholesome thoughts and emotions in the morning influences how you live the rest of the day, especially if you generate bodhicitta, which opens your heart to all sentient beings, and remember that people and things are transient and lack an independent nature, which reduces your grasping. If your schedule doesn't permit you to meditate in the morning, meditate at another time in the day when you can relax and will not be interrupted.

Although meditating for an hour is good, if that is not possible, do what is comfortable for you. Conclude before you feel tired so that you will have a positive feeling about meditation. Pushing yourself to meditate for longer than you are comfortably able to will make your mind resistant to future practice. Ten minutes of good-quality meditation is better than sitting for an hour with a distracted or sleepy mind. However, a person who is very busy and has little fortitude will find meditation almost impossible. He should do just a short prayer and then finish. That's best.

To get up early, we may have to sacrifice late-night activities in order to go to bed earlier. This may be easier for me to do because I live in a monastic environment in Dharamsala, an Indian town that is fairly quiet in the evening. In other places, there is entertainment and social life, so sticking to a regular schedule of daily meditation may be more challenging. Just as daily meals and exercise are necessary to keep our body healthy, daily spiritual practice is essential for our mental well-being and progress toward awakening.

Meditation sessions consist of three parts: the preparation, actual practice, and conclusion. The *preparation* involves taking refuge in the Buddhas,

Dharma, and Saṅgha; generating the bodhicitta motivation to attain full awakening for the benefit of all sentient beings; and purifying and creating merit. The *actual practice* is meditating on the lamrim topic for that session. At the *conclusion*, dedicate the merit created to attain buddhahood and lead all sentient beings to awakening as well.

Try to avoid developing bad habits in your meditation. As in other activities, correcting a bad habit in our meditation practice is more difficult than establishing a new habit. Pay attention to the meditation instructions and do your best to follow them; if necessary, you can adjust them slightly to suit your personal needs and situation.

The Six Preparatory Practices

When describing how to structure a meditation session, lamrim texts begin with the six preparatory practices that are done before the actual practice. These are: cleaning the room and arranging the altar, making offerings, sitting in the correct meditation position, taking refuge and generating bodhicitta, contemplating the seven limbs, and requesting inspiration from our root and lineage spiritual mentors

Cleaning the room and arranging the altar

Begin by cleaning the room and arranging the altar to enhance the environment in which you meditate and beautify the place where you will invite the buddhas and bodhisattvas to come. Cleaning the environment is analogous to cleansing your mind and making it more receptive. Meditating in an uncluttered and peaceful room is best, not in the same room as the television, computer, or your children's toys. However, if that is not possible, do your meditation session in whatever space is available. It is not necessary to have a separate room for meditation.

On a table, set up the symbols of the Buddha's body, speech, and mind: a statue, a Dharma text, and a stūpa, respectively. Place the image of Śākyamuni Buddha in the center, as he is the founder and source of the teachings. I am sad to see that nowadays some people place meditational deities and not the Buddha at the center of their altars, as if they value the meditational deities more than the Buddha. Seeing the Buddha's image reminds you of his qualities, which gladdens and motivates your mind. Avoid buying costly

Buddha images with the motivation to show them off to friends, and cultivate an attitude of respect for all Dharma items.

Making offerings

Making offerings enables you to create vast merit and cultivate the mind that delights in giving. Offer items that are pure in two regards. First, they are procured honestly, through right livelihood. Avoid obtaining offerings—or for that matter, daily life requisites—through the five wrong livelihoods of flattery, hinting, giving a small gift in the hopes of receiving a large one, coercion, or hypocrisy. Second, the offerings are given with a pure motivation—a sincere wish to practice the Buddhadharma for the sake of all beings—not simply to receive some benefit for this life alone or to have a beautiful altar.

We may offer things from our own culture and items easily available in the place where we live. It is not necessary to imitate Tibetan-style offerings. In Tibet we made food offerings and tormas (ritual cakes) out of tsampa (barley flour) because it was readily available. But in the West tsampa is hard to come by, and it seems strange to eat one thing and offer something else to the Three Jewels, so offer fruit, cookies, and other foods that you consider delicious instead of tormas made of tsampa. I do this too when traveling in other countries.

Most important, the offerings to the buddhas and bodhisattvas should be the same or better quality than what we eat. Avoid making lavish offerings with the hidden motivation of eating them later. Tibetans know that tsog offerings will later be distributed to the assembly, so they use delicious ingredients to make them. But the tormas that will not be eaten are made of cheap ingredients and sometimes taste so bad that no one would even want to eat them! This is not as it should be.

Arrange the offerings nicely with respect for the Three Jewels and with the motivation that the Buddhadharma long endure and sentient beings benefit from it. Whether we are able to offer a lot or a little, our motivation is most important because it is the purity of our intention that determines the value of our actions. Although Milarepa was impoverished, he gained high realizations because of his strong faith, correct motivation, and joyous effort.

Sitting in the correct meditation position

If you can, sit in the seven-point position of Buddha Vairocana as outlined in the *Explanatory Tantra Vajramālā*. Sitting in this way enables the body to remain firm and the mind steady. It also aids the flow of the subtle energies in the body.

1. Sit on a cushion of whatever shape and size works best for you with your legs in the vajra position—the left foot on the right thigh and the right foot on the left thigh. If this isn't possible, other cross-legged positions are fine. Some people find sitting on a slanted meditation bench enables their back to be straight and is easier on their knees. You may also sit on a straight-backed chair with your feet flat on the floor.

2. Put your right hand on top of the left, palms up. Touch the thumbs together lightly and put your hands in your lap near your navel.

3. Keep your shoulders level.

4. Straighten your back.

5. Tuck your chin in slightly so that the tip of your nose is aligned with your navel, but do not let your head droop.

6. Keep your lips and teeth natural, with your tongue on the upper palate to prevent thirst as well as excess saliva.

7. Direct your eyes toward the tip of your nose. If this is difficult, direct your gaze downward in front of you without focusing on anything specific. As your mind becomes more concentrated, you will cease to notice what comes into your field of vision.

Keeping your eyes slightly open when you meditate prevents drowsiness. If your eyes are focused on an attractive object, distraction will easily arise, so place them on a neutral object. Although your eye consciousness may see this object, do not focus on it or let the mental consciousness—the meditating consciousness—get involved with it. Do not intentionally close your eyes, but if they naturally close, it is fine. If you become accustomed to meditating with your eyes slightly open, restraining your senses in break time will be easier because you are already used to ignoring sense data. The position of the eyes may differ according to the practice. When doing the Kālacakra practice, the eyes are open and look up; in Dzogchen, the eyes are open and look straight ahead.

Your physical position should be firm yet relaxed; avoid tensing your muscles. Sitting erect helps the mind to be clear and alert, while lying down often leads to falling asleep. However, this may not be true for people with different habits or cultural backgrounds, so judge this for yourself.

Depending on the layout of the room, facing east is recommended because the sun rises there and light uplifts your mental attitude and dispels mental sluggishness. Sitting in a well-lit room also serves that purpose if you struggle with drowsiness. If your mind is easily excited, you may face the wall, but otherwise it is not necessary to do that.

The Vairocana posture is sometimes said to have eight points. In this case, calming the mind by observing the breath is added to the above seven. This is especially helpful to do if your mind is agitated. Breathe in and out in a natural, even rhythm without undue noise or effort. Do not force your breath. Place your attention on the breath, experiencing and observing each breath, without letting the mind stray to other objects. If you get distracted by a sound, thought, or physical sensation, simply acknowledge it, and then return your attention to the gentle flow of the breath. In this way, let your mind calm down in preparation for taking refuge and generating bodhicitta.

Meditation on the breath may be done in several ways and for different purposes in both Buddhist and non-Buddhist contexts. Here it is done to calm the mind before meditating on the stages of the path. Meditations to develop serenity and insight using the breath as the object of meditation will be discussed later.

After observing the breath for a few minutes, examine your mind to see if any afflictions are present. If they are, reflect that you have experienced so much misery in this and previous lives by following attachment, anger, and confusion. Make a firm determination not to get entangled with them, but to do your practice with focus.

Taking refuge and generating bodhicitta
The process of taking refuge and generating bodhicitta begins with visualizing the Buddha, Dharma, and Saṅgha in the space in front. You may do the simple visualization of Śākyamuni Buddha, thinking he is the embodiment of all the Buddhas, Dharma, and Saṅgha, or the complex visualization with the lineage teachers, deities, bodhisattvas, and so on surrounding

the central figure of Śākyamuni Buddha. When meditating mainly on the method side of the path—the cultivation of renunciation, bodhicitta, and the like—you may want to visualize Avalokiteśvara and Maitreya near the Buddha, and when developing wisdom, you can imagine Mañjuśrī next to the Buddha. When facing obstacles, such as illness or injury, visualize Tārā seated near the Buddha, and so on.

Visualization is an imaginative process done in our minds. Do not think you should "see" things as you do when your eyes are open; we are generating mental images in our mind's eye. For beginners these images will be vague, but as we progress and develop familiarity with visualization, they will become more vivid.

You may wonder why Tibetan Buddhism encourages visualization. Imagining the holy beings naturally makes us reflect on their awakened qualities; thinking that we are in their presence creates a feeling of closeness with them. All of this strengthens our faith and confidence in the Three Jewels, which are more important than the clarity of the visualization. To review, there are three types of faith: inspired, aspiring, and believing faith.[33] We cultivate inspired faith by discerning and reflecting on the wonderful qualities of the Three Jewels, making our mind inspired with a vivid reflection of their qualities. To this joyous state of mind, we add understanding of the four truths of āryas, which leads us to be convinced that the Three Jewels—particularly the Dharma Jewel, which consists of the third and fourth truths—are nondeceptive objects of refuge that we can fully rely on to guide us to liberation and awakening. This is believing faith. Strengthening this faith, we gain stronger determination and do not simply admire or believe in the Three Jewels but aspire to become like them. This is aspiring faith, which gives us great enthusiasm to practice.

To engage in the uncommon Mahāyāna practice of taking refuge, in addition to visualizing the Three Jewels in front, imagine all sentient beings surrounding you. Recalling that they are experiencing various types of duḥkha in cyclic existence, generate strong compassion that wants them to be free from all duḥkha. While chanting the refuge verse, think that you are leading them in turning to the Three Jewels for refuge.

Some people think that generating compassion is useless because it is impossible to eliminate suffering completely. Remembering that all afflictions can be eliminated and that all beings have the potential to become buddhas clears this misconception. Other people fear that thinking about others' suffering will cause them to feel hopeless and fall into despair. Should this happen, our focus has shifted from compassion for others to personal despair that wants to protect ourselves from witnessing anything discomforting. To renew our compassion, we should return our focus to sentient beings and recall the joyous and skillful ways in which the Three Jewels continuously work to benefit them. This gives us hope and inspires us to work for the welfare of others.

Reflecting in this way, our compassion for sentient beings and faith in the Three Jewels become so strong that we want to express them by reciting "I take refuge in the gurus. I take refuge in the Buddha. I take refuge in the Dharma. I take refuge in the Saṅgha." These words reflect our inner feelings of faith and determination.

Some people ask why "I take refuge in the gurus" is added, since Buddhists have three objects of refuge, not four. The spiritual master is the one who introduces us to the Three Jewels, and due to his or her kindness, we are able to learn and practice the path and eventually become the Three Jewels. To emphasize the importance and kindness of our spiritual mentors, especially in tantric practice we include them when taking refuge. Here the guru is seen as inseparable with the Buddha.

Recite each line of the refuge several times before going on to the next. This is more effective than reciting all the lines together several times. While reciting each line, focus on light streaming from that refuge object into you, purifying all negativities you have created in relation to that refuge object and bringing its inspiration into you. In this or previous lives, we may have angrily criticized our spiritual teacher or defamed the Buddha. We may have deprecated the Saṅgha with our sarcastic remarks.

Perhaps we criticized subtle points of the Dharma thinking they are just Tibetan culture, or said that the Dharma is not a correct path because it does not agree with our ideas. Before we can accurately discriminate what is Asian culture and what is the Buddha's teachings, it is unwise to dismiss certain teachings, "This doesn't pertain to me. It is only meant for Tibetans." Similarly, it is not wise to declare, "The Buddha didn't teach this and that" simply because we do not feel comfortable with that teaching. It is wiser to maintain an open mind and think, "I do not understand this point and will continue to learn and think about it until I reach a clear understanding. In the meantime, I will practice the teachings that I understand because doing so benefits me."

Negativities in relation to the Saṅgha are created by criticizing āryas or the monastic community. Since we ordinary beings are not capable of discerning the spiritual levels of others, it is wiser to avoid hostile judgment concerning anyone, as this interferes with our refuge and creates destructive karma. Avoid making sweeping statements about the Saṅgha, for example, saying that monasticism is useless and outdated, that monastics are parasites on society, or that celibacy is unhealthy. Such misconceptions make me sad. Our teacher, Śākyamuni Buddha himself, was a monastic, and he established the monastic community for a good purpose. Due to the kindness of the Saṅgha, the teachings exist in pure forms today and we are able to encounter them. Respecting the precepts that exist in the monastics' mindstreams enables us to benefit from their good example of ethical conduct.

When visualizing white light flowing from each refuge object into you and all sentient beings around you, think that the negativities created in relation to that refuge object are purified. Then imagine golden light streaming from them into you and all sentient beings, inspiring your minds with their good qualities. In this way, form a pure and strong connection to the Three Jewels.

After taking refuge, generate bodhicitta. Cultivating the proper motivation for our meditation is extremely important, because the result of our spiritual practice accords with our motivation for doing it. Although your bodhicitta may at present be contrived and generated only with effort, do not despair. By reflecting on bodhicitta repeatedly, you will gradually become more accustomed to it, until eventually this altruistic intention will arise effortlessly within you.

At this point, pause and be aware of the status of the I who is taking refuge and aspiring to awaken. How does this I exist: Does it have an inherent nature or does it exist dependent on other factors?

Now, with firm aspiration to follow the guidance of the Three Jewels for the benefit of all sentient beings and with a sincere wish to become the Three Jewels, dissolve the refuge objects into you by imagining that they melt into light and dissolve into the Buddha, who, in turn, dissolves into light that absorbs into your midbrow. The dissolving of the refuge objects into you is not like butter melting on a dish, where the butter and dish remain separate. Rather, reflect that we ordinary beings and the Buddha have the same nature. Just as the Buddha's mind is empty of inherent existence, our mind is also free from inherent existence. This is the meaning of the statement, "The buddhas and sentient beings are of equal taste in emptiness." Just as the buddhas were able to attain awakening because they had the natural Buddha nature and the transforming buddha nature, we have the same buddha nature that they have. Just as the buddhas were once ordinary beings who practiced the Dharma diligently, removed their faults, and developed all good qualities, we, too, can do this by putting energy into cultivating the path.

Reflecting on these similarities between the buddhas and sentient beings leads us to contemplate the ultimate nature of all existents—emptiness. This is the real meaning of the Buddha dissolving into us. At this point, do not focus on the qualities of the Three Jewels, but on their emptiness of inherent existence, which is the same as your ultimate nature. When meditating on emptiness, conventional objects such as buddhas and sentient beings do not appear to the mind, so do not see yourself and the refuge objects as separate; you have become nondual in emptiness. At this point, dwell in emptiness according to your present understanding of it.

After a while, within this emptiness of true existence, your wisdom realizing emptiness appears in the form of the Buddha with a body made of golden light. Imagine that, as the Buddha, you radiate light that purifies and inspires sentient beings, transforming them into buddhas and their environments into pure lands—places where all conditions are conducive for Dharma practice. Allow your mind to rest in this vision of all sentient beings being liberated from cyclic existence due to your having guided them with compassion.

Then reflect that sentient beings still live in conflict because they lack the four immeasurables—equanimity, love, compassion, and joy. Equanimity is the wish for all beings to be free from bias, attachment, and anger. Love is the wish for them to have happiness and its causes. Compassion is the wish that they be free from duḥkha and its causes. Joy is the wish that they never be separated from sorrowless bliss.

Meditate on these four immeasurables to reinforce your feeling of connection and involvement with others. This will help you to avoid harming them and to engage in benefiting them in your daily life. Although these practices are done at the level of imagination, they plant seeds in our mindstreams that enable us to act in this way.

Contemplating the seven limbs

Before contemplating the seven limbs, we imagine the merit field (*puṇyakṣetra*). A field of merit is so-called because in it we plant the seeds of virtue that will bring good results. Here the field of merit is the assembly of our root spiritual mentors, the lineage spiritual mentors, meditation deities, buddhas, bodhisattvas, solitary realizer and śrāvaka arhats, heroes (*ḍākas*) and heroines (*ḍākinīs*), and Dharma protectors. As the details of this visualization and the way to contemplate its meaning have been described extensively in other texts, I will not go into detail about them here.

Having imagined the holy beings in the space in front of us, we then cultivate the seven practices in their presence. These are prostrating, making offerings, confessing our negativities, rejoicing in goodness and virtue, requesting Dharma teachings, requesting the Buddha to remain in our world, and dedicating the merit.

The purpose of these seven limbs is to purify our mindstream and create merit so that our meditation session will be effective and we will gain deeper understanding and experience of the stages of the path. The importance of purification and creation of merit cannot be overestimated.

You may recite a long or short version of the seven limbs while contemplating its meaning. A short version is:

> Reverently I prostrate with my body, speech, and mind,
> and present clouds of every type of offering, actual and
> mentally transformed.
> I confess all my destructive actions accumulated since
> beginningless time,
> and rejoice in the virtues of all holy and ordinary beings.
> Please remain until cyclic existence ends,
> and turn the wheel of Dharma for sentient beings.
> I dedicate all the virtues of myself and others to the great
> awakening.

Prostrating reduces our pride and increases our humility. Making the excellent qualities of the holy beings vivid in our minds, it strengthens our aspiration to practice the path to develop those same qualities ourselves. Prostrations are done mentally by remembering the good qualities of the Three Jewels, verbally by praising these qualities with our speech, and physically by bowing down to show our respect.

Making offerings reduces attachment and stinginess and increases our generosity and delight in giving. Offer actual objects on the altar—fruit, flowers, lights, incense, water, perfume, and so on—and mentally offer beautiful objects that we possess or forests, wildflowers, and other places of natural beauty that are possessed by others. When making mental offerings, imagine objects of incomparable beauty that fill the universe, offer them to the Three Jewels, and imagine them experiencing bliss from receiving your offerings.

Offer your Dharma practice—your effort, understanding, and virtue—by imagining them in the form of magnificent objects that you present to the merit field. This is the supreme offering that pleases the buddhas and bodhisattvas because it contributes to their aim of liberating all sentient beings.

As Śāntideva stresses in *Engaging in the Bodhisattvas' Deeds* (*Bodhicaryāvatāra*), making offerings is necessary to accumulate the merit that supports us in generating bodhicitta and attaining full awakening. High bodhisattvas, such as Samantabhadra, emanate a vast display of sumptuous and glorious items that they offer to all the buddhas and bodhisattvas in all the pure lands throughout the universe. While we are currently unable to emanate these elaborate offerings, visualizing them brings great benefit because they are free from the attachment we may have for our possessions. In addition, since visualized offerings are mentally fabricated and do not exist in the way they appear, it is easier to contemplate that phenomena arise due to designation by name and concept and thus are empty of inherent existence. You may want to meditate using the verses of offering that Śāntideva wrote in chapter 2 of his inspiring book.

Confessing negativities is done through the four opponent powers. We have engaged in countless physical, verbal, and mental deeds motivated by ignorance, animosity, and attachment. The seeds of these misdeeds ripen in unpleasant or painful experiences, obscure our minds from gaining realizations, and limit our ability to benefit others. To purify them, first generate a sense of regret for the harm you have inflicted on yourself and others through your destructive behavior. Regret is the main cause to purify destructive actions, and the stronger it is, the stronger will be the second power, the determination to restrain from such actions in the future. This step gives you the inner strength to begin changing your ways and counteracting habitual harmful behavior.

Third, take refuge in the Three Jewels, which purifies destructive actions created in relation to the Three Jewels, and generate bodhicitta, which purifies negativities created in relation to other sentient beings. Taking refuge and generating bodhicitta transforms the harmful or ignorant attitude you previously had toward holy beings and sentient beings into a virtuous mental relationship with them. After confessing your faults, it is helpful to do the taking and giving (T. *tong len*) meditation, which will be described later.

Fourth, apply remedies to those destructive actions by engaging in constructive actions, for example, bowing to the Three Jewels, reciting mantras, making offerings, circumambulating holy objects, meditating on emptiness, generating bodhicitta, doing volunteer service at a charity, Dharma center, or monastery, or helping others in other ways.

Rejoicing in your own and others' virtue is the fourth limb. Doing this is an excellent method to fill your mind with hope and joy and overcomes competition and jealousy. Reflect with joy on the virtues you and others have created in this and previous lives and at all the goodness in the world. Rejoicing in your own virtue invigorates and multiplies it so that it will increase day by day. Also admire and rejoice in the virtues of people you know and those you don't, reflecting repeatedly on their constructive thoughts, feelings, words, and deeds. Rejoicing in the virtues and spiritual attainments of the buddhas, bodhisattvas, solitary realizers, and śrāvakas throughout all time and space creates vast merit. If you and others are of similar levels on the path, by rejoicing at their virtue you accumulate merit equal to theirs. If they are of lesser attainment, your rejoicing creates more merit than their original virtuous action. The practice of rejoicing is praised because through making a small effort, great merit is accumulated.

Requesting Dharma teachings counteracts abandoning the Dharma and creates the cause to receive teachings in the future. We must not take our present good fortune of encountering teachers and teachings for granted, but appreciate and take advantage of them; requesting teachings is one way to do this. Requesting the buddhas to turn the wheel of Dharma—to teach us the path to awakening—also creates the cause to receive teachings in the future. Whenever possible attend Dharma discourses given by qualified spiritual mentors. As a beginner, study books that give you a general overview of the path. As you advance, delve into the sūtras, the great Indian commentaries, and commentaries by other Buddhist sages.

Requesting the buddhas to remain until cyclic existence ends helps to purify negativities created in relation to our spiritual mentors and the buddhas and increases our understanding of the importance of having excellent spiritual mentors. With heartfelt sincerity, request the emanation bodies of buddhas not to pass into parinirvāṇa, but to remain in the world to guide sentient beings according to their various dispositions and tendencies.

To conclude the seven-limb prayer, *dedicate the merit* accumulated from the above practices for the full awakening of yourself and all others. Imagine your merit transforms into offerings that you present to the Three Jewels and to sentient beings.

Requesting inspiration

Requesting inspiration increases our connection to the lineage of practitioners who have preceded us and who have done what we aspire to do. It also invigorates our confidence and enthusiasm to practice the Dharma. While reciting the "Supplication for the Three Great Purposes," visualize light and nectar flowing from the lineage teachers into you and all the sentient beings around you (LC 1:98):

> Please inspire me and all mother sentient beings to quickly abandon all flawed states of mind, beginning with not respecting our spiritual mentors up to grasping the true existence of persons and phenomena. Please inspire us to easily generate all flawless states of mind, beginning with respecting our spiritual mentors up to knowing the reality of selflessness. Please inspire us to quell all inner and outer hindrances.

People ask, "If buddhas help sentient beings impartially and their awakening activities are spontaneous, why do we need to request inspiration?" Receiving the inspiration of the buddhas is a dependent process that relies on their ability to help as well as our receptivity. Our turning to them for refuge and making sincere requests opens our mind to receive their awakening influence. A large, shady tree naturally has the ability to protect us from the sun, but we have to go and stand under it. Receiving inspiration and the buddhas' awakening influence depends on the combination of the tree of their compassion and our sitting under it.

Now imagine that all the figures in the merit field dissolve into the central figure of Śākyamuni Buddha, who then comes on top of your head, facing the same direction as you. Again imagine light flowing from the Buddha into you. This light purifies all negativities and fills you with all the blessings, inspiration, and understanding of the Buddha. Feel Buddha's compassion for you and his willingness to guide you to awakening. As you meditate like this, recite the Buddha's name mantra, *om mune mune maha-muneya svāhā*, as much as possible.

After reciting the mantra, do a glance meditation on the stages of the path to awakening by reviewing the principal meditations in a brief form. Reciting a short lamrim text such as the "Foundation of all Good Qualities," "Parting from the Four Attachments," "Three Principal Aspects of the Path," or "Thirty-Seven Practices of Bodhisattvas" enables us to briefly reflect on all the stages of the path and imprint them in our mindstreams.

Then, with the Buddha on the crown of your head, begin the actual meditation session. With lowered eyes, turn your mind inward to reflect on the lamrim topic you have chosen for that session. Make examples from your life in which these teachings apply and could help you.

The Actual Session and Dedication at the Conclusion

The majority of meditations on the stages of the path involve analytical meditation on the topic followed by stabilizing meditation on the conclusion we have reached. Before meditating on a topic, have in mind an outline of the major points and then ponder them in order, one by one. Until you become familiar with a topic, make an outline of its points by referring to this book and add pertinent points from other lamrim books. If you read, listened to, or watched a teaching on the topic before the meditation session, jot down a brief outline of salient points to meditate on. Use reasoning and logic to understand the meaning of each point, and make examples from your life that pertain to the points. In this way, conviction in their veracity will arise. In addition, you will gain familiarity with the topics so that you will be able to remember and apply them during your daily life.

When you reach a conclusion through your reflection or a strong understanding of the topic arises in your mind, cease analytical meditation, and with stabilizing meditation focus your mind one-pointedly on the meaning you discovered or the experience you gained. Employing both analytical and stabilizing meditation to the topics in this way is important for gaining and sustaining an understanding of the path.

For example, to meditate on precious human life, first make an outline of the eight freedoms and ten fortunes and add other pertinent points. Then do the six preparatory practices. Next contemplate the points one by one, thinking about them logically and relating them to your life. When you feel a sense of appreciation for your life and an eagerness to use it for Dharma practice, you have reached the proper conclusion. At that point, stop thinking about the points and let your mind dwell on the fact that you have a precious human life and the feeling of being extremely fortunate.

When you are interested in the lamrim topics, your reflection and analysis will keep your attention on the subject. That helps bring your mind to a focused state. If you find stabilizing meditation difficult because your mind is easily distracted, put more emphasis on checking meditation.

Near the end of the session, it is helpful to relate the topic to the method and wisdom aspects of the path—bodhicitta and the wisdom realizing emptiness, respectively. For example, if your meditation topic is the ten nonvirtues, first reflect on them in terms of your own life. Then reflect that like you, other sentient beings have engaged in these nonvirtues and will have to experience their results. Generate the wish to become a buddha in order to lead them on the path to liberation so they will be free from experiencing painful results and the afflictions that cause them. Then reflect that all these karmas and their results are empty of true existence. They arise and function dependently, like a dream, and do not exist in the way they appear.

When you have meditated on a particular topic sufficiently, imagine the Buddha on your head dissolves into you, merging with your mind at your heart cakra at the center of your chest. Feel that your mind and the Buddha's mind are inseparable.

As mentioned previously, do not expect instant results or fantastic peak experiences. Instead, be satisfied with gradual growth in your compassion and wisdom and seek stable, steady change. By meditating consistently, your understanding will deepen over the months and years.

At the conclusion of a session, dedicate the merit created from your meditation to attain awakening for the benefit of all sentient beings. The primary purpose of dedicating the merit is to make the results of our virtue inexhaustible, lasting until all sentient beings attain full awakening. While the merit can still bring good results before awakening, it will not be exhausted until awakening is attained. By connecting even small virtue to the wider vision of the awakening of all sentient beings, you bring an extraordinary dimension to this small action. It immerses your mind in bodhicitta, increases your generosity, and expands your rejoicing at virtue.

In addition, seal the dedication by reflecting that you as the agent, the merit you are dedicating, the awakening you are dedicating to attain, and the sentient beings you wish to benefit are all empty of existing from their own side, but exist dependently. As Nāgārjuna says in *Praise to the Supramundane* (*Lokātītastava* 9):

> There exists no agent, no subject too;
> no merit [exists], they arise through dependence.
> "Though dependently arisen, they are unborn,"
> so you have proclaimed, O Master of Words.[34]

While none of the elements of a dedication—the person, merit, and so forth—exist inherently, they exist nominally by being merely designated by name and concept. Their emptiness of inherent existence and their conventional existence are not contradictory. Reflecting in this way increases our understanding of the compatibility of emptiness and dependent arising and prevents us from becoming arrogant.

Interrelationship of the Lamrim Topics

Analytical meditation on these lamrim topics is critical at all levels of the path. It transforms our mind by giving us an overview of the entire path and establishing the Buddhist worldview firmly within us. It engenders great conviction in the path and a correct motivation for spiritual practice. While other forms of meditation may make us feel good in the moment, if they do not increase our understanding of the undesirable nature of cyclic existence and our wish to be free from it, our motivation and enthusiasm for practice will flag. Analytical meditation makes our motivation strong and stable, and with such a motivation our analytical and stabilizing meditation on emptiness will bear fruit. We will be able to enter the Vajrayāna, practice it correctly, and attain awakening.

The order of the topics in the stages of the path are skillfully arranged to gradually lead your mind to deeper understandings, so try to meditate on them in order. Of course, if you face a certain problem and know that a particular meditation will help calm your mind, do that meditation even if it isn't in sequence.

Repeatedly cycle through the sequence of meditations. Grounding yourself in the initial meditations will facilitate understanding the later ones. Going directly to the advanced meditations is not helpful for our overall development. Once you have a heartfelt understanding of one topic, don't just leave it be and go on to the next. Continue to review your understanding and stabilize your experience, even though your focus has shifted to the next topic.

The meditations of the three levels of practitioners are intertwined and cross-fertilize one another. Our understanding of the earlier topics sets the stage for the later ones, and our understanding of the later ones enriches our experience of the earlier ones. For example, precious human life appears early in the lamrim, but the more we have a feeling for the bodhicitta meditations, the more we will see our human life as precious because it provides us the opportunity to develop bodhicitta. While the perfection of fortitude is explained in the path of the advanced practitioner, we must learn and practice fortitude from the beginning because we must lessen our anger in order to abandon destructive actions.

Some lamrim topics come up repeatedly in the sequence each time we explore them in more depth. Ethical conduct first appears in the topic of karma on the initial level; it appears again as the higher training in ethical conduct on the intermediate level, and again on the advanced level with the bodhisattvas' perfection of ethical conduct. Each time our understanding of what to practice and abandon is refined.

After gaining a firm understanding of the lamrim through study, reflection, and meditation, some practitioners may wish to direct more energy to developing serenity through perfecting their stabilizing meditation. Others may wish to focus more on the meditations regarding the thirty-seven harmonies with awakening, while others may prefer to emphasize insight into emptiness or tantric practice. These decisions are best made in consultation with a spiritual mentor.

Breaks between Meditation Sessions

Our meditation sessions and our daily life activities flow together, one following the other without pause. To indicate this relationship, the great masters call our daily life activities "break times between meditation sessions." Both play a role in our spiritual life. Meditation sessions give us the opportunity to practice in a more focused way. Daily life activities provide the chance to test how well we have integrated the meditation topics into our lives. We may meditate on fortitude in the morning, but the real test is when we have to deal with a difficult person. Observing the thoughts and emotions that arise in our minds during the day will give us an idea of the qualities we need to strengthen in order to counteract the afflictions that arise frequently in our minds.

Spiritual practice does not occur only when we recite a text or meditate, but also while we walk down the street, clean our room, and interact with others. Dharma practice involves watching our mind and keeping it in a wholesome state no matter what we are doing. We can practice anywhere and at any time.

What we do during the break times between meditation sessions influences our meditation sessions. For this reason, great practitioners advise moderation in food and sleep, guarding the sense doors, and acting with introspective awareness while engaging in daily life activities.

Food

What we eat influences our mental state. The food should be nutritious and easily digestible. We should eat a moderate amount: eating too much makes the mind drowsy; eating too little makes the body weak. In *Middle Stages of Meditation* (*Bhāvanākrama II*) Kamalaśīla encourages practitioners to have a vegetarian diet. In general, this is conducive for being clear-minded when meditating, although depending on someone's physical condition, taking meat may be necessary. Drinking alcohol, taking recreational drugs, or misusing prescription drugs are out of the question if we want to concentrate the mind, and smoking is similarly to be abandoned.

If attachment to food arises, as it can easily do when we limit other distractions, think of what the food looks like after it is chewed and after it is digested; think of the excrement that food produces. Contemplate how much of our precious human life is involved in procuring, preparing, and eating food as well as cleaning up afterward. Some people spend hours discussing the foods they like and planning what to eat, yet we often hardly taste the food because we are talking to a friend or reading while eating. The pleasure of eating ends quickly, and sometimes we feel worse from having overeaten.

Offering our food to the Three Jewels before we eat is meritorious and allows us to pause and reflect. In the Chinese tradition, five points are recited before eating and are contemplated while eating:

1. I contemplate all the causes and conditions and the kindness of others by which I have received this food.
2. I contemplate my own practice, constantly trying to improve it.
3. I contemplate my mind, cautiously guarding it from wrongdoing, greed, and other defilements.
4. I contemplate this food, treating it as wondrous medicine to nourish my body.
5. I contemplate the aim of buddhahood, accepting and consuming this food in order to accomplish it.

In the Tibetan tradition, verses of homage and offering are commonly recited before the main meal.

Great compassionate Protector,
all-knowing Teacher,
field of merit and good qualities vast as an ocean—
to the Tathāgata, I bow.

Through purity, freeing from attachment,
through virtue, freeing from the unfortunate states,
unique, supreme ultimate reality—
to the Dharma that is peace, I bow.

Having freed themselves, showing the path to freedom too,
well established in the trainings,
the holy field endowed with good qualities—
to the Saṅgha, I bow.

To the supreme teacher, the precious Buddha,
to the supreme refuge, the holy precious Dharma,
to the supreme guides, the precious Saṅgha—
to all objects of refuge we make this offering.

May we and all those around us
never be separated from the Three Jewels in any of our lives.
May we always have the opportunity to make offerings to them,
and may we continuously receive their blessings and inspiration
    to progress along the path.

By seeing this food as medicine,
I will consume it without attachment or complaint,
not to increase my arrogance, strength, or good looks,
but solely to sustain my life.

At the conclusion of a meal Tibetan monastics make offerings to the
hungry ghosts and recite homages to the buddhas. We then dedicate for the
welfare of those who offered our food.

May all those who offered me food attain the happiness of total peace. May all those who offered me drink, who served me, who received me, who honored me, or who made offerings to me attain happiness that is total peace.

May all those who scold me, make me unhappy, hit me, attack me with weapons, or do things up to the point of killing me attain the happiness of awakening. May they fully awaken to the unsurpassed, perfectly accomplished state of Buddhahood.

By the merit of offering food, may they have a good complexion, magnificence, and strength. May they find foods having hundreds of tastes and live with the food of samādhi.

By the merit of offering drink, may their afflictions, hunger, and thirst be pacified. May they possess good qualities such as generosity and take a rebirth without any sickness or thirst.

The one who gives, the one who receives, and the generous action are not to be observed as truly existent. By giving with impartiality, may the benefactors attain perfection.

By the power of being generous, may they become buddhas for the benefit of sentient beings, and through generosity may all the beings who have not been liberated by previous conquerors be liberated.

By the merit of this generosity, may the nāga kings, gods having faith in the Dharma, leaders who support religious freedom, benefactors, and others living in the area live long, enjoy good health and prosperity, and attain lasting happiness.

Due to this virtue, may all beings complete the collections of merit and wisdom. May they attain the two buddha bodies resulting from merit and wisdom.

Sleep

Sleep allows the body to rest, which makes it more serviceable for engaging in virtuous activities. Sleeping in moderation produces good results. Too much sleep makes the mind dull, and too little is also not good. Sleeping during the middle part of the night is advised, as is rising early. It is best to sleep in the "lion position," on your right side, with the left leg on the right, and your right hand under your right cheek. This helps to maintain mindfulness during sleep and to prevent nightmares and nonvirtuous dreams.

Sleep is a changeable mental factor; it becomes virtuous when we fall asleep with a positive thought or intention. Meditating, reading a Dharma book, or contemplating a wholesome topic before going to sleep helps us do that, as does thinking, "I will sleep to rest my body and mind so that I can wake up refreshed and continue practicing the Dharma."

If an affliction arises as you are falling asleep or when you are dreaming, notice it and let it go. Do not indulge in thoughts of attachment or anger while falling asleep. If you do, those thoughts and images will occupy your mind for many hours while you sleep, making your sleep nonvirtuous. In addition, your mind will be restless or in a bad mood when you awake.

When you lie down, imagine the Buddha sitting on your pillow and lay your head in his lap. Visualize very gentle, peaceful light flowing from the Buddha into you as you fall asleep. This will prevent your sleep from being too heavy and enable you to awake without grogginess. Make a determination to arise when you are rested, without oversleeping. Also generate the intention to maintain a wholesome mental state the next day.

The *Flower Ornament Sūtra* contains verses that bodhisattvas contemplate as they fall asleep, dream, and wake up:

> "May all sentient beings attain the dimension of reality of
> a Buddha."
> This is the aspiration of a bodhisattva when going to sleep.

> "May all sentient beings realize the dreamlike nature of things."
> This is the aspiration of a bodhisattva while dreaming.

> "May all beings awake from the sleep of ignorance."
> This is the aspiration of a bodhisattva when waking up.

> "May all beings attain the buddha's form bodies."
> This is the aspiration of a bodhisattva when getting up.

If you have received empowerment and instructions in highest yoga tantra, do the practice of transforming sleep into the truth body, dreaming into the enjoyment body, and waking up into the emanation body. Training in this practice now is of great benefit at the time of death.

Activities

During your daily activities, continue to contemplate the lamrim topics. Some people go through the lamrim topics sequentially, seeing everything they encounter in a day in terms of the topic of meditation that morning. Doing this makes it easier to return to the experience of these topics in meditation sessions. In break times, be mindful of your precepts and ethical values—remembering them throughout the day—and apply introspective awareness to monitor if you are living according to them. In this way your mind will be in a wholesome state when you next meditate. However, if break times are passed in distraction—gossiping, singing, reading magazines, or watching violent films—these images and memories will plague your meditation. Please observe your own experiences to see if this is true.

Making Requests, Receiving Blessings, and Gaining Realizations

The topic of requesting and receiving inspiration from the buddhas is not easy to understand, so I would like to explain it further. To gain realizations of the path, we need to create the causes—both the principal causes and the cooperative conditions that support the principal causes. The principal causes to progress on the path are receiving teachings from a qualified teacher, reflecting and meditating on them, and putting them into practice in daily life. Creating these main causes is essential. Without our sincere and consistent practice, our mind won't be transformed even if all the buddhas came before us.

The cooperative conditions that help the principal causes to ripen into the resultant realizations of the path may be external or internal. External cooperative conditions include being in the presence of our spiritual mentor, staying at a holy place such as a monastery or temple, living with other sincere Dharma practitioners, and meditating in front of an image of the Buddha.

An analogy is helpful to understand how an external condition can help to deepen our Dharma understanding. If we know nothing about ecology, we won't understand much by hearing an expert respond to questions about it. But if we already have some background yet lack clarity on this subject, the words of an expert will dispel our doubts and clarify our understanding.

Similarly, we may have some knowledge about a Dharma topic, but don't understand it well. If someone who has meditated deeply on the topic discusses it, the combination of our knowledge and the words of a compassionate and wise person will give rise to an understanding that we did not have before. The basic cause is our own knowledge; the other person's words lift our understanding to another level.

Our daily Dharma studies and practices establish the groundwork so that being in holy sites or in the presence of our spiritual mentors will effect experiences and realizations in our minds. We may recite the verses to generate bodhicitta every day, but not feel much when we do, even though we have admiration for bodhicitta. Then one day, while repeating the same verses in the presence of our spiritual mentor, the words have a totally new effect on our mind and deep feelings of compassion and altruism blossom in us. Similarly, we may study and reflect on emptiness often but reach a mental roadblock that we cannot seem to get beyond. When we meditate on emptiness under the bodhi tree in Bodhgaya, that obstacle disappears and our understanding of emptiness becomes clearer. The inspiration of our spiritual mentor and the blessing of the site of the Buddha's awakening are cooperative conditions; the indispensable principal cause is our effort to practice sincerely. Without this, such experiences do not magically happen.

If we have knowledge of the Buddha's qualities as well as strong confidence that awakening is possible, our mind is more receptive to the Buddha's awakening influence at pilgrimage sites. We cannot force ourselves to have faith in the Three Jewels; stable faith is gained through learning and reflection. If a person has little interest in the Dharma or minimal faith in the Buddha, although a good imprint is left on her mindstream by going to Bodhgaya, very little else will happen. She may spend a lot of time drinking tea and visiting tourist shops!

Internal cooperative conditions include purification and collection of merit, as explained above in the seven-limb prayer, as well as requesting our spiritual mentors, buddhas, meditation deities, and bodhisattvas to bless and inspire our minds. Several factors, such as the qualities of the person(s) we request and how we make the request, play a role.

Realized beings possess marvelous qualities that enable them to influence others in a positive way. In contrast, ordinary people and worldly gods cannot inspire our mind very much. If you visualize President Franklin Roosevelt and make a strong request to realize great compassion, what happens? Maybe psychologically someone could be helped a little, but aside from that, nothing else occurs because the person you request for spiritual inspiration is an ordinary being. Contrariwise, due to their great accumulation of merit and the force of their boundless compassion, buddhas and bodhisattvas have a certain power or energy that can affect our minds in a positive way.

People who accept the Mahāyāna doctrine of the four buddha bodies have a sense of the abilities the awakened ones possess to guide and inspire us. Even if we see the Buddha as a historical person who lived on this earth, it is clear that he was an extraordinary human being who accumulated great merit and had profound realizations. The depth of the Buddha's compassion and the extent of his skillful means and wisdom are evident in his life story. A person of such magnificent qualities must have abilities to benefit others that the rest of us lack.

In our daily practice, we request all holy beings in the merit field to come to the place where we meditate. From their side, invitations are unnecessary. These requests are done to benefit us, so that we turn our attention to them and feel their presence. But beings who lack spiritual realizations cannot come even if we invite them, unless we send a car to pick them up! We may sincerely pray for President Roosevelt to come to our meditation place, but he cannot do so. If we invite worldly gods and spirits to come, they will not know an invitation has been extended, and even if they know, there is not a lot they can do to help us gain Dharma realizations.

How does someone gain the ability to bless another's mind? On the mundane level, we see that some people have unusual abilities, such as the ability to hypnotize others. From the Buddhist viewpoint, this is due to karma they created in previous lives. If some ordinary people have the ability to influence the minds of others in an unusual way, then surely those with great spiritual realizations and compassion must be able to do so. By means of their awakening activities, buddhas spontaneously and effortlessly act to benefit all beings according to their level of receptivity.

The power of the buddhas' realizations, compassion, and awakening activity alone is not enough to effect change in us. If the conditions are not ripe within us, very little occurs. Just as the sun shines everywhere, but only upturned vessels are filled with sunlight, the buddhas' awakening influence is always present, regardless of whether we believe it exists, practice the teachings, or visualize the buddhas and request their inspiration. From our side, doing these activities makes our minds more receptive to receive their awakening influence. Receiving inspiration is a dependent arising; it depends on the state of our mind as well as on the wisdom, compassion, and power of the awakened ones.

How we make the requests is also important. The more focused and clear our visualization of the Buddha is, the more we feel that we are in his presence. This facilitates our experiencing the Buddha's inspiration and blessing.

The Buddhist concept of "blessing and inspiration" cannot be understood with sensory direct perception. It depends in part on our conviction in the possibility of awakening, and thus the possibility of developing the effortless, spontaneous awakening activities that can spark realizations in receptive beings. If we have confidence that we can awaken, it is not difficult to know that others have awakened before us and have gained these special abilities. In short, the deeper our refuge in the Three Jewels, the more we will make effort to transform our minds and the greater our receptivity to the buddhas' awakening activities will be.

Requesting the Buddha for inspiration to generate bodhicitta or realize emptiness is different than requesting an external creator for blessings. Buddhists with a proper understanding see the Buddha as our Teacher. We know that the Buddha is not omnipotent, that our past actions condition our present experiences, and that we are responsible for our actions. Those petitioning an external creator believe that everything is in his hands and depends on his will. Although both Buddhists and those of other faiths may request inspiration or blessing from holy beings to become more loving, their way of requesting, their notion of to whom they pray, and their understanding of the process of prayer differ.

7 | Mind, Body, and Rebirth

B ECAUSE OUR MIND is the ultimate source of our happiness and suffering and by transforming the mind we attain awakening, understanding the mind is essential. The topic of the mind and its potential was introduced in *Approaching the Buddhist Path*, the first volume of the Library of Wisdom and Compassion, and in this chapter we will explore the nature of the mind, its relationship with the brain, and rebirth more deeply.

Sentience, Mind, and Brain

The mind's nature is clarity and cognizance. *Clarity* refers to the immateriality of the mind, the fact that it cannot be apprehended by our physical senses and is not made of atoms. Clarity also indicates the mirror-like quality of the mind, the fact that it can reflect objects. Dharmakīrti says (PV):

> Therefore my own mind is clear
> by virtue of its own nature of clarity;
> by virtue of other (objects) being transferred and illuminated in it,
> this makes it clear too.[35]

In addition, clarity means the fundamental nature of the mind is not affected by defilement (PV 2.208a–b):

> The nature of mind is clear light.
> The defilements are adventitious.[36]

Cognizance refers to the mind's ability to engage with its object. Together clarity and cognizance allow for the appearance of objects to arise and for objects to be known and experienced. The presence of a mind is the difference between a living being and a corpse. In his struggle to clarify how we know anything exists, Descartes said, "I can doubt the existence of the body, but I know I exist because I am conscious." In short, the nature of consciousness is to be aware and to know objects (PV):

> Consciousness apprehends objects,
> apprehending them as they exist;
> it arises in the nature of the objects,
> it is generated by them as well.

A sentient being (*sattva*) is any being with a mind who is not a buddha. Everything that is biologically alive is not necessarily sentient. Bacteria and viruses are biologically alive, but we do not know whether they have mind, the presence of which is indicated by the ability to experience pain and pleasure. Most Buddhist thinkers believe they do not. Animals and insects, however, do. Computers may have artificial intelligence that enables them to respond like a human being, but they do not experience pain and pleasure and are not sentient beings. However, if one day computers become capable of being a physical support for consciousness and a sentient being creates the karma to be born in one, a computer could be a sentient being!

Some material substances, such as plants, may appear to have consciousness although they do not. A Venus flytrap—a flower that catches and ingests insects—is able to detect the presence of flies and moves to trap them. However, movement is not a sufficient indicator for the presence of mind. Some plants may grow better when people talk to them, but that too isn't proof that they cognize phenomena and experience pleasure and pain as sentient beings do. Their growth could be due simply to biological functions, just as a sunflower turning toward the sun is explained through biological functions.

Some sūtras mention that in a few cases spirits are born in trees, rocks, or wood. These are the spirits' homes, not their bodies. Still, those sentient beings may be disturbed if their home is damaged.

While the brain is material in nature, the mind is not. The mind lacks shape and color and cannot be perceived by scientific instruments. Like other produced phenomena, the mind is impermanent in that it changes moment by moment, although it is eternal in that it has no end. When it is obscured by afflictions and other defilements, it is said to be the mind of a sentient being; when all obscurations have been removed, it becomes the mind of a buddha.

Just as our body has many parts—arms, legs, internal organs—and diverse characteristics—hardness, fluidity, mobility, heat, and space—so too there are many types of mind: gross and subtle levels of mind, primary consciousnesses and the mental factors that accompany them, sense consciousnesses and the mental consciousness, and so forth. In the case of human beings, many of these types of mind depend on the body and brain, but some do not seem to. Our sense consciousnesses depend on the sense faculties, nervous system, and brain as well as on an external object. Due to the contact of a flower with a healthy eye faculty, a visual consciousness that sees its color and shape arises. If the eye faculty malfunctions or is absent, the visual consciousness cannot arise. Likewise, if the area of the brain that is related to visual consciousness is damaged, we cannot see. Here I speak generally, for as far as I know, scientists have not determined whether just one part of the brain facilitates sight or if other parts of the brain can assume that function if the first part is damaged. Buddhist science adds that the arising of visual consciousness also depends on a preceding moment of mind; physical elements alone cannot cause or constitute cognition.

Other mental states seem to arise through a different process. Memories of the past or imagination of the future often seem to pop into our mind without an external object stimulating them. Once we remember or imagine something, the brain responds. Here the mental function appears to come first and the effects on the brain and the body follow. The scientists I have spoken with affirm this sequence, but according to current scientific belief that the mind is an emergent property of the brain, it should not occur. Scientists are also baffled by the case of a forty-four-year-old French civil servant who is missing 90 percent of his brain but functions normally.[37] This does not accord with their theory that consciousness is an emergent property of the brain.

In one study neuroscientists observed people's brains before and after they were taught a certain meditation practice. They detected noticeable changes in their brains after doing the meditation practice for some time. Scientific studies have also shown that some aspects of the brains of experienced meditators differ from those of ordinary people. These findings demonstrate that just as changes in the brain may affect the mind, training the mind can effect changes in the brain. Causation can go both ways.

Distinctions between mental states cannot be made at the level of brain functions only. Experiments have demonstrated that the same area of the brain is activated when a person sees an object and when he mentally thinks about that object. Similarly, the pain centers in the brain are activated both when we actually experience pain and when we see someone else in pain. Clearly there is a real experiential difference between seeing something with our eyes and thinking about it, although the brain does not seem to distinguish the two. This indicates that brain functions alone are not responsible for everything about human experience and perception.

When a meditator practices one-pointed concentration and attains serenity (*śamatha*), she develops physical and mental pliancy and experiences a particular type of physical and mental bliss. Through this, she attains deep levels of meditative absorption, such that she does not hear a loud sound nearby. Although she did not make a special effort to change her brain, because her brain plays a role in the development of serenity, some changes may have taken place in its function and structure owing to the development of physical and mental pliancy and bliss. Using scientific instruments to investigate this would be intriguing.

Along this line, genes received from our parents may have some influence on our mental disposition. However, I do not believe that the diversity of human dispositions, interests, and attitudes is due principally to our genetic composition. The habitual thoughts, emotions, and actions of a person's mind earlier in this life and in previous lives, as well as the imprints left on his mindstream, play a role. The vast majority of parents tell me that each of their children has a different personality and habits from birth. They say that babies are not blank slates conditioned only by their genes and the events of this lifetime.

Events at the time of death also make us question if the mind always depends on the brain. Within a few minutes of the breath stopping, brain functions also cease, and the person is pronounced clinically dead. However, I know of many cases in which consciousness is still present. In 2001 someone who appeared to be an ordinary monk died at Delek Hospital, just down the road from where I live in Dharamsala. After his breath stopped, there was no rigor mortis and seven days passed before his body began to decay. Only then did they realize that he was meditating during this time.

Tibetans have observed that experienced meditators may remain in meditation for several days without their body decaying. My senior tutor, Kyabje Ling Rinpoche, remained sitting upright in meditation for thirteen days after his breath, heart, and brain functions stopped. Once he had completed his meditation, his body slumped over and death occurred. I also saw a picture of an elderly Mongolian monk who stayed in meditation (T. *thug dam*) for twenty-five days after his breath ceased.

Buddhists attribute this to the existence of the subtlest mind, the mind of clear light, which can function separate from the brain and may remain in the body for some time after physical death. If the subtlest mind did not exist, it would be difficult to account for the fact that when one person's vital signs cease, the body decays immediately and when another's cease, it does not. It would be good for scientists to investigate this.

Some years ago, some scientists brought an instrument to Delek Hospital to observe the brain functioning of proficient meditators while they were dying and after their vital signs ceased. But as often happens, things do not turn out as planned, and no meditators died during the time the scientists were there!

However, one time they were successful. After some scientists set up equipment in a Tibetan hospital in India, a previous Ganden Tripa (head of the Geluk tradition) died. His body remained fresh without decaying for three weeks. During this time, scientists put electrodes on his head and recorded data about his brain functions. This made them think that a subtle "energy" that does not depend on the body might exist.

A few people have clear memories of previous lives and on occasion some have prescience of future events. These extraordinary events are beyond current scientific theories, but they support the Buddhist explanation that different types and levels of mind exist. Some are related to and dependent on the body, while some can function independently of the body and physical sense organs. This is because the mind and body have different continua: the body is material, whereas the mind is not.

Although science and Buddhism share many similarities, such as the investigative approach, some of their underlying premises differ. First, the source or foundation of cognitive processes is seen differently. Science believes that all mental processes derive from the physical organ of the brain, whereas highest yoga tantra asserts that all mental processes—sense perceptions, emotions, intellect, coarse as well as subtle mental functions—derive from the primordial mind of clear light, the subtlest mind that is independent of the brain.

This leads to a second difference. Buddhism doesn't see the mind as limited to the body and accepts past and future lives. It believes that our actions (karma) in one life can affect our future circumstances, perceptions and emotions, and can influence which body, with its unique genetic makeup, we take in future lives. Science currently states that either the mind is the brain or it is an emergent property of the brain. Since the brain exists only in this life, most scientists have not considered investigating the possibility of the influence of past and future lives and focus only on what is noticeable in this life.[38] If their basic assumptions were different, scientists might make unexpected discoveries.

The differences between Buddhism and science should not be points of contention, but rather areas in which we come together to do further research and investigation. Both Buddhism and science have the common aim to know the truth about how things exist and to conduct research that can be verified by experience. Both seek to benefit people, and neither follows blind belief.

Due to recent scientific discoveries of correlations between the body—especially our genes and brain—and the mind, there is a trend in society to think of mental and emotional difficulties as caused by these physical components. Although alcoholism and certain mental illnesses may correlate with particular genes or certain neurological functions, I (Chodron) believe that it could be damaging to assume that these are causal factors and minimize the social, mental, and emotional factors involved. An alcoholic could easily come to think, "It is hopeless to try to quit drinking because my alcoholism is due to my genetic makeup, which cannot be changed." Someone who loses his temper and behaves violently could believe, "My brain is wired this way. There's not much I can do to change until medical scientists make a pill that will alter my brain chemistry."

Physical and mental disorders and their causes are multifaceted. The more we remain open to this, the more we will be successful in treating them. Genetic factors, biochemical processes, brain structure and functioning, as well as social, economic, dietary, mental, and emotional factors must all be factored in. Remedies, too, can be multifaceted. Such an approach, I believe, leads to more social and personal reflection and responsibility.

The Nature of Mind

While we may easily say the words, "the mind is mere clarity and cognizance," it is difficult to actually have a notion of what the mind is—let alone to perceive its clear and cognizant nature. Although the clarity and cognizance of the mind are present in every moment of mental activity, we are not aware of them. What prevents this? A consciousness is usually identified in relation to its object—the visual consciousness perceiving blue or the mental consciousness thinking about a table. When a consciousness engages with its object, it appears in the aspect of that object.[39] Because of the mind's involvement with that object, it is obscured from perceiving the actual nature of the mind.

The mind is usually invaded by a host of constructive and destructive thoughts that concern external objects and people we have perceived or experienced. These cloud the clear and cognizant nature of the mind, preventing us from perceiving it. When the flow of thoughts slows down, it is possible to see into the depths of the mind—its clear and cognizant nature that is like a still pool of water. One technique for discovering the conventional nature of mind is to prevent the mind from arising in the aspect of those objects and to stop all conceptual thoughts regarding past and future events. To do this, first generate a strong determination not to let your mind be disturbed by sense perceptions such as sounds or thoughts. Let your mind rest without being overrun by sensory perceptions or ideas. At first it may seem that more thoughts than usual arise, but this is not the case. It is simply that in your daily life you do not pay much attention to how many thoughts there are!

Continuing to meditate in this way, you will gradually be able to keep the mind at a distance from sense objects, and the barrage of thoughts will diminish and eventually cease. By the mind not arising in the aspect of those objects, the clear nature of mind will become apparent. When you experience your mind in the absence of thoughts about the past and the future, you will have a sense of vacuity, which is the gap between the mind and those objects. This vacuity is not the ultimate nature of mind—the mind's emptiness of inherent existence—nor is it nothingness as in blank-mind meditation.

Once you experience that vacuous state of mind, try to meditate or remain in it. Eventually you will have a feeling that the mind is something like a mirror with infinite dimensions. At that time, the nature of the mind itself is clear. Yet whenever the mind contacts an object, a reflection immediately arises. In this way, understand the mirror-like clarity of the mind. The mind remains clear by nature even though reflections of phenomena may appear in it.

In addition, practice being aware of the moment when you are just beginning to sleep and the moment just after waking up. At both these times, the cognitive faculties are not fully engaged. In the moment just after waking, sleep has ceased. Your mind is in a neutral state, not crowded with thoughts and emotions. If your physical condition is normal and fresh, you may have some feeling of the clarity of mind at that time. Try to remain in that state, although it is not easy. Experiment with this and see what happens. Some experience of the mind should come, perhaps even an experience of the grosser level of clear light.

Having some experience of the conventional nature of mind is valuable for knowing that mind exists, which helps you to understand the continuity of mind from one life to the next. It also gives you a better idea of what is meant when we say that Dharma practice is about working with our mind. Although meditating on the clear nature of the mind is not a unique Buddhist practice—it is common with Hindus and perhaps some other religious traditions as well—it is useful for showing us another aspect of our experience.

Some years back I did a one-month retreat in Ladakh, India. When I meditate, I usually have a statue of the Buddha in front of me. The Buddha is my "boss," a very loving and gentle boss. This particular statue was painted gold, and while colorful areas in general are attractive and can stir up the mind, the gold had come off of one part of the statue. Initially I focused my attention at this more neutral area. Then I lowered my eyes, let go of memories of the past, and stopped imagining and planning the future. Eventually, a little experience of the clarity and cognizance of the mind came. This is an experience; we are not saying to ourselves in words, "The mind is clear and cognizant." With that little glimpse, I was then able to be aware of when my mind began following a sound or chasing a thought. I could recognize where the mind was going and what was distracting it, as well as when it was at rest—clear and concentrated. But after that one-month retreat, I resumed my usual busy duties and came back to my original state! Nevertheless, this experience was valuable.

Rebirth: Past and Future Lives

The mind of each individual forms its own continuum with one moment of mind producing the next moment of mind. As an impermanent phenomenon, it is produced by causes that precede it. The substantial cause of one moment of mind—the main cause that actually transforms into the resultant next moment of mind—is the previous moment of mind in the same continuum. Although the gross body and gross mind influence each other, they cannot be the substantial cause of each other because they do not share the same nature. The body is material in nature, the mind is not. Dharmakīrti tells us (PV 2.165):

> That which is not a consciousness itself
> cannot be the substantial cause for another consciousness.

This can be understood by three principles of causality from Asaṅga's *Compendium of Knowledge*:
1. An effect cannot arise without a cause, and every effect is preceded by its own cause. There is no absolute creator that is the original source of all existents because such a creator would not have a cause and would have arisen causelessly, which is impossible. This refutes causeless production.
2. An effect cannot arise from a permanent cause. Permanent phenomena do not change, and to produce an effect, change is necessary. The cause must cease for the effect to arise.
3. A cause must have the potential to produce a particular effect; an effect cannot arise from a discordant cause. Daisies cannot grow from

tomato seeds. The substantial cause of form is previous moments of matter or energy, and the substantial cause of mind is previous moments of mind. These last two principles refute cases of impossible production: a permanent cause cannot produce a result, and a discordant cause—something that does not have the ability to produce a particular result—cannot produce that result.[40]

Applying these principles to the arising of consciousness, we find that the sperm and egg, which are the substantial cause of the body, are unsuitable to be the substantial cause of the mind, which is not form. The substantial cause of the sperm and egg can be traced back to the Big Bang (or to space particles if we use the Buddhist paradigm), in which case the Big Bang would also be the ultimate substantial cause of our mind. In this case, consciousness would have been present in the dense matter preceding the Big Bang. Since it was the ultimate cause of the entire physical universe, everything—rocks, water, fire, and so forth—should be conscious and would experience pleasure and pain. But we would feel quite strange accepting that each and every rock, water molecule, or carbon atom has consciousness and is a living being.

If we said instead that consciousness emerged from matter after a period of time, then did consciousness appear in all material particles? If not, what would make consciousness emerge from some particles but not others? Along this line, if scientists could construct a brain, would that brain be conscious? Would it be a person who experiences happiness and suffering?

If our mind came from our parents' minds or if our mind were a collection of different parts of the minds of people who died before our birth, many logical inconsistencies would arise. Because each individual has his or her own mindstream or mental continuum, we can remember events from our past and will experience the results of our own actions, not those of another person. These would be impossible if our mind were composed of fragments of our parents' or other peoples' minds. Instead we should be able to remember their past. We should also have the knowledge they have accumulated thus far in their lives and our emotional makeup would closely resemble theirs. But we see that this is not the case.

If an external creator or prior intelligence created the universe, that creator would not have a cause because it would have preceded all existence.

Without a cause, how could such a creator arise? If it did not arise due to a cause, it would be permanent and could not create effects, such as the universe and the beings in it. A permanent creator cannot change, and creation involves change. If we said the creator was both permanent and impermanent, that too is contradictory, for one thing cannot simultaneously possess opposite traits. If we said the creator or prior intelligence alternated being permanent and impermanent, that too would present problems: a permanent phenomenon would need a cause to become impermanent, and no such cause exists. Further questions also arise: why would a creator or prior intelligence create suffering?

Someone once asked me if neural pathways could be the means by which karma was imprinted on the mindstream, such that the deeds of one life would influence events in another life. This is not possible because brain activity ceases at death. The brain does not come with us into the next life.

Applying these principles of causality to matter and consciousness, rebirth can be established without having to resort to blind faith or reliance on scriptural authority. The only possible cause of our mind is a previous moment of mind, the mind of the person we were in our previous life.

REFLECTION

1. Everything that functions arises from a cause. Just as our body arose from a cause, so did our mind.

2. Consider the three principles of causality. The only cause that could produce a moment of mind is a previous moment of mind.

3. The mind that joined with the fertilized egg to create a living being must have been a mind from a living being who had lived before and had recently died.

Human beings have long discussed the beginning of the universe and of mind in particular. From a Buddhist perspective, there is no beginning to either of these because all functioning things arise from their causes.

Those causes arise from their causes, and so on, back ad infinitum. Positing a first moment of consciousness is logically untenable. If there were a first moment, it would either arise without a cause or arise from a discordant cause. Neither of these is possible.

If we assert a beginning point before which nothing existed, we must say that sentient beings were born without cause. That is difficult to accept, for without causes producing effects, nothing could operate. Farmers would not have to plant seeds to grow a crop, children would not need to be educated, and we would not take medicine to cure our illnesses. Although we may not know all the causes and conditions of a particular thing or event, it definitely arose due to them.

Some people reject past and future lives, for the reason that they do not see them. However, not perceiving something does not negate its existence. Cats and birds see things and dogs smell odors that we do not. On the other hand, evidence exists for future lives. If we investigate the nature of mind, we understand that it is a continuity. Like all things, the mind exists because its causes exist. The continuity of a thing ceases only when its causes are exhausted or when a strong counteractive agent that can stop it is applied. In the case of a mindstream, neither of these is the case. No agent exists that can cease the continuity of mind. When it separates from this body, its continuity goes on to the next life. At the time of death, the coarser levels of mind, which depend on the physical body, dissolve. An extremely subtle consciousness—the primordial clear light mind—which can function apart from the coarse body, manifests, and this acts as the substantial cause for the mind of the next life. In the end, the only plausible explanation is the beginningless and endless continuity of moments of mind.

Another factor that supports the existence of rebirth is that people remember past lives. Although I have no clear memories of my previous lives, according to my mother and members of the search party who identified the Fourteenth Dalai Lama, when I was very young I spoke quite clearly about my past life. Sometimes I have had the same dreams; they are vague recollections of some previous lives—as a Tibetan, Indian, and on one occasion Egyptian. But then the memory faded.

Our not remembering previous lives does not refute their existence. I don't think any of us remembers our experience in the mother's womb, yet we were undoubtedly there. It is difficult to recall experiences from previous lives because memory is formed with the gross levels of consciousness, which are dependent on the body and brain. The latencies of memories going with our mental consciousness may not be very strong, and upon taking a new rebirth, our attention is directed toward the present life, not the previous one.

Nevertheless, the accounts of many people who remember their previous lives have been verified. I heard of an Indian girl who described her previous life. She was a young girl in that previous life and died suddenly, so the natural process of dissolution of the levels of consciousness did not take place, which may be a factor in her being able to remember her previous life. Being very young, her memory was clearer, whereas older children may not remember their previous life because their grosser-level mind is fully developed and their subtle mind has become inactive.

It is possible through meditation to make grosser-level minds inactive and to activate subtler levels of mind. I met a Kagyu lama who was a very nice monk. Although he was not learned, he was very sincere and jovial and we became close friends. One time he was very serious and told me stories about studying with his tutor as a child. Even though he would deceive his tutor and play tricks on him, after his tutor passed away he remembered him with gratitude. One time, he had such a strong experience when recalling his tutor's tremendous kindness that he almost fainted. At the time of fainting, the coarser level of mind became inactive and a subtler mind arose. This mind then remembered his previous life.

We don't need to prove the existence of previous lives to someone who is able to recollect past lives; for her they are evident phenomena. However, for people who do not have such recollection, the existence of previous lives is a slightly obscure phenomenon, which can be proven with reasoning. Dharmakīrti does this in chapter 2 of his *Commentary on Reliable Cognition*, based on the continuity of consciousness. This is the argument I made above.

For something to exist, it is not necessary that the majority of people know about it and agree on it. There may be certain species of plants and animals that only very few people on the planet know, but they exist. Similarly, not everyone needs to agree that rebirth exists in order for it to exist.

Even if you cannot ascertain the existence of future lives, you can tentatively accept it without any harm. Wishing to create the causes for fortunate future lives, you will endeavor to subdue your afflictions and cultivate your good qualities. This, in turn, will help you to be happier in the present because you will experience things freshly, without the confusion of attachment and anger. If you find it difficult to accept past and future lives, set the topic aside and focus on being a good person in this life. Do not create trouble for others, and use your life to bring calm and peace in your own mind and in the world. This is more important. If, at the time of death, you find there is no future life, nothing has been lost. But if you find there is, at least you have prepared for it by living a good life now. This is better than someone who accepts future lives but does not behave properly in his daily life and thus makes problems for himself and others.

The Kālāmas were a people confused by the claims of various teachers and unsure what to believe. The Buddha taught them meditation on the four immeasurables—love, compassion, joy, and equanimity. Once they experienced for themselves the immediate benefits of these, they were joyous. The Buddha then pointed out the benefits they accrue by cultivating positive states of mind, whether or not rebirth exists (AN 3.65):

> This noble disciple, Kālāmas, whose mind is in this way without enmity, without ill will, undefiled and pure, has won four assurances in this very life . . . (1) If there is another world, and if there is the fruit and result of good and bad deeds, it is possible that with the breakup of the body, after death, I will be reborn in a good destination, in a heavenly world . . . (2) If there is no other world, and there is no fruit and result of good and bad deeds, still right here, in this very life, I maintain myself in happiness, without enmity and ill will, free of trouble . . . (3) Suppose evil [results] befall one who does evil. Then, when I have no evil intentions toward anyone, how can suffering afflict me, since I do no evil deed? . . . (4) Suppose evil [results] do not befall one who does evil. Then right here I see myself purified in both respects.

In essence, if there turns out to be no future lives, we do not have to worry that we have wasted our time cultivating beneficial mental states through practicing the Buddha's teachings, because we have already experienced benefits in this life. Furthermore, if future lives exist, we have made good preparation for them and need not fear at the time of death.

REFLECTION

1. Tentatively accept the existence of past and future lives.

2. Do you see any disadvantages to doing this?

3. Does it help you to understand certain events, memories, or thoughts in your life?

The Buddha Responds to Questions about Rebirth

In the *Sūtra Responding to a Query about What Happens after Death* (*Āyuṣpatti-yathākāra-paripṛcchā Sūtra*), the Buddha responds to questions that his father, King Śuddhodana, poses about death, dying, and rebirth. The following is a summary of their exchange.[41]

After death, do we cease to exist like a fire that has burned out?
No, one life follows the next, just as the sun rises again after it has set and new plants grow in an area after a natural disaster. If there were no rebirth, all living beings would have been completely extinguished by now.

Will sentient beings be born in similar forms in their future lives, or can they be born in other forms that are different from their present ones?
Sentient beings are born according to the force of their virtuous and non-virtuous actions. Depending on which karmic seeds ripen at the time of death, their next rebirth may be in any realm. Human beings whose virtuous karma ripens may be born as devas, while those whose nonvirtuous karma ripens at the time of death may be born as animals.

In their future lives, do sentient beings have the same family members
as in this life?
No, we consider ourselves relatives and recognize each other based on our
present bodies. When we pass away, we relinquish these bodies and take
new ones. We will be unable to recognize each other and have no basis on
which to consider ourselves relatives then.

Are people born in the same economic class with the same wealth
or lack thereof as in this life?
Even within this one life, we see affluent people become poor and the poor
become wealthy; our socioeconomic status is temporary and impermanent.
Generosity is the cause of wealth, whereas miserliness and theft are the
causes of poverty. Some people, both the rich and the poor, practice generosity continuously. Those whose financial status vacillates considerably
may practice generosity sporadically or may regret their previous acts of
giving. Persistent miserliness and stealing—including embezzling money,
cheating others in business deals, and so forth—can result in poverty over
many lifetimes. However, if someone regrets and purifies these actions, the
results will not be experienced.

Sometimes people dream about their deceased relatives and friends. Are their
relatives actually appearing and communicating with them in these dreams?
When we dream of deceased loved ones, it is just a case of past latencies
being activated. The person we dream about is not present. He or she is
not having the same dream, and even when alive, we don't experience each
other's dreams. If someone dreams about us, we are not in his dream doing
what he dreams we are doing. The dream is due to the ripening of latencies
on his mindstream.

Suppose someone lives in a very luxurious house and later moves to
another place. Her previous house is torn down to build another building.
She may have a very clear dream of the house, so clear that she feels that she
is actually in it. Yet this is just her dream; it is a product of activated latencies. Dreaming of the deceased is similar. That dear one no longer has his
previous body; he has already taken rebirth in accordance with his karma.
Our dream of him is simply the maturation of latencies on our mind.

Sometimes people offer and dedicate food and drink to their dead
relatives so they will have these to consume for a long time. Does this help
the deceased relatives?
It is not possible for the deceased to consume these things gradually over
time for centuries and eons, since there is no cause that can make these
things last that long. We may put food out in our home for people in distant
lands who are hungry, but they do not receive it. It is even less likely for
someone who is separated from their previous body to partake of the food
and drink their living relatives dedicate to them.

Does that mean that all acts of dedicating useful items such as food,
vehicles, clothes, and ornaments to the deceased are meaningless?
The best way to benefit deceased loved ones is to do virtuous activities
and dedicate the merit for their good rebirth and progress on the path to
awakening.

Sentient beings who commit nonvirtuous actions such as killing their
parents are certain to experience horrible consequences of their actions.
Is there a way for them to attain a happy rebirth?
If they genuinely believe in the law of karma and its effects and sincerely
purify their wrongdoings, those nonvirtuous actions will be purified. At
the time of death, if they regret their past unwholesome actions and generate genuine admiration and take refuge in the buddhas and bodhisattvas,
the unwholesome actions will be purified and they could take rebirth in
the higher realms.

Do not think that there are no future lives. Do not cling to worldly pleasures or anything in cyclic existence. When we transmigrate from one life
to the next, there is nothing permanent that goes on to the next life. Nor
does everything discontinue, becoming nonexistent. Our future rebirth
is not the work of an external creator, it is not a whim of the self, and it
does not occur without any cause. Rebirth takes place due to the coming
together of causes and conditions, such as afflictions and the karma created
by them.

How rebirth occurs without a permanent self or soul and without the work of an external creator is difficult to understand. It is also hard to comprehend that everything does not cease at death and that rebirth isn't simply random and causeless. Please give some examples to help us understand.

Having some basic information about the rebirth process first will help you understand the examples:

- Everything about this life does not discontinue and cease altogether in order for rebirth to exist.
- No permanent entity transmigrates to the next life.
- Transmigration to another life occurs in dependence on this life.
- We are not born in this life because we wished for it.
- We are not born in this life because of having prayed to an external creator.
- We are not born due to wishing to be born wherever we like.
- We are not reborn due to wishing that causes and conditions don't affect our rebirth.
- It is not the case that nothing remains after death when the physical and mental aggregates disintegrate.
- There is no "kingdom of death" in which people reside forever after death without taking rebirth.
- The consciousness of the next life is connected to the consciousness of the present life in that it is a continuation of that mind.
- The body of the present life and of the future life do not exist simultaneously. Neither do the mental aggregates of the two lives.
- We are not reborn with similar physical characteristics in one life after the next; someone who is beautiful in one life will not necessarily be beautiful in the next.
- We are not necessarily born in the same realm in the next life; a human being will not necessarily be reborn as a human being. The future life depends on the karma created in this life and the karma that ripens at the time of death.
- A virtuous action cannot propel an unfortunate rebirth, and a nonvirtuous action cannot propel a fortunate one.
- Many consciousnesses do not arise from a single consciousness.
- Someone cannot be born in a fortunate realm without having engaged

in virtuous actions and cannot be born in an unfortunate state without having created nonvirtuous actions.

• A birth is not the handiwork of an independent, external creator.

Eight examples seen together will convey an idea of how rebirth occurs:

1. A student learning from her teacher's lectures represents the next life being affected by the present one.

2. A lamp being lit from another lamp indicates that while a new life begins, nothing permanent is transmitted and that the next life depends on a cause.

3. A reflection in a mirror illustrates that the next life comes about due to the existence of the previous one. Although nothing is transferred from one life to the next, the next rebirth is assured.

4. Embossed impressions and designs emerging from stamps indicates that we are reborn according to the actions we have done.

5. Fire produced by a magnifying glass demonstrates that the next life could be in a realm different from this life, just as the fire is different from the magnifying glass.

6. Sprouts growing from seeds shows that one doesn't disintegrate and cease to exist at death.

7. Salivating from the mention of something that tastes sour indicates taking rebirth by the force of our previous actions, not by choice, wish, or whim.

8. An echo illustrates that we take rebirth when conditions are ripe and no obstacles are present. Also, the future life is neither identical with nor completely different from the present one.

Although each example illustrates an important point about rebirth, there is the possibility that we misunderstand it. Therefore, one example acts to correct the possible misinterpretation of another:

1. From the example of a student learning from the lectures of a teacher, we may think that a being takes rebirth into the next life without its previous consciousness having ceased. To counteract this, the example of the seed shows that the cause must change to produce its result. Similarly, a permanent self or soul does not transmigrate from one life

to the next. Rather the last moment of consciousness in this life must cease for the first moment of consciousness in the next life to arise.

2. From the example of both lamps being present when one is lit from the other, we may think that the same body and mind exist in both this and the next life. The example of the echo prevents this misunderstanding because an echo is neither produced without someone making a noise nor simultaneous with the noise. The initial noise is not the same as the echo of it.

3. From the example of a reflection in a mirror, we may think that we have the same physical characteristics in previous and subsequent lives. The fire being produced by the magnifying glass corrects this because the fire and the magnifying glass look quite different.

4. From the example of embossing stamps, we may think that we are born in the same realm after death. The example of the student learning from the lectures of a teacher remedies this because the teacher, who represents this life, and the student, who represents the next life, are not the same.

5. From the example of the magnifying glass, we may believe that a virtuous action could lead to birth in an unfortunate state and a nonvirtuous action to rebirth in a fortunate state. The example of one lamp being lit from another remedies this by showing that the result is concordant with the cause. Just as one light gives rise to another, virtuous and nonvirtuous actions propel results concordant with them, a fortunate or unfortunate rebirth, respectively.

6. From the example of the seed, we could infer that one consciousness could give rise to numerous consciousnesses. The example of an embossing stamp prevents this misinterpretation by showing that regardless of the design of a stamp, it impresses that very same design, not many other signs on the clay.

7. From the example of sour taste, we may think that someone could have a good rebirth even if he had not acted virtuously and someone could have an unfortunate rebirth without having acted nonvirtuously. The example of the mirror counteracts this by illustrating that the image in the mirror exactly reflects the object.

8. From the example of an echo, we may think that no one is born unless the creator wished it, just as an echo is not heard unless a person has

made a noise. The example of the sour taste counteracts this because only someone who has eaten something sour before would salivate at the mention of sour food. Likewise, only someone who has earlier indulged in afflictions and created polluted karma would be subject to a conditioned birth, not others.

Having a basic understanding of rebirth, we see our present life as one among many—it is a product of our previous lives, and during it we create causes for our future lives, liberation, and awakening. We will now look at the great opportunity this present life presents us for spiritual practice.

REFLECTION

Contemplate each of these examples to get an accurate idea of how rebirth occurs, remembering that since they are examples, they do not correspond in all aspects with what they are exemplifying.

8 | The Essence of a Meaningful Life

VISUALIZING THE BUDDHA during the preparatory practices prompts us to reflect on his ultimate attainment—full awakening with its magnificent physical, verbal, and mental qualities. This, in turn, causes us to contemplate the path leading to that state, a path that Śākyamuni Buddha taught from his own experience. Since attaining the awakened state is our ultimate purpose, we want to learn and practice the same path the Buddha did. Cultivating bodhicitta is an essential element of this process.

Within the three levels of being—initial, intermediate, and advanced—the method to cultivate bodhicitta and the bodhisattva's deeds is contained in the advanced level. To make ourselves capable of engaging in these more advanced practices, we must first train in the preceding practices. Of these, the most important center around ceasing our obsession with the pleasures of cyclic existence and aspiring for liberation, which are contained in the intermediate level. But to relinquish attachment to all of cyclic existence, we must first stop attachment to the pleasures of this present life and aspire to have a good rebirth in the future. To do this, we engage in the initial-level practices.

Although liberation and awakening are our ultimate purposes, attaining them in one life is extremely difficult, although not impossible. Certain tantric practices, when done by well-prepared and qualified practitioners, can bring awakening in this life. But generally speaking, completing the path requires many lifetimes. For our spiritual development to proceed smoothly, we need to ensure that we have a series of successive precious human lives in order to practice the Dharma continuously over many

184 | THE FOUNDATION OF BUDDHIST PRACTICE

lifetimes. For this to occur, we must create the causes, which are included in the practices of the initial practitioner. For this reason, too, the initial practices are extremely important to obtain our ultimate goal.

Precious Human Life

Whatever activity—mundane or spiritual—we do in life, self-confidence is a crucial internal factor to accomplish it. We must have conviction and trust ourselves, believing that we can successfully complete that work. Developing self-confidence and appreciation of our potential are the chief purposes of contemplating our precious human life. As we do this meditation, the conviction that we can definitely transform our mind and gain spiritual realizations will grow.

Recognizing the potential of our precious human life is essential; without it we may spend a lot of time complaining about upsetting events around us, from personal problems to environmental destruction and war. Consistently focusing on misfortune prevents us from seeing the good in the world, and this narrow and unrealistic vision hinders our well-being as well as our enthusiasm for Dharma practice.

Not every human life is a precious human life. A variety of conditions must be present in order to have a precious human life that can be used in a meaningful way. When the Buddha was alive in India, people had access to an awakened teacher, but not everyone was interested in hearing his teachings, and among those who were, some had previous commitments or health conditions that impeded them from doing so. Sadly, these people had human lives, but not precious human lives.

A precious human life is free from eight impediments and endowed with ten fortunes.[42] Of the eight unfavorable states, four are rebirth in nonhuman states. Although these rebirths are temporary, the person is impeded from practicing for their duration.

1. Facing intense physical torment, hell beings (*nāraka*) are unable to direct their minds to spiritual practice.
2. Hungry ghosts (*preta*) are distracted from spiritual practice by extreme hunger and thirst, as well as by their constant search for food and drink and the frustration of not being able to procure them.
3. Animals are eaten by other animals higher on the food chain, often

mistreated by humans, and are mentally incapable of understanding Dharma teachings.

4. Those born as discriminationless (*asaṃjñika*) gods—a type of god in the fourth dhyāna of the form realm—have almost no mental activity during that life. Born there because of having cultivated the meditative absorption without discrimination in the previous life, their only moments of clear discrimination occur at the time of their birth and death.[43]

A precious human life is also free from four disadvantageous human conditions:

1. Living in a barbaric, uncivilized society or in a country where religion is outlawed.
2. Living where the Buddha's teachings are not available or during a time when the Dharma has not been taught.
3. Being severely mentally or physically impaired, so that our ability to learn and practice the teachings is extremely restricted.
4. Instinctively holding wrong views, making our mind unreceptive to examining new explanations of duḥkha, its causes, cessation, and the path leading to that cessation.

When meditating on the eight unfavorable conditions, do not simply think of other people born in those states, but imagine living in those circumstances yourself. Then recall your current freedom from those limitations and appreciate the excellent conditions you now have.

Then reflect on the ten fortunes you presently have. Five of these are personal and five come from society. The five personal fortunes are:

1. Being a human being with human intelligence that enables you to learn, reflect, and meditate on the Buddhadharma.
2. Living in a central Buddhist region, one where the four types of Buddhist disciples are found—male and female fully ordained monastics and male and female lay followers with the five precepts. In terms of Vinaya, a central country is one where a sangha of four or more fully ordained monks or nuns lives and performs the three major Vinaya ceremonies: fortnightly confession, rains retreat, and the invitation for feedback at the conclusion of the retreat.

3. Having a healthy body and mind.
4. Not having committed five actions of immediate retribution (*ānan-taryakarma*): killing one's father, mother, or an arhat, drawing blood from a buddha, or causing a schism in the saṅgha.
5. Having belief in things worthy of respect, such as the Vinaya as the basis of Dharma practice, and the Three Baskets of teachings on ethical conduct, concentration, and wisdom.

The five fortunate factors coming from society are living at a place and time when:

6. A buddha is present in the world.
7. The Buddha has taught and is still teaching the Dharma. Although these two conditions are not strictly fulfilled now, there are presently qualified spiritual mentors who give the teachings of Śākyamuni Buddha, and this suffices for fulfilling these two conditions.
8. Those teachings still exist and are flourishing. The transmitted Dharma of the Three Baskets exists and is propagated, and the realized Dharma of true cessation and true paths exists in the mindstreams of living practitioners. There is a living tradition of spiritual mentors who can impart the teachings orally and through their example.
9. There are spiritual mentors, monastics, and other like-minded people who follow the Buddha's teachings and inspire us by showing that the Buddhadharma is a living tradition.
10. There are benefactors who offer the four requisites for life: food, shelter, clothing, and medicine.

Reflect individually on each of these points and see that you have an advantageous situation and all the necessary conditions for serious practice. Allow this to gladden your mind and give you great enthusiasm and self-confidence.

People who have not thought about rebirth very much may not be able to clearly ascertain the freedoms and fortunes of a precious human life. Nevertheless, there are common points on which everyone can agree. We know that Śākyamuni Buddha lived and taught in ancient India and that many Buddhist sages such as Nāgārjuna, Asaṅga, and Śāntideva gained extraordinary qualities by following in his footsteps. Their pure ethical conduct, meditative experience, wisdom, and great humility are evident in their life stories and the treatises they authored. These and many other Buddhist sages did not become renowned by becoming war heroes or financial tycoons. Rather, they observed a life of restraint and humility and benefited others. Through this, without seeking fame, they became well-known role models for subsequent generations of practitioners.

If we reflect on the nature of their precious human lives and our own, we do not find much difference. Everyone has the same human potential. As human beings, we have unique intelligence compared with other life forms, regardless of our nationality, gender, race, ethnicity, sexual orientation, social class, religion, and so on. Everyone has the same Buddha nature. Siddhārtha Gautama was an ordinary person just like us. By tapping into and using his human potential in the right way, he became a buddha and was able to greatly benefit sentient beings living at that time as well as those in many centuries to come. Even today, we hear of and encounter people who offer great service and benefit to humankind. We have the ability to do the same.

I have found in my discussions with people that many suffer from low self-esteem and self-hatred. When we reflect on our spectacular good fortune in having a precious human life, these distorted conceptions vanish. We have all eighteen factors of a precious human life, so obviously we are a worthwhile and adequate person. We created tremendous constructive karma in previous lives to have our present opportunity, so we are capable of Dharma practice. We have all necessary conditions to progress on the path and accomplish our spiritual aims in this life, so seeing the future as bleak is unrealistic. Consistent meditation on precious human life prevents us from such self-defeating and inaccurate ways of viewing ourselves. To the contrary, it generates great enthusiasm for Dharma practice.

Rare and Difficult to Attain

The Buddha did not exaggerate when he said that receiving all the conditions necessary for a precious human life is not easy. Looking at the current world population, we may think a human life is easy to come by. However, not all human beings have the eighteen qualities of a precious human life that give them the best opportunity to practice the Dharma. Some people lack interest in spiritual matters, others cannot meet qualified teachers and teachings. Some people live without religious freedom, others face hindrances, such as starvation, war, illness, and injury, that make practice extremely difficult. Contemplating that lacking even one of the eighteen conditions interferes with all others bearing fruit helps us to see that we are extremely fortunate and must not take this opportunity for granted, but use it to create the causes for full awakening. *Array of Stalks Sūtra* speaks of the difficulties of attaining each condition of a precious human life.

> It is hard to avoid unfavorable conditions. It is hard to find a human birth. It is hard to remove error and doubt about the right opportunity. It is hard also to find a buddha in the world. It is hard also to have all our sense faculties in order. It is hard also to hear the Dharma teaching of a buddha. It is hard also to meet people of truth (holy beings). It is hard also to find authentic spiritual masters. It is hard also to receive genuine guidance and instruction. It is hard also to live right in the human world (have right livelihood). It is hard also to carry out the Dharma in all respects.[44]

We must look inside and ask ourselves, "Do we have all the factors that guarantee having a similar precious human life in the future?" Firm ethical conduct, training in the six perfections, and sincere dedication prayers are needed, as are cultivation of stable faith and correct wisdom. Ethical conduct is the cause for a human rebirth. Training in the six perfections results in having the conducive circumstances to practice the Dharma—generosity in this life results in receiving food, shelter, clothing, and medicine in future lives, and joyous effort in this life enables us to accomplish our goals in future lives. Sincere dedication prayers to have a series of precious human lives so that we can attain full awakening direct our merit so that it will ripen accordingly.

In this context, living in pure ethical conduct refers chiefly to abandoning the ten destructive pathways of actions—killing, stealing, unwise sexual behavior, lying, creating disharmony, harsh words, idle talk, coveting, maliciousness, and wrong views. It also involves taking and keeping any of the prātimokṣa ethical codes—those for monastics or lay followers. Doing this requires some conviction in the infallibility of the law of karma and its results.

We know that every conditioned phenomenon arises due to its preceding causes and conditions. This is the general interdependent nature of causes and effects. Within that exists one type of cause and effect—karma and its results. Karma—sentient beings' volitional physical, verbal, and mental actions—depends on our virtuous and nonvirtuous motivations and produces our experience of happiness and suffering.

All sentient beings—except those in the formless realm—have a body. While the body itself is produced by external causes, such as the sperm and egg of our parents, which body our mindstream is born into depends on the quality of our mind and the kinds of karmic seeds left on our mindstream in the past. By acting constructively in this life, we create beneficial mental habits and leave many seeds of virtuous actions on our mindstream. When we die, some of these will ripen, enabling us to take a precious human life for many lifetimes to come, enabling us to continue our spiritual development with minimum interruption. For this reason, spiritual practice, which concerns working with our mind and its intentions, is important. We are responsible for accumulating sufficient causes to produce future precious human lives like the one we have now.

Reflecting in detail on the specific causes for a specific rebirth leads us to the very subtle and profound functioning of karma and its effects—the specific action an individual did in a certain lifetime that is now ripening in a particular event. This is an extremely obscure topic, one only omniscient buddhas know clearly and perfectly. At present, we must depend on scriptural authority to understand it.

Nevertheless, we can understand the general functioning of karma and its results. We know that constructive acts bring happy results and destructive acts bring suffering results. Reflecting on the actions we've done throughout our lives and the various intentions that motivated them, can we say with conviction, "I definitely have created all the causes and conditions for a precious human life and have purified all opposing ones?" Most of us find it difficult to say this with complete conviction because we have done actions we now regret. Transforming our mind by practicing the Dharma affords us the opportunity to change this situation by accumulating merit, purifying negativities, and gaining realizations. Understanding the potential and preciousness of human life to do this and the difficulty of receiving this opportunity in the future, we should avoid wasting our life in frivolous pursuits and engage in Dharma practice now.

Taking the Essence of Our Precious Human Life

If something is true but does not have much to do with our daily experience, knowing it is not important, and our lack of understanding does not bring great problems. But knowing the great value of our precious human life is crucial to this and future lives. Unaware of this fact, we will not see our present lives as significant and filled with opportunity, and risk wasting the chance to create the cause of happiness for a long time to come. Instead, we will mindlessly follow our self-centered thoughts, which will lead us to unfortunate rebirths. But once aware of the rarity of a precious human life, the difficulty of attaining it, and the amazing things we can do with it, we will no longer think our lives are meaningless.

All living beings seek happiness and peace, and I believe attaining this is the purpose of human life. Happiness and peace depend on hope. People lose hope when their lives do not go smoothly or they fail to actualize their expectations. Some people become depressed and some look to suicide for relief, which doesn't stop their pain. But when we understand that creating the causes for peace and happiness are within our ability, despondency cannot take root.

There are two types of happiness: temporary and long-lasting. Experienced while we are in cyclic existence, temporary happiness includes the attainment of higher rebirth as a human being or god. Long-lasting happiness is liberation and awakening, which are attained through spiritual practice. The way to make our life meaningful and to attain these two kinds of happiness is by engaging in sincere spiritual practice, specifically the practices of beings of initial, middle, and advanced levels; that is to say, we must aspire to attain liberation, generate bodhicitta, and ascertain the correct view of emptiness. If we have learned the Dharma and are skillful, no matter our situation in life, where we are, or what time it is, the potential to enrich ourselves through Dharma practice is always present.

Spiritual practice involves some form of renunciation. Misidentifying what to renounce, some people think they must give up happiness and undergo hardship and suffering by accepting extra problems and miseries that they did not have before. If this were so, no sensible person would want to practice the Dharma.

The Buddha does not direct us toward suffering; rather, he shows us the path to be free from misery. He does this by explaining that the roots of suffering—ignorance, animosity, and attachment—are to be renounced, and the causes of happiness—generosity, fortitude, compassion, and so on—are to be adopted. He teaches a gradual path so that we can practice according to our capability at any particular moment. In this way, his followers embrace a way of life in which they eliminate all suffering and its causes step by step, beginning with gross ones and proceeding to subtle ones. In addition, they cultivate happiness, starting with temporary happiness and progressing up to the ultimate happiness of buddhahood.

From this, we see that the purpose of spiritual practice is to bring a sense of internal peace, well-being, and fulfillment. Although our ultimate goal is full awakening, the most urgent and immediate happiness to work for is that of future lives, and for that reason practitioners endeavor to create the causes and conditions to have precious human lives and abandon causes that create the contrary.

Eight Worldly Concerns

Although we have such precious potential, we often fail to recognize it, or even if we do, we are often distracted and do not utilize it. Our tendency to pay more attention to gaining immediate happiness and avoiding unpleasant situations is often stronger than a clear awareness that sees the value of creating the causes for a fortunate rebirth, liberation, and awakening. Our chief obstacles at present are subsumed in the eight worldly concerns—four pairs of delight and dejection that produce attachment and anger. The Buddha said (AN 8.6):[45]

> Gain and loss, disrepute and fame, blame and praise, pleasure
> and pain. These eight worldly concerns revolve around the world,
> and the world revolves around these eight worldly concerns.

Attachment arises toward one part of each pair: material or financial gain, good reputation or image, praise and approval, and pleasure, especially from sights, sounds, smells, tastes, and tactile sensations. Aversion arises toward the other part of each pair: lack of money and possessions, a notorious reputation, blame and criticism, discomfort or pain.

Illustrations of these eight abound in our daily lives. We try to arrange our lives to come in contact with attractive objects and people, tantalizing sense experiences, sweet ego-pleasing words, money, possessions, and so forth. We complain when these do not meet our standard or when we encounter their opposite. Being preoccupied with these eight—which center on our own happiness in only this life—we become very reactive to our environment and the people in it. This emotional reactivity—clinging to what we like, pushing away what we don't—brings difficulties in this life and impedes actualizing our long-term Dharma goals.

Financial and material gain and loss
The first pair of delights and dejections involves our relationship with money and possessions. We are elated when we have a lot of money, nice clothes, a comfortable house, a new car, and good sports equipment, and we become upset when we are unable to procure the things we desire, when they are destroyed, or when they are taken away from us. Sadly, many people measure their success in life by their material wealth. No matter how much they have, they are never satisfied and never feel fully successful.

Of course we need to take care of the practical aspects of our lives, but if we pay undue attention to material possessions and finances, we become a slave to them. Once we are entrapped by their lure, contentment evades us; quarrels ensue as we try to procure more and better and protect what we already have. We become arrogant toward those who have less, jealous of those who have more, and compete with equals, trying to prove our worth by having more than them.

Attached to financial and material gain, we work long hours and plan big projects to make us rich. Unless we are able to use the money wisely to benefit others, the process of gaining wealth consumes our time and energy so that we have little left for practicing Dharma. In the process of accumulating wealth, our ethical discipline is easily corrupted. Those who are greedy become involved in activities that harm individuals and society and that result in scandals and prison terms.

Unfortunately, some lamas and geshes initially live a simple life, studying and practicing diligently. They are very humble and not at all arrogant. Later, when they have many disciples, especially wealthy ones, they become ostentatious. They forget the many years of sacrifice they went through for the Dharma and are corrupted by seeking wealth and fame. We must be attentive not to do this ourselves.

Good and bad reputation and image
We feel elated when we are well-known and have a good reputation and dejected when our image is damaged. Continually preoccupied by what others think of us leads to self-preoccupation and emotional instability. We pay a lot of attention to appearances, and lacking sincerity, we use others for our own advantage. Many people succeed in achieving a good reputation or a high rank, but lack internal peace and true friendships.

People are attracted to a famous person because of his or her reputation. Whether or not that person has something valuable to contribute to society is another question. Without being impressed with titles, honors, or power, we are better off looking at each person as another human being who has the Buddha nature and seeks happiness and not suffering, just like us.

As a monastic, I am not so concerned about gain and loss of wealth. However, as the Dalai Lama, I sit on a high throne when I teach, and sometimes in a corner of my mind the thought arises, "I hope people respect me." When explaining the Dharma, I sometimes wonder, "Does the audience like this talk?" Sometimes our minds are invaded by defiled thoughts: "What a great practitioner I have become! I hope others notice!" It is important to free our minds from expectations of receiving offerings, respect, and appreciation when we share the Dharma. We should talk about our faults and let others speak of our good qualities.

Of course we must prepare before giving a Dharma talk, but if we are too concerned with our delivery or how the audience receives the teaching, there is danger that our talk is for show. Instead of being apprehensive about what others will say about us, we should generate a sincere motivation at the beginning: "Although I do not know much, I will explain what

I understand." Then we will not be nervous and will speak truthfully. If people ask questions that we cannot answer, we simply say that we do not know and use it as an opportunity to learn more.

A member of my staff chided me, saying that I don't prepare my speeches well enough. Perhaps he would like me to make more astute comments about complex topics. However, I feel more genuine when I talk about what I practice and live myself. When I do that, I'm not worried about whether or not others like my talk.

One time a reporter from an important paper in New York interviewed me and asked how I would like to be remembered in history. I told her, "This is not my concern. I am a Buddhist practitioner and am not interested in such things." But she kept asking me until I got impatient and said, "I don't think about that!"

Being concerned with present reputation or our name in history is foolish. We will not be alive to enjoy our reputation in history, so why worry about it? A good reputation doesn't get us any closer to awakening. Our image is not important, but our motivation is. If our motivation is insincere, then even if everyone praises us, the glory will not last long. But if we are sincere and straightforward, we will communicate well with others. Eventually they will accept and appreciate our intentions, and that respect will last over time.

Buddha Śākyamuni was never concerned about his name or fame, but after nearly twenty-six centuries, people still love and respect him. Even non-Buddhists appreciate his message of nonviolence and compassion. Great masters such as Nāgārjuna remained simple Buddhist monks, however learned they became. Of course, when they debated the meaning of the teachings, they became animated and spoke forcefully; but this was not done out of arrogance or desire. Some present geshes are like that. In their ordinary life, they are so humble that we may even doubt whether they can walk properly. But when they go into the debating courtyard, they suddenly become active and assertive.

Look at the great Indian sage Śāntideva. From his writings we know that he was an intelligent, realized practitioner. But in his daily life, he was so humble that people thought he only ate, slept, and defecated. However, we see in the ninth chapter of *Engaging in the Bodhisattvas' Deeds* that in debate he could be relentless and fierce in counteracting wrong conceptions.

Once when he taught emptiness, he floated upward in space until he finally disappeared and only his voice could be heard, displaying a superpower that flabbergasted the audience!

Praise/approval and criticism/disapproval
We love when people we like comment on our good qualities or competent work and we become depressed when they point out our faults, criticize us, or blame us for things we may or may not have done. Due to this delight and dejection, our emotions vacillate drastically, as does our self-image.

In an effort to win the approval of others and avoid their disapproval, we may sacrifice our ethical standards to win their favor, succumb to peer pressure to fit in, and make unwise decisions that have long-term consequences. In the hopes of winning someone's approval, we try to become what we think they think we should be. In the process of doing so, we lose touch with what we really think and feel, and live in fear of accidently doing something that would annoy the other person and garner their criticism.

When meeting new people, we usually present our good side and may exaggerate our qualities to win their approval and affection, often not realizing the extent of our deceit and pretension until later. Once they like us, we may take their friendship for granted and stop being so considerate of them. As a result, they criticize us, we feel hurt and resentful, and difficulties in the relationship ensue. Our self-confidence plummets because it was based on the praise of others and not on our honest self-assessment. Sometimes we become confused and don't know what to believe about ourselves because one person praises us and another criticizes us for the same action, in quick succession.

I have found that it is better for everyone involved to be sincere, frank, and natural with others. I show what I am and do not pretend to be otherwise, no matter what others think or say about me. Being free of attachment to praise and reputation gives us the ability to relate as one human being to another.

When I was in China in 1954, I met with some members of the Communist Party. They spoke to the point, our discussions were very frank, and I liked some of them, at least for a while. But other officials were too polite. They were trying to impress me, and that made me suspicious of their purpose.

The eight worldly concerns are sneaky, even when we try to create virtue. Excellent practitioners will sometimes notice in the back of their minds the thought wishing to receive praise, respect, or offerings. Worse yet are those who try to impress others with their knowledge or ability to perform rituals. Some get enamored with their own charisma. In fact praise doesn't benefit us in a substantial way: it doesn't increase our longevity, intelligence, or good health, nor does criticism impede these. The law of karma and its effects is our true witness: others may sing our praises, but we still have to experience the results of the destructive actions we created. Other people may criticize us, but they cannot destroy our merit or cause us to be reborn in an unfortunate rebirth. Our infatuation with praise and accolades is like thinking a rainbow has some substance. The great Nyingma practitioner, Longchen Rabjam, said:

> See the equality of praise and blame, approval and disapproval,
>   good and bad reputation,
> for they are just like illusions or dreams and have no true existence.
> Learn to bear them patiently, as if they were mere echoes,
> and sever at its root the mind that clings to an I or a self.[46]

Pleasure and pain

So many of our actions are fueled by attachment to pleasurable sights, sounds, odors, tastes, and tactile sensations, such as feeling warm on a cold day and cool on a hot day, and aversion for their opposites—grating noises, disgusting food, sleeping on a bed that is too hard or too soft, and witnessing alarming sights. Securing the former and avoiding the latter becomes the purpose of most of our daily life activities. Yet as hard as we try, we are never able to make our lives entirely comfortable, which leaves us feeling grouchy and complaining. Our unhappiness does not come from inability to control the environment so that we have only pleasant sensory experiences, but from internal emotions of strong craving and aversion. Minus the craving and aversion, we may still have preferences, but are able to accept what life brings us. Our frustration and worry decrease, giving way to enjoying what is instead of pining for what isn't.

This pair may also be described as attachment to success and aversion to failure. Rather than allow our mind and self-esteem to vacillate according to these, we can maintain a balanced attitude by contemplating interdependence. Success does not depend on us alone; the efforts of many people are involved, so arrogance is uncalled for. Failure may be due to mistakes or to external circumstances that we cannot control. Learning from our mistakes is useful and accepting that we cannot control the world is practical. Both of these will calm our mind.

Disadvantages of the Eight Worldly Concerns

When we speak of Dharma as distinct from non-Dharma, the line of demarcation is the presence or absence of the eight worldly concerns. If our action is motivated by attachment to only the happiness of this life, it is considered non-Dharma. Actions motivated by the aspiration to have a fortunate rebirth, to attain liberation, or to attain buddhahood are Dharma actions. This does not mean that secular people or those of other religions do not create virtue. Anyone can refrain from harming others, cultivate a kind heart, and create merit through generosity, forgiveness, and compassion.

In the Pāli canon (AN 8.6) the Buddha explains that the eight worldly concerns are encountered by both uninstructed worldly people and by knowledgeable āryas, but there is a big difference between how these two groups respond. When ordinary people receive gain, fame, praise, and pleasure, they do not reflect on these as being impermanent and subject to change; they do not know them as they are in reality. Instead ordinary beings are delighted and their common sense is swept away by elation. When they meet with the opposite of these four—loss, disrepute, blame, and unpleasant sensations, they become dejected. Obsessed with their likes and dislikes, they continue to revolve in cyclic existence, with its birth, ageing, sickness, and death, and to be tormented by pain, grief, and despair. Their minds are never peaceful, as they desperately try to procure everything that appears to bring them happiness and vehemently reject the reality of painful situations.

When instructed āryas come upon these concerns, however, they understand the four pleasant ones to be transient and changing. Understanding them as they really are—impermanent, unable to provide lasting happiness, and lacking their own independent essence—their minds remain balanced. They do not become upset when loss, blame, disrepute, and unpleasant sensations come their way. Giving up attachment to likes and aversion to dislikes, they seek a higher happiness—that of liberation—and create the causes to be free from cyclic existence. Speaking of the eight worldly concerns, the Buddha observes (AN 8.5):

> The wise and mindful person knows them
> and sees that they are subject to change.
> Desirable conditions don't excite his mind,
> nor is he repelled by undesirable conditions.
>
> He has dispelled attraction and repulsion;
> they are gone and no longer present.
> Having known the dustless, sorrowless state,
> he understands rightly and has transcended [cyclic] existence.

The eight worldly concerns center around attachment to the pleasures of just this life. While this life is important, clinging to its pleasures is problematic. The Buddha does not say that pleasure is bad or evil. Pleasure is what it is—a nice experience that lasts a short while. It is fine to enjoy the good things we encounter. But becoming attached to them is another matter, because the attachment—and the aversion that arises when we cannot get what we like—causes problems in this and future lives and distracts us from fulfilling our spiritual yearnings. For this reason, the Seventh Dalai Lama said:[47]

> Fantasies about material objects and the winds of [tendencies toward] the eight worldly concerns are completely misleading. Because of clinging to things that give only temporary fulfilment, at death one is weighed down with the pain of a mind empty [of virtue].

The Fourth Paṇchen Lama, Losang Chokyi Gyaltsen, said true practitioners of Mahāmudrā see that the eight worldly concerns are like dramas of madness and prefer solitude—"solitude" meaning separating the mind from ignorance, animosity, and attachment.

In our attempts to obtain the four factors that superficially seem to bring happiness in only this life and to distance ourselves from the four undesirable ones, we create a great deal of negative karma. To protect our reputation, we talk behind others' backs; to get more money, we cheat others or get involved in illegal business dealings; to win someone's approval or praise, we lie, hiding our mistakes and making up successes that we lack. In the long run, due to the functioning of karma and its effects, these actions bring suffering on us. Although seeking the eight worldly concerns seems to bring us happiness superficially, in the long term it brings more misery. The eight worldly concerns make our viewpoint very narrow and self-centered. We become blind to karma and its effects and ignore the need to create the causes for well-being in future lives. Aspiring to liberation or awakening is far from our mind.

The eight worldly concerns obstruct us from genuine Dharma practice. Most of our distractions in meditation involve the eight worldly concerns. When our mind wanders while listening to teachings, our attention has strayed to one of these eight. We postpone positive deeds, such as generosity or helping others, because our time is occupied with these eight. For these reasons, Dharma practitioners are warned about seeking the temporary happiness of *only* this life, not because it is bad or "sinful" but because it impedes us from actualizing the spiritual realizations that will bring long-term happiness.

Attachment to the pleasures of only this life breeds dissatisfaction. However much we have, it is not enough. Even wealthy people don't feel satisfied with what they have. No matter how much our loved ones praise us, we still want more. We long for another reward, trophy, or public acknowledgement of what we have accomplished. True satisfaction eludes us.

When we have worldly success, we easily become arrogant and haughty, flaunting our success and ignoring the needs of others. Therefore mind training texts say that it is better to meet difficulties, for they make us humble and more compassionate. Difficulties flatten our haughtiness, and we learn to respect the concerns and feelings of others. Difficulties also deepen our refuge in the Three Jewels and spur us to be mindful of karma and its effects.

Giving up attachment to the pleasures of only this life and the eight worldly concerns does not mean that we neglect ourselves and become a pauper. Some people make a big display of having renounced the world, but remain attached to their reputation as a renunciant! We need a certain amount of possessions and financial support to function in society. Having wise friends and maintaining our health facilitate Dharma practice. Problems arise when we are attached to these and seek them to the exclusion of all else.

Relinquishing attachment and aversion does not entail having a dull and boring life. Rather, our life becomes fuller because being free from the push and pull of delight and dejection, we are able to appreciate whatever comes our way. Instead of thinking, "I can only be happy when I'm near this one special person," we become more open and enjoy the company of many others.

In brief, the problem does not rest in the experience of pleasure or the objects that seem to bring pleasure. It is clinging to the pleasure that is the troublemaker. The Buddha says (AN 6.63):

> They are not sensual pleasures, the pretty things in the world;
> a person's sensual pleasure is lustful intention;
> the pretty things remain just as they are in the world,
> but the wise remove the desire for them.

In the *Inquiry of Ugra Sūtra* (*Ugraparipṛcchā*) the Buddha gives excellent guidance on how to deal with our addiction to the eight worldly concerns:

> Being free of attachment and aversion [the bodhisattva] should attain equanimity with respect to the eight worldly concerns. If he succeeds in obtaining wealth, or a spouse, or children, or valuables, or produce, he should not become arrogant or over-joyed. If he fails to obtain all these things, he should not be downcast or distressed. Rather he should reflect as follows: "All conditioned things are illusory and are marked by involvement in fabrication. Thus my father and mother, children, spouse, employees . . . friends, companions, kinsfolk, and relatives—all are the result of the ripening of actions. Thus they are not mine, and I am not theirs.
>
> "And why? Because my father, mother, and so on are not my protector, refuge, resort, place of rest, island, self, or what

belongs to the self. If even my own perishable aggregates, sense sources, cognitive faculties and their objects are not me or mine, how much less are my father, mother, and so on me or mine, or I theirs? And why? Because I am subject to my actions and heir to my actions, I will inherit [the results of] whatever I have done, whether good deeds or bad. I will taste the fruit of every one of them and will experience the ripening of each one. Because these people are also subject to their actions and heir to their actions, they too will inherit [the results of] whatever they have done, whether good deeds or bad. They will experience the ripening of every one of them and will taste the fruit of each one.

It is not my business to accumulate nonvirtuous deeds for their sake. All of them are a source of pleasure now, but they will not be a source of pleasure later on. Instead, I should devote myself to what is really mine—to the virtues of generosity, discipline, self-restraint, fortitude, good character, exertion, vigilance, and the accumulation and production of the [seven] awakening factors. That is what is actually mine. Wherever I may go, these qualities will go with me."[48]

Using our human intelligence to accomplish long-term benefit for ourselves is valuable, whereas focusing on just our own short-term interests is limited. Even businesspersons who are nonbelievers know that being short-sighted and impatient is a disadvantage to achieving their goals. If this is true for obtaining good results in this life, it is even truer for actualizing our spiritual goals. Thus when we experience suffering and are deprived of sensory pleasures, wealth, praise, and fame, we should maintain a long-term perspective and practice fortitude so that we can tolerate these temporary situations in cyclic existence. Such fortitude maintains our spiritual resolve without feeling defeated or upset, no matter what we encounter. But when we are focused on only our immediate happiness and benefit, we are perpetually dissatisfied and create much destructive karma.

Our precious human life presents us with great opportunities. If we use our energy only to get delicious food, attractive clothing, a good income, a great reputation, and popularity, we waste our human potential. Using our human intelligence to improve only our external situation but not the state of our mind and heart does not do justice to our extraordinary intelligence. Simply helping our friends and harming our enemies wastes our human potential and does nothing to distinguish us from animals who also care for their dear ones and harm those who threaten them. We must not limit our human life to just these activities. Spending our lives striving only for the eight worldly concerns leaves us regretful at the end of our lives, for none of these is of any use to us at the time of death or afterward. We regret wasting a little money, but we should regret even more wasting our lives seeking only comfort, prestige, romantic love, and so forth.

What, then, can human beings do that animals and insects cannot do? We can transform, discipline, and train our minds and hearts. We can understand teachings on ethical conduct and the method to cultivate love and compassion. We can realize the nature of reality, which will liberate us from all duḥkha. Channeling our energy into actualizing our peerless potential is truly worthwhile.

Each sentient being wants happiness. A worldly perspective leads us to believe that it is found by possessing certain things, being close to specific people, and gaining acceptance and reputation. A Dharma perspective proposes seeking happiness in transforming our mind and heart and cultivating our wisdom and good heart. Dharma practitioners seek happiness in a more reliable way by expanding our motivation to include the long-term welfare of all sentient beings. The Buddha speaks of the joy a sincere practitioner derives from Dharma practice (MN 27.14–15): by living ethically, "he experiences within himself a bliss that is blameless." Living an ethical life enables us to be free from guilt and remorse and to feel good about our actions. By restraining the sense faculties so that the mind is not continuously running here and there in search of temporary pleasure, "he experiences within himself a bliss that is unsullied," that arises from acting with mindfulness and introspective awareness.

By cultivating contentment, we experience the internal peace of accepting ourselves. The practice of bodhicitta opens our hearts with love and compassion toward all beings, producing great joy in the mind. By acting for the benefit of others, we gain the satisfaction of making a positive contribution to the welfare of others. The practice of stabilizing meditation leads to the attainment of higher states of concentration. The joy and bliss that arise in them are free from attachment to the desire realm and invigorate the mind. Realizing the true nature of all phenomena and integrating it in our lives brings a peace that cannot be destroyed. The union of clear light mind and illusory body in tantric practice produces the magnificent bliss of full awakening. The Buddha spoke of giving up attachment to the pleasures of this life in order to lead us on the path to more stable and profound states of fulfillment that can be actualized only by Dharma practice. Sentient beings naturally seek happiness and there is nothing wrong with having it. We want to free ourselves from attachment to inferior states of happiness that are in the nature of duḥkha. Rather than seek situations and things that at first appear wonderful but eventually become troublesome, it is wiser to generate spiritual happiness that is based on more stable, realistic, and beneficial states of mind.

9 | Looking beyond This Life

To attain a fortunate rebirth, liberation, and full awakening, we must have heartfelt aspirations and a firm commitment to engage in the practices that bring these about. Understanding the benefits of attaining those aims and the disadvantages of not attaining them fosters a pure motivation. Contemplating the drawbacks of being born as one of the three unfortunate classes of beings and the opportunities for spiritual progress with a fortunate rebirth will motivate us to keep good ethical conduct, practice the six perfections, and dedicate the merit for a precious human life. Reflecting on the faults of cyclic existence and the difficulties of being under the power of afflictions and karma motivates us to counteract these. Contemplating the kindness of sentient beings and their duḥkha generates the aspiration for awakening.

As described above, the biggest obstacle to attaining our spiritual aims is our obsessive preoccupation with the eight worldly concerns, which lead us to engage in destructive actions and distract us from creating virtue. The most effective way to initially subdue the eight worldly concerns is to reflect on impermanence and death. The *Dhammapada* counsels (168–74):

> This world is blind! There are so few who see things as they truly are. Come, take a good look at this world, pretty like a king's chariot. Though fools become immersed in it, for the wise there is no attachment. See how it is like a bubble! See how it is like a mirage! The king of death does not see one who regards the world in this way. Rouse yourself and don't be lazy! Follow the good ways of Dhamma.

Gross and Subtle Impermanence

As the first of the sixteen aspects or key points of the four truths and the first of the four seals that mark a teaching as Buddhadharma, impermanence is an essential point to contemplate on the path. Impermanence has two levels: subtle and gross. Subtle impermanence refers to the fact that every conditioned phenomenon changes and does not endure to the next moment. Its very nature is transient: the subtle particles composing an atom are in constant motion; each moment of mind ceases and gives way to the next.

Gross impermanence refers to the ceasing of the continuity of an object: a chair breaks, a human being dies. Initial-level practitioners meditate on gross impermanence to help them to evaluate their priorities in life by seeing the impermanent nature of the happiness of just this life and the eight worldly concerns. Not thinking that we will die one day, we think, "I need this and that because I'm going to live." Focusing on the pursuit of money, fame, praise, success, and comfortable experiences—all of which do not last long—we neglect to prepare to depart this life and go on to the next. Awareness of the fleeting nature of life spurs us to engage in what is beneficial for this life as well as what is meaningful for lives to come. A lamrim text encourages us to think of impermanence in five ways.

1. The *impermanence of destruction* refers to the annihilation of something that existed. For example, the twin towers in New York were decimated, and death is the cessation of a person's life force.

2. The *impermanence of cultural trends and attitudes* points to the changes occurring in society. One hundred years ago, women had few options in life outside of marriage and family. Now more opportunities are available to them and society benefits from their contribution. Centuries ago democracy was virtually unheard of. Now it is a value in many cultures.

3. The *impermanence of separation* indicates that whatever comes together must separate; it is impossible to always remain together. Relationships transform over time, and people who were close at one time later go their own ways. Organizations and companies form and dissolve, their employees going in many different directions.

4. *Sudden impermanence* is the fact that circumstances can change quickly and unexpectedly. We get up in the morning expecting to

have certain experiences and meet particular people, but plans change on short notice. While we can easily adapt to some sudden changes, others, such as a mass shooting or the death of a dear one in a car accident, are difficult to adapt to.

5. The *nature of impermanence* refers to the fact that everything that arises due to causes and conditions is transitory in nature. Whether we want it to be stable and predictable or wish it to change quickly, change is its very nature.

REFLECTION

1. Review the five points above one by one and make examples of them from your life.

2. Notice the effect this has on your mind.

Learning from Our Own Mortality

Contemplating death is neither morbid nor unrealistic. To the contrary, it helps us prepare for death and live with more wisdom and kindness. This meditation has three points: death is definite, its time is uncertain, and at the time of death only the Dharma can help us. Each point has three subpoints and a conclusion; together these lead us to a realistic and beneficial perspective on what is important in life.

Death is definite.
Death is the cutting off of the life faculty; it occurs at the time that the continuities of body and mind are disjoined. The continuity of the body is a lifeless corpse; in general, the continuity of the mind enters an intermediate state, and then ordinary beings take rebirth in another coarse body. The only exceptions are meditators who have deep concentration and are reborn in the form or formless realms, a person who will be born in a pure land, a tantric practitioner who gains spiritual realizations at the time of death, or an ārya who has control over the rebirth process. Death occurs owing to four situations: (1) Exhaustion of the life span. The karma that

brought about that life is exhausted, and that lifetime ceases. (2) Exhaustion of merit. Merit is required to stay alive once we are born, and when it runs out, death occurs. The karma that maintains the life span may still be intact, but the person lacks the merit to receive food, shelter, clothing, or medicine, and death occurs. (3) Both of the above occur simultaneously. (4) Ripening of destructive karma. Even though the life span and merit may not be exhausted, the seed of a strong destructive karma ripens and cuts short the life span, bringing an untimely death due to an accident or unexpected illness.

The three subpoints that help us understand the certainty of our death are:

1. Everyone who is born dies; death is a natural result of birth. Death is common to all beings; it is the great equalizing factor, for no one can avoid it. Wealth, fame, intelligence, love, or power—none of these can prevent death—and even holy beings and great leaders die.

2. When the time of death arrives, our life span cannot be extended. There is nowhere to go to avoid death; beings in every realm of cyclic existence die. Moving to another place, finding another doctor, and changing our medicine may prolong our life awhile, but cannot prevent death.

3. We will die even if we have not had the time to practice the Dharma. As each moment passes, we approach the end of our life, and the time available for Dharma practice is brief and consumed with other activities. When we're young we go to school and play, in our adult years we have a family and work, in our senior years we spend time caring for our health.

While most of us intellectually know that we will die, our inner feeling is that death will not come to us: "Others will die, but not me." How wrong that is! Śāntideva cautions us (BCA 2.39):

> Remaining neither day nor night,
> this life is always slipping by
> and never lengthening.
> Why will death not come to one like me?

Given that there is no way to avoid death, wouldn't it be beneficial to prepare for death so that we will not be caught unawares when it happens? The best way to prepare for death is to practice the Dharma—to transform our mind by pacifying afflictions and cultivating good qualities. Doing this, we will be more peaceful at the time of death and our future rebirth will be better.

The conclusion to reach from this meditation is: Since death is definite and practicing the Dharma will benefit us in this life, at the time of death, and in future lives, we resolve to definitely transform our minds through putting the Buddha's teachings into practice.

The time of death is uncertain.
Although we feel we will not die anytime soon, in fact we do not know when death will come. Although we plan for our old age, we may not live that long; there is no guarantee that we will be alive tomorrow. Contemplate:

1. The life span of human beings in our world is indefinite, and people die at all ages. We may believe that death will come only after we have accomplished certain career goals or after we've enjoyed watching our children grow up or traveling to faraway places, but in fact we don't know when we will die. Whenever it is, we will surely be in the middle of doing something that will be left unfinished. Some people die on the way to work, others while eating, some simply between one breath and the next.

2. Many circumstances lead to death and fewer lead to survival. Great effort is required to stay alive: we must feed our body and protect it from heat, cold, disease, and injury. It takes a lot of planning and effort to keep this body alive, whereas if we did nothing, our body would simply die of dehydration or starvation.

3. Even things meant to protect life, such as medicine, food, shelter, and transportation, can inadvertently cause death. Microscopic viruses and bacteria may cause death, small pieces of metal can kill us. Our physiological systems are delicate and easily become unbalanced, leading to illness and death. While medical science has made tremendous advancements, it has not been able to stop death, and sometimes the treatment we take for illness has side effects that hasten death.

It is to our advantage to prepare ourselves for death, whenever it will come. The way to do this is by developing a stable spiritual practice now so that we will accumulate as much virtue and Dharma understanding as possible while alive. This also makes it more likely that we will have a virtuous mental state should death come suddenly. Āryaśūra warns us:

> Between the two—tomorrow and the next life—
> which will come first is uncertain.
> Therefore, do not make effort in the means for tomorrow;
> it is right to make effort for the welfare of the next life.[49]

Conclusion: Seeing that the time of death is uncertain let's start transforming our minds today. Since death may come at any time, we cannot afford to postpone our Dharma practice until conditions are more suitable. The only time we will ever have for practice is now.

Only Dharma helps at the time of death.
At the time of death, our wealth, fame, friends, relatives, social status, awards, and even our body cannot help us. None of them can come with us into our future lives; they are all left behind as we separate from everything that is familiar. However, the karmic seeds of destructive actions that we have done to procure and protect our wealth, dear ones, and body follow the mindstream (*cittasaṃtāna*) as it goes on to the next life. Only the positive mental qualities we have built up during our lives and the karmic seeds of constructive actions are able to ease our mind at the time of death and ensure fortunate future lives. To understand this, reflect:

1. Money and possessions are of no help at the time of death. We may work very hard while alive to amass money and material goods, but all of them remain behind. We may have created great destructive karma to procure and protect our money and possessions, but our wealth in this life is useless in the next. We go to the next life with only the karmic seeds and habitual tendencies we have built up while alive.

2. Friends and relatives cannot prevent our death no matter how much they love and respect us. We may have been constant companions for decades, but separation is guaranteed because everything that comes

together must separate. Separation at the time of death can be excruciating when we are very attached to others.

3. Not even our body is of benefit. We have spent so much of our lives taking care of this body, but at the time of death it abandons us, becoming a corpse that remains here while the mindstream goes on alone to future lives. All the pleasures this body enjoyed are last night's dream, but the karma we created to secure them goes with us.

Śri Jagan-mitrananda's *Letter to King Moon* (*Candrarājalekha*) says (LC 1:158):

Divine one, no matter what fortunes you have gained,
when you depart to another rebirth,
as though conquered by an enemy in the desert,
you are alone without children or queen,
without clothing, without servants,
without kingdom, and without palace.

Though you have limitless power and armies,
you will not see or hear them.
Eventually not even one being or thing
will follow you in an everlasting way.
In brief, if you lack even a name at that time,
what need is there to speak about anything else?

Śāntideva counsels (BCA 2.33, 34, 36, 38):

The untrustworthy lord of death without waiting
whether or not something has been done;[50]
whether one is sick or otherwise, suddenly comes;
do not be complacent about life.

Leaving all behind, I must depart alone.
Through not having understood this
I committed various kinds of negativities
for the sake of my friends and foes...

Just like an experience in a dream,
whatever things I enjoy
will become a memory.
Whatever has passed will not be seen [again].

Thereby, through not having realized
that I will suddenly vanish,
I committed many negativities
through ignorance, attachment, and hatred.

Our worldly actions are like ripples in water, one leading to the next. Our mind distracted by the endless worldly activities in our lives, we have little time for Dharma practice before death arrives. At that time regret overwhelms us as we realize that time could have been spent cultivating wisdom and cutting the root of saṃsāra.

In addition, many of our constructive actions are polluted by the eight worldly concerns; creating the image of being an excellent practitioner, we hunger for praise, offerings, and reputation. Unaware, we miss the chance to prepare for death. There is a story about a man who slipped while walking on the edge of a cliff. He broke his fall by catching hold of a root. Looking up, he saw a strawberry, and yearning for the pleasure of its taste overwhelmed him. Meanwhile a rat was busy gnawing the root. Distracted by desire for the strawberry, he did not protect himself and fell to his death as the root broke.

Oblivious of the effects our actions have on others and ourselves, we often act impulsively and grasp whatever will fulfill our needs and wants in the present moment. But when we arrive at the end of our lives and look back—or even if we look back now at what we did for the last ten years—which of our actions were really valuable? I have never heard of a dying person regretting that they did not work more overtime. Remembering this, let's be mindful and make wise decisions now, steering our energy toward Dharma practice, an activity that will bring ourselves and others benefit for a long time to come.

Although many great masters may recite prayers for our good rebirth, perform *powa* (transference of consciousness) after our death, or give us instructions to recognize the bardo (intermediate state between one life and the next) after the breath has stopped, it is far more effective to have studied and practiced the Dharma we learned while alive. If we don't pay attention to these masters' instructions while we are alive, what makes us think that we will listen to them when we're dying?

We can pay people to do many things for us—to mow the lawn or to prepare a report. But we cannot hire someone who will eat for us so that we feel nourished. As with eating and sleeping, creating virtue and abandoning nonvirtue are activities we must do ourselves. Knowing that only the Dharma benefits us at death, generate the determination to practice it purely, free from the influence of the eight worldly concerns.

Whereas death arrives effortlessly, spiritual development requires effort. We cannot wait and hope that with the passage of time we become more disciplined, loving, and compassionate. Only through careful training can we develop these qualities. Although our body may get old, weak, and eventually stop functioning, our afflictions will not decline and disappear with time. In fact sometimes they grow stronger, and some people become more bitter, angry, or emotionally dependent as they age. The afflictions remain fresh and energetic unless we make an effort to counteract them.

Years ago I visited Thailand, where many monasteries have a skeleton near the meditation hall. One monastery had a display with photographs of the stages of a rotting corpse. Seeing these reminded me that I too will die, and keeping that vividly in mind spurs me to transform my mind.

Other Life Forms

After death, the continuity of our consciousness does not stop. Although the coarse sense consciousnesses cease as we go through the death process, the extremely subtle mind continues to the next life. What kind of life will we have in our next rebirth? We don't need to ask a fortune teller; the Buddha explained that according to the law of karma and its effects, virtuous actions bring fortunate rebirths as human or celestial beings (*devas*), whereas nonvirtuous ones lead to unfortunate ones as an animal, hungry ghost, or hell being. Since none of us wants an unfortunate rebirth, it behooves us to create the causes for a good rebirth now.

We may wonder: We know that humans and animals exist, but do the other classes of beings actually exist? Is the description of the unfortunate states to be taken literally? Neither reasoning nor direct experience is able to establish the nonexistence of these realms. Using reasoning to establish their existence is difficult, and we ordinary beings do not have the clairvoyance to determine whether such rebirths exist. In this case, we can rely on reliable scriptural quotations.

Sūtras in all three Buddhist canons—Pāli, Chinese, and Tibetan—speak of other life forms in the universe: in the *Jewel Sutta* (*Ratana Sutta* Sh 2.1), one of the most well-known sūtras in the Pāli canon, the Buddha addresses spirits who are making trouble for the Licchavi clan. The *Sutta of Fools and Wise Men* (*Bālapaṇḍita Sutta* MN 129) speaks of rebirth as hell, animal, and deva or celestial beings, and the *Sutta of the Divine Messengers* (*Devadūta Sutta* MN 130) describes the hell beings in detail.

If you have difficulty accepting scriptural quotations, I recommend remaining undecided yet open-minded. Continue to study and practice the Buddha's teachings, implementing what is useful in your life and leaving the rest aside for the time being. However, if you say, "I don't believe that other realms exist," consider the I that states this. Is that I omniscient? Is whatever that I thinks always accurate?

Personally speaking, although I do not take the descriptions of the hellish states in the *Treasury of Knowledge* literally, I believe the possibility that such states exist is real. From my own experience, I know that when the mind is disciplined and its positive qualities enhanced, having special experiences is possible. Similarly, when the mind is undisciplined and obscured by negative tendencies, suffering and problems occur. By seeing the interrelationship of the mind and our experiences, I have an inkling that other life forms—those in both pure lands and hellish states—exist.

In some cultures, people accept the existence of spirits and hungry ghosts, and some people even report seeing them. Although this is not generally the case in the West, some Westerners talk about UFOs and report being visited by beings from outer space. In other cultures, people who have similar experiences describe them as encountering spirits or hungry ghosts. In Tibet some people had a special capacity to see some of these spirits that are not normally seen by people. One of my childhood bodyguards could do this.

We may not believe in the existence of other classes of beings because we do not see them; but once we see them, we will have already been born there and it will be too late. Therefore, although we may not be convinced that hell beings and hungry ghosts exist, I recommend provisionally accepting their existence because doing so will make us more mindful of the consequences of our actions before doing them. Should such rebirths exist, we do not want to create the causes leading to them. On the other hand, if such rebirths do not exist, we have not lost anything by refraining from destructive actions!

We know the animals exist and can observe animals' lives. They are clouded by ignorance, and many are exploited by human beings or killed for food or hides. Domestic pets may have comfortable lives, but they are incapable of studying, thinking about, and meditating on the Dharma. If we try to teach our pet cats the value of abandoning killing, they cannot understand at all!

We also see people and events right now that resemble life in these other states. Some human beings act worse than animals, inflicting harm and suffering on others far beyond what any animal could do. Consider those who ran concentration camps during World War II, those behind the Cultural Revolution, and those conducting terrorist activities internationally. That human beings inflict such harm on other human beings leaves us stunned; we cannot find any suitable explanation for such horror. Yet we know that it is a reality. Likewise, we may not easily believe in the existence of unfortunate states and the suffering experienced in them, but these exist. Since powerful destructive actions produce strong suffering in future lives, it makes sense that human beings who inflict great pain on others would be born in unfortunate states.

In the *Sutta to the Dog-Duty Ascetic* (*Kukkuravatika Sutta* MN 57), the Buddha speaks in a compassionate yet matter-of-fact way about the possibility of rebirth in unfortunate states as a result of our destructive actions and shows that this can be prevented. As did many others, two ascetics in ancient India acted like animals, thinking that it would bring them fortunate rebirths. Approaching the Buddha, Seniya, acting like a dog, and Puṇṇa, behaving like an ox, asked him what their future lives would be. The Buddha did not want to answer, but when pressed he explained (MN 57.5):

> Here, someone develops the ox-duty...the ox-habit...the ox-mind...the ox-behavior fully and uninterruptedly. Having done

so, on the dissolution of the body, after death, he reappears in the company of oxen. But if he has such a view as this: "By this virtue or observance or asceticism or holy life I shall become a [great] god or some [lesser] god," that is a wrong view in his case. Now there are two destinations for one with wrong view, I say: hell or the animal state. So if his ox-duty succeeds, it will lead him to the company of oxen; if it fails, it will lead him to the hellish state.

These ascetics had faith in karma and its results, and by hearing that their practice was based on wrong views that would lead them to horrible rebirths, they sobbed and had deep regret for their actions. The Buddha then taught them about karma and concluded, "Thus I say beings are the heirs of their actions." Both of them became the Buddha's disciples, and by meditating with strong determination Seniya became an arhat in that life.

The purpose of contemplating the suffering of these migrations and the possibility of being reborn there is not to fill us with irrational panic, emotional fear, and immobilizing dread. Rather, it impels us to practice so that we will not create the causes for such births and will direct our energy in a positive direction instead.

If we are reborn as a hell being, hungry ghost, or animal, will we be able to endure the sufferings? Unpleasant as it may be, contemplating such topics is essential because we can act to prevent these types of rebirth. If we do not think about them and consequently do nothing to prevent them, once we are born in those unfortunate states very little can be done to ease the suffering.

Thinking that unfortunate migrations are in some faraway place and have nothing to do with us is unwise. None of us knows when we will die, and as ordinary beings without spiritual realizations, we have no guarantee that we will not take birth in one of these unfortunate states. Looking carefully at the actions we have done throughout our lives, we see there is a real possibility that we will face an unfortunate rebirth, one where there is not only great misery but also no opportunity to meet the Dharma. We have the opportunity now with our precious human lives to engage in abundant constructive actions that will lead to future happiness in cyclic existence and the ultimate happiness of liberation and awakening. Please keep this in mind and let it motivate you to live with wisdom and compassion now. Reflect on impermanence and death and make a strong determination to overcome the eight worldly concerns that could impede you from doing this.

The Buddha once asked his disciples, "Which is greater, the little bit of soil under my fingernail or the great earth?" They responded that the soil under his fingernail is trifling, whereas the earth is huge. The Buddha then advised them (SN 20.2):

> So too, those beings who are reborn among human beings are few. But those beings who are reborn elsewhere than among human beings are more numerous. Therefore you should train yourselves thus: "We shall dwell diligently."

Fear or Hope at Death?

If our lives have centered primarily around the eight worldly concerns, our mind becomes familiar with nonvirtue. While dying, attachment to self arises, and wanting security and not suffering, we cling to what is familiar—our body, mind, and so forth. Then fearing that we will cease to exist at death, we crave another body.

In contrast to this panicked fear, if while we are alive we generate a "wise fear" of death, we will be able to set our priorities wisely and make our lives meaningful. The wise fear is aware of the danger of destructive karma ripening at the time of death and propelling us to an unfortunate rebirth. It sharpens our mindfulness, motivates us to practice virtue, and enables us to prevent that danger. This "fear" is similar to the mental state when we merge our car into highway traffic: aware of the possibility of having an accident, we are cautious, which prevents an accident. Wise fear inspires us to set clear priorities, so that we make our life meaningful and do not waste it on unimportant activities. Our life becomes very vibrant and vital as we live each moment fully, aware that the only time we can practice the Dharma is now. Due to practicing diligently, we will be free of fear and regret at the time of death. As the great yogi Milarepa said:

In horror of death, I took to the mountains—
again and again I meditated on the uncertainty of the hour of death.
Capturing the fortress of the deathless unending nature of mind;
now all fear of death is over and done.

Upon seeing a stray horse and an empty chariot, the Buddha's disciple
Mahānāma noted that his mindfulness of the Three Jewels became mud-
dled. He remembered that he too would die, and although he was a stream-
enterer and had no reason to fear death, he became concerned about his
future rebirth. The Buddha assuaged his fear by reminding him that the
virtue he had created will propel his mind upward on the path (SN 55.21):

> Don't be afraid, Mahānāma! Your death will not be a bad one,
> your demise will not be a bad one. When a person's mind has been
> fortified over a long time by faith, ethical conduct, learning, gen-
> erosity, and wisdom, right here . . . [his body may be destroyed].
> But his mind, which has been fortified over a long time by faith,
> ethical conduct, learning, generosity, and wisdom—that goes
> upward, goes to distinction.

Death is a normal part of life, something that we must face as long as we
are in cyclic existence. To me, leaving this body and going to the next life
resembles shedding old clothes and putting on new ones. For practitioners
who have trained their minds well while alive, the experience of death can
be profound and transformative. Our present body feels solid, heavy, and
burdensome. In addition, our gross consciousnesses are dependent on the
brain, which limits our mental functions. When our mind separates from
the body, it is freer and can be utilized more effectively if we are well trained.
Practitioners with very deep meditative experience can control their death
and the process of rebirth. Although these people are rare, they show us the
potential of the mind. As mentioned before, my teacher, Kyabje Ling Rinpoche, meditated sitting upright for thirteen days after his bodily functions
had ceased. Death was joyful and spiritually satisfying for him.

Highest yoga tantra includes a meditation in which death, bardo, and
rebirth are taken as the path to the truth body, enjoyment body, and emanation body of a buddha. In the generation stage this is done by imagina-

tion; by working with the subtlest wind and mind during the completion stage, these three buddha bodies can be actualized. In my daily practice, I do this meditation at least six times a day to prepare for death, making my mind very familiar with the natural process of death. However, if I was in an airplane that is going down, I don't know how I would feel! I am curious to discover how much of what I am currently practicing I will be able to implement at the time of death. I have no doubt that the force of serious training during life, complemented by pure ethical conduct, bodhicitta, and some understanding of emptiness, will be beneficial at that time.

The Death Process

Highest yoga tantra explains the death process in great detail. Eight steps occur as the body gradually loses its ability to support coarse levels of consciousness and as the mind becomes increasingly subtler until the subtlest mind, the fundamental, innate clear light mind, dawns. That is the actual moment of death. In the next moment, the mind leaves the body and enters the bardo; at that time, the person is dead.

As each element dissolves—that is, as it loses its ability to support consciousness—our aggregates weaken and we have an inner appearance to the mind.

1. When the earth element dissolves into the water element, the body becomes thinner, the form aggregate—the body—weakens, and the person has an inner shimmering appearance like a mirage.
2. When the water element dissolves into fire, the mouth becomes dry and the skin puckers. The feeling aggregate loses the ability to experience pleasant, unpleasant, and neutral feelings, and the person has an inner appearance of smoke.
3. When the fire element dissolves into the wind element, the heat in the body diminishes. Sometimes the heat leaves beginning with the feet and going upward, other times from the head down. The aggregate of discrimination subsides, and the inner appearance is of sparks of light, like fireflies.
4. When the wind element dissolves into space or consciousness, the external breath stops. The aggregate of miscellaneous factors loses power, and there is an appearance of a small, dim candle flame about

to go out. At this point, breathing has stopped completely, the body grows cold, and the coarse consciousness has been absorbed. Doctors pronounce the person dead, but from a Buddhist viewpoint, the consciousness has not yet left the body.

5–7. Now the coarser winds—inner energies that serve as the mount of consciousness—begin to dissolve. As with the previous stages of dissolution, the time it takes to pass through the next three phases varies with the person, the cause of death, and the person's spiritual training. These three phases are inner appearances to the mind, named: (5) the vivid white appearance, which resembles the bright light of the full moon; (6) the red increase appearance, like the orange-red color of the sky at sunset; (7) the black near attainment of complete darkness.

8. Now the subtlest mind, the fundamental, innate clear light mind, manifests—this is the actual moment of death, although the subtlest wind-mind is still present in the body—and a well-trained practitioner will meditate on emptiness. There is no rigor mortis and there may be a slight sense of heat if we hold our hand above the person's heart cakra at the center of her chest. During this time, the relationship between the body and mind has not been severed, and the body does not decay. It is better to avoid touching or moving the body at this time.

Most sentient beings do not recognize the clear light of death and this phase passes quickly. When the mind leaves the body, small traces of a white or red substance at the nostrils or sexual organ may be seen. The body begins to decay and can safely be moved. For ordinary beings, this usually occurs within three days after the breath has stopped. If a person dies in an accident, the consciousness generally leaves the body quickly.

Some practitioners, especially those who have practiced highest yoga tantra, may meditate in the clear light for several days. I heard of some Tibetans monks who, after being tortured in Chinese prisons, sat cross-legged in their cells and remained meditating in the clear light of death for some time. Thinking that Buddhism was just blind faith and superstition, the Chinese Communist guards were surprised and speechless. For people who practice the Dharma sincerely and continuously, dying is not a frightening event but a joyful experience and an optimal time for meditation.

After separating from the body, the eight signs occur in the reverse order as a slightly coarser mind arises in the bardo. If we will be born in a fortunate birth, it will seem like we are walking on a luminous path surrounded by beauty. If we are headed toward an unfortunate birth, we will have the vision of walking in a gloomy place with fearful images and will experience fear and suffering. It is said that butchers who have not purified their acts of killing will see the images of animals they have slaughtered running toward them.

Bardo beings can travel uninterruptedly from one place to another. Those who will be born in similar realms can see one another, and people with clairvoyant powers can also see bardo beings. For ignorant sentient beings, the bardo can be a frightening and confusing time.

Helping Ourselves and Others at the Time of Death

Our attitudes shape our experiences. Some people avoid thinking about difficulties such as illness, aging, and death. But these are bound to happen, and accepting and preparing for them in advance enables our mind to be calmer when they occur.

There are different levels of preparation for death. While some rare and exceptional practitioners with deep meditative experience can control the process of death and rebirth, ordinary people like me prepare for death as part of our daily meditation practice. If death comes in the next few months or years, I am not afraid and even have some confidence. According to reasoning and some unusual experiences I've had, I have a 95 percent belief in future lives. But there's still a little doubt about the various experiences at the time of death.

As creatures of habit, we tend to die in the way we live. If we are not in the habit of acting kindly during our life, it will be unlikely that we will think to hold virtuous thoughts in mind or engage in virtuous actions as we are approaching death. For that reason, leading a good life by not harming others and helping them as much as possible is the best preparation for our death and future lives and enables us to die without regrets. In our daily life, and especially as we approach death, we should forgive people who have harmed us, engage in purification practice, recollect the Buddha, and meditate on love, compassion, and wisdom.

The best way to help friends and family prepare for death is to encourage them while they are alive to abandon nonvirtue and engage in purification to avoid unfortunate rebirths, and to create virtue to ensure that they have causes for a good rebirth. Encourage them to be generous and kind to others and to forgive others and not hold grudges. Avoid involving them in divisive speech, harsh speech, or idle talk. In this way, they will create merit and will have no regrets when they die.

The most prominent thought while we are actively dying yet still conscious stimulates the ripening of a karmic seed that will project us into a specific rebirth. If we die with strong attachment for our loved ones, possessions, or reputation, or with great anger toward our enemies, seeds of destructive karma will ripen. If our mind is virtuous owing to having trust in the Three Jewels, cultivating compassion for sentient beings, or contemplating the nature of reality, constructive karma is activated, and we will take a fortunate rebirth. Once the dying person has passed through the first four stages of the death process, the mind is in a neutral state and the karma projecting the next life is already beginning to ripen.

Vasubandhu said that consciousness can be virtuous, nonvirtuous, or neutral at the moment of death, depending on the person's thought at that time. His half-brother Asaṅga explained that whereas the coarser states of mind can be virtuous, nonvirtuous, or neutral, the subtle consciousness present at the time of death is neutral. In tantric texts, the Buddha explains that whereas the coarse consciousnesses can be virtuous, nonvirtuous, or neutral, the subtlest consciousness can never be nonvirtuous. This is because the eighty conceptual thoughts—most of which are nonvirtuous—function only in coarse states of mind, which cease before the subtlest mind arises at the actual moment of death. Through profound yogic methods, the subtlest consciousness, also called the fundamental, innate mind of clear light, which is ordinarily neutral, can be transformed into a virtuous state.

The best procedure to follow at the time of death depends on the person. In general, as someone approaches death, avoid disturbing her mind with unnecessary emotional outpourings, spiritual ideas that will confuse her, or idle talk. Help her to recall something virtuous—the Three Jewels, compassion, generosity, and so on—with which she is already familiar. Encourage her to rejoice in her own and others' virtues. If she has no religion, gently speak to her about forgiveness, love, compassion, and hope—qualities that everyone appreciates and that will make her mind virtuous.

No matter what religion a dying person follows, encourage her to do the practices with which she is familiar. Encourage a Christian to forgive others, develop a kind heart, pray to God, and think of Jesus's benevolent qualities. Speak to a Jew, Hindu, or Muslim according to the beliefs and concepts of his religion. These are more familiar and comforting to the dying person, and will facilitate his leaving this life peacefully. Never try to convert another person on his deathbed.

Some people have heard of the *Tibetan Book of the Dead* (*Bar do thos grol chen mo*), which describes a specific meditation done in the Nyingma tradition for those who have received empowerment into that practice and practiced it while alive. It is not the case that the visions of peaceful and wrathful deities and maṇḍalas described in this text occur to everyone at the time of death or in the intermediate state. Practitioners familiar with the practice described in the *Tibetan Book of the Dead* may have those appearances after death and use them in meditation. Hearing this text could possibly confuse a dying person who is unfamiliar with that practice. Therefore I recommend encouraging dying people to think of the religious figures and the qualities of the holy beings that inspire them personally and to develop a kind heart toward all sentient beings. It is not appropriate to introduce a complex meditation with unfamiliar and often fierce-looking figures to a dying person.

Buddhists can do a variety of practices, depending on their level of practice. Remind a dying Dharma friend of a practice she has trained in and guide her through it if she wishes. When it is our turn to die, we should likewise focus on a familiar practice. Since our mental power and alertness decrease at the time of death, forcing ourselves or others to do a new practice at that time will be confusing. Beneficial practices for Buddhists to do while dying include taking refuge in the Three Jewels, which enables our mind to relax and rest in a virtuous state, which is conducive for the ripening of constructive karma, which in turn will propel our mindstream to take a good rebirth. Developing a kind heart, generating bodhicitta, and doing the taking and giving meditation at the time of death also places our mind in a positive and fearless state. Reflecting on emptiness calms grasping and fear, enabling us to peacefully let go of this life.

We may also think of the Buddha or our meditational deity and imagine light and nectar flowing from that Buddha into us, purifying our destructive karma and inspiring our mind with realizations. Advanced practitioners, who have the proper empowerments and have practiced tantra during their lifetimes, should reaffirm the bodhisattva and tantric ethical codes and then do deity yoga, meditate with the wisdom of inseparable bliss and emptiness, or meditate to take death, bardo, and rebirth into the path to the three buddha bodies.

We should dedicate all the merit we have created during our lifetime for the awakening of ourselves and all sentient beings. We should pray to be born in a body and environment where we can meet and properly rely on fully qualified Fundamental Vehicle, Mahāyāna, and Vajrayāna spiritual mentors, learn under their guidance, and practice without obstacles. In short, we must do what is suitable to our level of mind and to the circumstances we are in. Whatever we do, we should be content and focus on that practice as best as we can without having doubts that perhaps we should be doing another, more effective practice.

In the *Sutta on Reappearance by Aspiration* (*Saṅkhārupapatti Sutta*), the Buddha offers advice on how to direct the mind toward the type of rebirth we seek (MN 120.2–3). He begins:

> Monastics, I shall teach you reappearance in accordance with your aspiration...A monastic possesses faith, virtue, learning, generosity, and wisdom. He thinks, "Oh, that on the dissolution of the body, after death, I might reappear in the company of well-to-do nobles!" He fixes his mind on that, establishes it, develops it. These aspirations and this abiding of his, thus developed and cultivated, lead to his reappearance there.

This is an example for someone who wishes to be born in an upper socioeconomic class as a human being. The Buddha says the same for those who want to be reborn as various gods in the desire realm. In all these cases, to intentionally direct our mind toward a specific rebirth, it is necessary to cultivate five qualities—faith, virtue, learning, generosity, and wisdom—during our life. Faith is confidence in the Three Jewels and the law of actions and their result. Virtue is the collection of merit created by keeping precepts, making offerings, sharing our wealth, cultivating fortitude, and so forth. Learning is gained by listening to teachings, reading Dharma books, reflecting on their meaning, and discussing the Dharma with others. Generosity is based on lack of attachment to material goods and distancing ourselves from the eight worldly concerns. Wisdom is the wisdom understanding karma and its effects and the emptiness of inherent existence. Having cultivated these qualities and become familiar with them when alive, at the time of death we generate a strong aspiration for a particular type of rebirth.

To be reborn in any of the four dhyānas or four formless absorptions, we must attain that specific level of dhyāna or meditative absorption as a human being. If we wish to be born in one of the pure abodes where nonreturners dwell, we must develop the union of serenity and insight on selflessness and attain the fruit of a nonreturner before death. If we complete the path to arhatship, we will attain the elimination of all pollutants at the time of death. Those wishing to be reborn in the pure land of Amitābha or another buddha will generate that aspiration at the time of death, thus directing their minds to that rebirth. Lower-level bodhisattvas will direct their aspirations toward whatever rebirth seems most conducive for accomplishing the bodhisattva path, while ārya bodhisattvas will be able to voluntarily choose their reappearance for the benefit of sentient beings.

Having these precious instructions, we should do our best to implement them now in order to prepare for death. Since death is certain, but its time uncertain, let's be prepared.

During the death process and for seven weeks afterward, meditations and prayers done for the deceased can positively influence their consciousness so that the virtuous karma the person had previously created will ripen. This is most effective when the people have a good karmic connection—for example, spiritual mentor and disciple, parent and child, relatives or friends. It is also helpful to donate the person's belongings to his or her spiritual mentors, charities, monasteries, or Dharma centers, and dedicate the merit of this generosity for the person to take a fortunate rebirth with all conducive circumstances to practice the Dharma.

Powa, Transference of Consciousness

Powa is a practice for transferring the consciousness at the time of death so that it will take a precious human life or be reborn in the pure lands. Pure lands are places created by the unshakable resolve and merit of buddhas where all external conditions are conducive for Dharma practice. There are two forms of powa, one found in the mind-training teachings, the other in tantra.

In the *Seven-Point Thought Transformation*, the fourth point, "elucidating a lifetime's practice," describes a practice of transference of consciousness based on bodhicitta called the five forces. Familiarizing ourselves with the five forces while alive will make practicing them at the time of death much easier and give us a sense of joy at the time we die. Bodhicitta gives us courage to work for sentient beings; it makes our life meaningful and dispels all despair. Who wouldn't want to have this mental state when dying?

The first of the five forces, the white seed, is done before actively dying when the mind is clear and can make decisions. Create merit and free your mind from attachment to possessions by giving them away. Forgive all those who have harmed you intentionally or unintentionally and apologize to all those whom you have harmed. If it is not possible to apologize directly to a person, reconciling with them in your mind is more important. Also recall that there is no sense worrying about what happens to your body after death; it is simply a lump of organic matter. Accept death as a natural part of life.

Second is the force of aspiration. Do the seven limbs: visualize prostrating and making offerings to your spiritual mentors and the Three Jewels, confess and restore all broken precepts and degenerated ethical restraints, and dedicate all your merit by aspiring, "During death, bardo, and rebirth, may I never be separated from the practice of bodhicitta. May I always be guided by qualified spiritual mentors who lead me to cultivate bodhicitta."

Third is the force of destruction. Seeing that grasping the self, possessions, friends, and relatives as inherently existent is the chief cause of cyclic existence, try to eradicate it by contemplating impermanence and emptiness. Make a strong determination not to let your mind fall under the influence of ignorance, animosity, and attachment.

Fourth is the force of motivation. This is a strong intention to practice bodhicitta during death, bardo, and rebirth. Develop a strong motivation to practice the two bodhicittas: conventional bodhicitta (the altruistic intention), and ultimate bodhicitta (the wisdom realizing emptiness). Aspire never to be separated from the mind-training practice and the two bodhicittas in any of your lives.

Fifth is the force of acquaintance or familiarity. At the time of death, do the taking and giving practice to increase your love and compassion. Especially think of taking on the pain of others who are dying and transforming your body and merit into whatever others need and giving it to them. Meditate on emptiness, especially the absence of an inherently existent person who is dying. Meditation on the empty nature of mind is also helpful, so recognize all that appears as simply appearance to the mind, not as things to react to or grasp onto.

The *King of Concentration Sūtra* says:

> Migrators in cyclic existence are like dreams;
> no one is [inherently] born here and no one [inherently] dies;
> no [inherently existent] sentient being, human, or living being
>   is found.
> These things are like bubbles, plantain trees,
> illusions, flashes of lightning,
> [reflections of] the moon in water, and mirages.
> In this world, no one [inherently] dies and passes,
> or transmigrates to another life.

If possible, lie in the lion position—the position the Buddha rested in when he passed away: Lie on your right side with your right hand under your cheek. Extend your legs and place your left hand on your left thigh. Then relax the mind and practice as outlined above.

The tantric powa practice involves a practitioner ejecting his or her consciousness out of the body through the top of the head and transferring it to a pure land. Among the different levels of powa, the supreme is when a realized yogi on the completion stage of tantra actualizes the clear light and then arises in the impure illusory body instead of the bardo. This is a rare occurrence.

Powa enables a skilled practitioner to take a rebirth with excellent conditions for Dharma practice. After 1959, some Tibetans who were to be imprisoned by the Chinese communists made their consciousnesses leave their body through powa rather than be subjected to imprisonment. By means of meditation and visualization techniques, they severed the connection between their body and subtlest mind and projected the subtlest mind into a pure land where they could continue practicing the path.

As taught in the tantric texts, powa is to be done by the practitioner himself when he is about to die. To be able to meditate in this way at the time of death, one must receive empowerment and train in powa while one is healthy and alive. While training in powa, it is also essential to do the practice of a long-life deity. A person who has not practiced powa consistently while alive will not be able to perform it when dying.

When a practitioner, through meditation, has attained some control over the wind-energy in the body and mastery over his mind and feels that death is imminent and cannot be avoided, he transfers his consciousness to a pure land. He does this while he still has enough physical energy and mental concentration to properly perform the practice. If he waits until the body is weak, transferring the consciousness could be difficult. But doing it too soon resembles suicide, so great skill is required to perform powa at the proper time. If the powa practice is done irresponsibly or without the proper motivation, there is danger of inadvertently shortening one's life. Although the person does not go through the eight dissolutions in a prolonged manner, they do occur in the proper sequence.

Powa is not a substitute for practicing the Dharma daily. Tantric practitioners should continue practicing taking death, bardo, and rebirth into the three buddha bodies. If, at the time of death, they are not able to actualize the path itself, they do powa in order to carry on Dharma practice continuously in their future life. Powa is specifically for those who have engaged in serious tantric practice during their lives. If you neglect to purify negativities, accumulate merit, and meditate on renunciation, bodhicitta, and emptiness while alive, and at the time of death ask a lama to do powa for you, it is difficult. Without your own effort to practice the Dharma, if you want someone to miraculously transfer your consciousness to a pure land when you die, you will be disappointed. You should be very careful.

Many Tibetan families, and now some non-Tibetan ones, ask a practitioner to perform this ritual at the time of their loved one's death. Although it is customary to do this in the Tibetan community, realistically speaking it has little value if the dying person lacks familiarity with the powa practice and the person doing it lacks a deeper experience of it. Under these circumstances, doing powa becomes a dry ritual. Of course it still has some value because people repeat mantras and recite holy scriptures, which creates a peaceful feeling in the room of the dying person and can help him or her let go of this life more easily.

Although powa is principally meant for a practitioner to transfer his own mind at the time of death, an experienced powa practitioner may be able to help a dying person transfer his consciousness. Powa is done just before the person dies or at the time he is dying. As a result of the expert powa practitioner's influence, the dying person may develop some determination or inspiration, or may have a new spiritual experience. If the dying person has trained in powa when he was alive and healthy, it is easier for the expert powa practitioner to help him at the time of death. This is a proper way to practice powa.

Some people become excited at the prospect of powa, especially because the physical signs such as fluid or swelling at the crown can appear when they practice. This is due to the impact of the winds in the body. It is not indicative of high realization. The real determination of our future rebirth is the karma we create. Observing proper ethical discipline, applying the antidotes to the afflictions, purifying destructive karma, and practicing the six perfections are guaranteed methods for having a good rebirth. If we do not do these, even if a very high lama does powa at our bedside as we die, he can do very little to help us. He can say *hic* and *phey* to transfer our mind to a pure land many times during the ritual, but if we have not created merit and purified destructive karma while alive, these just become the cries of a miserable dying person.

In short, depending on the person, different meditations could be practiced at the time of death. People who are more familiar with the five forces will do that. Others who have trained well in taking death, intermediate state, and rebirth into the path to the three buddha bodies will practice that. Those who are well-trained in powa can rely on that method. The main point is that whatever practice we do should be done with bodhicitta. It should transform our mind and place it in a virtuous state at the time of death.

10 | Karma and Its Effects

H AVING FOUND a precious human life, we now have a choice: Will we create the causes for suffering or will we create the causes for happiness? If we decide to do the latter, the most urgent thing to do is abandon the ten nonvirtues and engage in the ten virtues—to observe karma and its effects. Doing so will bring happiness in this life and fortunate rebirths in future lives, and will establish the foundation of liberation and full awakening.

Since karma and its effects is a very obscure topic, traditional lamrim texts speak of refuge at this point because knowing the qualities of the Three Jewels generates faith in the teachings. This, in turn, helps people to accept the teachings on karma. However, many people nowadays find the qualities of the Three Jewels to be subtle and difficult to understand and the cause-and-effect approach of teachings on karma to be practical. For this reason, we will discuss karma and its effects now, and the qualities of the Three Jewels when we discuss true paths and true cessations.

There are many types of causality—biological, chemical, psychological, and so forth—of which the law of karma and its effects is one. *Karma* literally means action and refers to sentient beings' intentional physical, verbal, and mental actions. Our actions matter: they not only influence others in this life but also result in our own experiences in this and future lives. The results of our actions depend on our intentions, in that actions done with a virtuous intention bring happy results and those motivated by nonvirtuous intentions bring unpleasant results.

Human intelligence makes us particularly qualified to discriminate between constructive and destructive, beneficial and harmful, what to practice and what to abandon. Animals do not have such discriminative wisdom. As human beings, simply surviving or seeking a healthy, happy life is not fully making use of our potential. We must look deeper and ask, "How did this human being—me—come into existence? How can I make my life meaningful? What happens after I die?" This leads us to investigate causality—both the external systems of cause and effect detailed in science and the internal system of cause and effect—the law of karma and its effects. These two systems are harmonious, and I do not find any contradiction between the laws of nature, scientific findings on Darwinian evolution, and the law of karma and its effects.[51]

The Law of Karma and Its Effects

It is helpful to review the three characteristics of all systems of causality mentioned in chapter 7: (1) Effects arise from causes and cannot arise without causes. A tree grows from a seed and cannot grow without a seed. (2) Causes are impermanent because the arising of an effect necessitates the cessation of the cause. The seed ceases and changes into a sprout and then a tree. (3) Effects must be concordant with their causes; only a specific cause can produce a specific result. Pine trees grow from pine seeds, not from daisy seeds. Furthermore, one cause alone cannot produce an effect; cooperative conditions are needed. The seed grows into a tree only when there is sufficient water, fertilizer, and heat.

We can see the specific causes of many external things. However, if we search for the causes of those causes, and the causes of those causes, going back to the origin of this universe, we will not be able to pinpoint precisely each and every cause and condition. Although the details of all the causes of the Big Bang are too vast and complex for us to understand, we would not feel right saying that the universe arose without causes. We know that its development follows particular laws of nature—certain systematic ways of growth and decay—even though we may not be able to discern each unique cause and condition.

Similarly, on the internal level sentient beings' experiences of happiness and suffering arise from preceding causes and conditions. Secular society usually traces these to genetic or environmental factors and does not consider the law of karma and its effects. Bringing in the ethical dimension of our mental intentions gives us a fuller picture of both sentient beings' experiences and the environment they inhabit.

As a natural process that functions whether or not a person believes in it, the law of karma and its effects was not created by the Buddha. Nor does the Buddha judge people according to their actions and punish or reward them. When someone suffers from illness in which his unwholesome karma plays a causal role along with other factors, it does not mean that he deserves to suffer or that he made himself sick. Nor should we ignore those who are injured or oppressed by unjust social structures, thinking that helping them would interfere with their karma. This is a poor excuse for our lack of compassion. Needless to say, those holding such attitudes create destructive karma themselves.

It is important to avoid superimposing concepts from theistic religions on the Buddhadharma. The Buddha is not a creator. Karma and its effects are not a system of reward and punishment. It is simply a natural law: happiness is a result of virtue; suffering is the result of nonvirtue.

Nowadays we may hear the word "karma" used in a flippant way. For example, when asked, "Why did my business fail when it seemed to have everything required for success?" someone may dismiss it by replying, "It's karma," meaning, "I don't know. It was fated and nothing can be done about it." These are inappropriate usages of the word "karma."

The principal meaning of karma is volitional action—a physical, verbal, or mental action done with intention. The Buddha says (AN 6.63):

> It is intention, bhikkhus, that I call kamma. For having willed, one acts by body, speech, or mind.

All karmic paths originate with the mind (*Dhammapada* 1.1–2):

> Mind is the forerunner of all [miserable] states.
> It is mind that leads the way.
> Just as the wheel of the oxcart follows
> the hoof of the ox,
> so suffering will surely follow
> when we speak or act impulsively
> from an impure state of mind.

Mind is the forerunner of all [happy] states.
It is mind that leads the way.
Just as our shadow never leaves us,
so well-being will surely follow
when we speak or act
from a pure state of mind.

Not every instance of the mental factor of intention (*cetanā*) creates karma, but intention (volition) is always necessary for the creation of karma. Mental factors such as anger, attachment, and love also play a role in the creation of karma. While karma may be physical, verbal, or mental, all actions can be traced back to an intention in our mind. Our body and mouth do not move on their own, they act spurred by an intention in our mind. The mind is the root of all our actions and the source of the happiness and suffering that result from them. When we carefully observe our own experience, we will see how true this is. For example, with a particular intention we adopt a certain behavior in the early part of our life. While some of its effects may manifest immediately, some may ripen only decades in the future. Likewise, our motivation in the morning sets the stage for what we experience and how we act later in the day. When we're in a bad mood, we meet more obnoxious people (funny that they all show up that day!) and we act rudely. These examples illustrate causality within this life. When we talk about karma and its effects, it primarily concerns causes created in one life bringing results in future lives. In both cases, we see that our happiness and suffering are not the effect of an external creator, nor are they causeless. They come about because of our intentions and actions. Our experience of happiness and suffering is in our own hands.

An understanding of karma and its effects will have a direct effect on our choices, decisions, and actions in daily life. We will become more conscientious and mindful. Instead of putting energy into overcoming adversaries and competing with rivals, we will choose to cultivate cooperation, tolerance, and forgiveness.

The Buddha has vast knowledge and understanding of the functioning of karma. While we limited sentient beings do not have the capacity to specify the exact interplay of karmic forces and other causes and conditions at work in a specific event, we can gain a general understanding by studying and reflecting on the teachings. This topic is very practical and directly applicable to our lives. The Buddha emphasized the importance of understanding karma (MN 135.20):

> Beings are the owners of their kamma, heirs of their kamma; they originate from their kamma, are bound to their kamma, have their kamma as their refuge. It is kamma that distinguishes beings as inferior and superior.

With compassion, the Buddha shared his understanding of karma with us by recommending we abandon certain actions and engage in others. When we put his advice into practice, we become empowered to stop the causes of suffering and create the causes of happiness.

General Characteristics of Karma

Karma has four general characteristics. Understanding these provides us the basic framework to understand karma and its effects.

1. *Karma is definite* in that happiness comes from previously created constructive actions and suffering comes from previously created destructive ones. It never occurs the other way around. An action is not inherently good or bad, but is designated as virtuous (*kuśala*), nonvirtuous (*akuśala*), or neutral in relation to the result it brings. Abhidharma (ELP 597) says:

> Karma that yields happiness is virtuous karma. Karma that yields the unhappiness of suffering is nonvirtuous karma. The other karma, which creates a neutral feeling, is the other, neutral karma.

Pāli commentaries explain nuances of the terms *virtue* and *nonvirtue*. From a psychological and spiritual viewpoint, nonvirtue (*akuśala*) indicates something that is psychologically or spiritually unhealthy. From an ethical perspective, it is to be censured and shown disapproval. From the standpoint of its cause, it is produced by defilements, and from the viewpoint of its result, it produces suffering. Contrarily, virtue is spiritually and psychologically healthy and beneficial, ethically commendable, not produced under the influence of gross defilements, and leads to fortunate results. The Buddha explains (SN 22.2):

> If, friends, one who enters and dwells amid unwholesome states could dwell happily in this very life, without vexation, despair, and fever, and if, with the breakup of the body, after death, he could expect a good destination, then the Blessed One would not praise the abandoning of unwholesome states. But because one who enters and dwells amid unwholesome states dwells in suffering in this very life, with vexation, despair, and fever, and because he can expect a bad destination with the breakup of the body, after death, the Blessed One praises the abandoning of unwholesome states.
>
> If, friends, one who enters and dwells amid wholesome states would dwell in suffering in this very life, with vexation, despair, and fever, and if, with the breakup of the body, after death, he could expect a bad destination, then the Blessed one would not praise the acquisition of wholesome states. But because one who enters and dwells amid wholesome states dwells happily in this very life, without vexation, despair, and fever, and because he can expect a good destination with the breakup of the body, after death, the Blessed One praises the acquisition of wholesome states.

The *Questions of the Bodhisattva Suratā Sūtra* (*Suratāpariprcchā Sūtra*) says:

> As in planting, happiness and misery
> are effects from the deeds performed.
> How can a bitter seed
> yield a sweet fruit?
>
> Seeing this universal truth,
> the wise should think:
> evildoing brings painful effects,
> while good deeds always lead
> to peace and happiness.[52]

It may seem that some people experience satisfaction after engaging in destructive actions such as taking revenge on another person. The immediate pleasure they experience is due to their distorted way of thinking while the result of their present action will be suffering in the future. Similarly, someone may go through physical difficulties doing prostrations but the long-term result of this action will be happiness.

2. *Karma is expandable* in that a small action can bring a large effect in the same way that a small seed can produce a large tree. Understanding this protects us from being complacent, thinking, "This is only a tiny action. I don't need to bother with it." Instead, we will take care to avoid small destructive actions and engage in small constructive ones. The *Groups of Utterances* (*Udānavarga*) counsels (LC 1:211):

> Like a poison that has been ingested,
> the commission of even a small negativity
> creates in your lives hereafter
> great fear and a terrible downfall.

> As when grain ripens into a bounty,
> even the creation of small merit
> leads in lives hereafter to great happiness
> and will be immensely meaningful as well.

3. *We will not experience the effect of an action we have not done.* If we have not created the cause to experience a contagious disease, we will not contract it, even though others around us may. If we do not create the causes to attain awakening, we will not, even though we make many prayers to the Buddha to gain realizations. Udbhaṭṭasiddhasvāmin's *Praise of the Exalted One* (*Viśeṣastava*) says (LC 1:214):

> The brahmins say that virtue and negativity
> may transfer to others, like giving and receiving a gift.
> You [Buddha] taught that what one has done does not perish
> and that one does not meet with the effects of what one
>   has not done.

4. *Karmic seeds do not get lost or magically vanish.* The effect of an action will be experienced unless it is counteracted. *Bases of Discipline (Vinaya-vastu)* says (LC 1:214):

> Even in one hundred eons
> karma does not perish.
> When the circumstances and the time arrive
> beings surely feel its effects.

Unless a karmic seed is counteracted, it will one day bring its result. Seeds from destructive actions are inhibited from ripening by the four opponent powers explained below. Seeds from constructive actions are thwarted by anger and wrong views.

Although karmic seeds do not get lost, events are not predetermined. The ripening of karma is an interdependent occurrence, with many contributing factors and variables. We do not know what the future will be until it happens.

Specific Characteristics of Karma

The main focus of initial-level practitioners is to bring about a series of precious human lives in the future so that our Dharma practice can continue without interruption. This entails understanding the specific characteristics of karma: harmful karmic paths that cause unfortunate rebirths or otherwise hinder our ability to practice, and constructive karmic paths that bring fortunate rebirths and circumstances conducive for Dharma practice. In this light, the Buddha outlined ten nonvirtues to abandon and ten virtues to practice. These ten subsume the significant karmic paths to pay attention to, although they do not encompass all physical, verbal, and mental actions. The Buddha set these out (AN 10.178):

> What is the bad? The destruction of life, taking what is not given, unwise sexual conduct, false speech, divisive speech, harsh speech, idle talk, covetousness, maliciousness, and wrong views... And what is the good? Abstinence from the destruction

of life, from taking what is not given, from unwise sexual conduct, from false speech, from divisive speech, from harsh speech, from idle talk, noncovetousness, goodwill, and right views.

The Buddha continues, describing these two sets of karmic paths respectively as ignoble and noble, harmful and beneficial, non-Dharma and Dharma, polluted and unpolluted, blameworthy and blameless, tormenting and untormenting, leading to suffering and to happiness, building up the round of rebirth and diminishing it, to be abandoned and to be cultivated.

Of the ten nonvirtues, three are done physically: killing, stealing, and unwise and unkind sexual behavior. The Buddha describes them (AN 10.211):

> There is a person who destroys life; he is cruel and his hands are blood-stained. He is bent on slaying and murdering, having no compassion for any living being.
>
> He takes what is not given to him, appropriates with thievish intent the property of others, be it in the village or the forest.
>
> He conducts himself wrongly in matters of sex: he has intercourse with those under the protection of father, mother, brother, sister, relatives, or clan, or of their religious community, or with those engaged to a fiancé, protected by law, and even with those betrothed with a garland.

Four nonvirtues are done verbally: lying, divisive speech, harsh speech, and idle talk. The Buddha expounds on these (AN 10.211):

> There is one who tells lies. When he is in the council of his community or in another assembly, or among his relatives, his guild, in the royal court, or when he has been summoned as a witness and is asked to tell what he knows, then, though he does not know, he says, "I know"; though he does know, he says, "I do not know"; though he has not seen, he says, "I have seen"; and though he has seen, he says, "I have not seen." In that way he utters deliberate lies, be it for his own sake, for the sake of others, or for some material advantage.

He utters divisive words: what he hears he reports elsewhere to foment conflict there; and what he hears elsewhere he reports here to foment conflict here. Thus he creates discord among those united, and he incites still more those who are in discord. He is fond of dissension, he delights and rejoices in it, and he utters words that cause dissension.

He speaks harshly, using speech that is coarse, rough, bitter, and abusive, that makes others angry and causes distraction of mind.

He indulges in idle chatter: he speaks what is untimely, unreasonable, and unbeneficial, having no connection with Dhamma or Vinaya. His talk is not worth treasuring, it is inopportune, inadvisable, unrestrained, and harmful.

When these four are done by writing, signaling, typing, or nodding the head, they are considered nonvirtues of speech because they involve communication.

Three nonvirtues are done mentally: covetousness, malice, and wrong views. The Buddha describes these (AN 10.211):

> There is a person who is covetous; he covets the wealth and property of others, thinking, "Oh, that what he owns might belong to me!"
>
> There is also one who has malice in his heart. He has depraved thoughts such as, "Let these beings be slain! Let them be killed and destroyed! May they perish and cease to exist!"
>
> He has wrong views and perverted ideas, such as, "There is no ethical value in a gift, offering, or sacrifice; there is no result or recompense from constructive or destructive deeds; there is neither this world nor another world (i.e., no rebirth); there are no duties toward mother and father; there are no spontaneously reborn beings; and there are no ascetics and brahmins in this world, living and conducting themselves rightly, who can explain this world and the world beyond, having realized them by their own direct knowledge.

While covetousness, malice, and wrong views are associated with attachment, animosity, and confusion, respectively, they are more specific and intense forms of those afflictions. The mental factor of attachment becomes the karmic path of covetousness when it has the wish to take possession of property belonging to others. Covetousness is not a random thought of attachment, but the greedy desire to possess something that belongs to someone else. This desire has been cultivated and increased by repeatedly thinking how nice it would be to have that object and planning how to obtain it. This thought now has the power to generate a rebirth. It may also instigate someone to steal or lie to obtain the object coveted.

The mental factor of anger becomes the karmic path of malice when it wishes to inflict harm on another living being or wishes that person to suffer by another means. The milder anger that simply wants to avoid someone we just quarreled with is not the karmic path of malice.

The mental factor of wrong views becomes the karmic path of wrong views when it strongly holds an incorrect view, such as believing the Three Jewels, the four truths, and the law of karma and its effects do not exist. Here someone defiantly thinks, "It doesn't matter if I exploit the other person. I won't suffer any consequences," "Killing heretics is virtuous," or "Neither rebirth nor liberation exists." Such ignorant views lead to unfortunate rebirths in future lives.

The first six nonvirtues directly harm others. Although idle talk does not directly harm others, it provokes people to act in ways that do. The harmful effects of the ten nonvirtues are evident, even to animals. If someone takes away an animal's food—an act that resembles stealing—the animal is miserable. If someone shouts at an animal, it is unhappy. Once someone begins to covet the possessions of others, even his or her close friends are wary and keep a distance. Someone who uses their sexuality unwisely or unkindly loses the trust of others. This is the experience of sentient beings in general; it doesn't matter if they are religious practitioners or not. To stop engaging in the nonvirtuous actions that no one likes, we have to counteract the three poisons that motivate them. Since doing that takes time, we begin by restraining our physical and verbal actions that directly harm others.

Four branches must be present for a complete destructive karmic path to be committed: (1) the *basis* is the object or sentient being acted on, (2) the *attitude* has three parts: correct discernment of the object, the presence of an affliction, and the motivation to do the action, (3) the *performance* of the action, and (4) the *completion* of the action, which entails our accomplishing our purpose and being satisfied with the outcome.

Killing

1. Basis: A sentient being other than yourself who is alive. A sentient being is any being who has a mind—excluding a fully awakened buddha—who feels happiness and pain.

2. Attitude: (a) Discerning a living being as a living being and correctly identifying the living being to be killed. (b) Any of the three poisons of attachment, animosity, and confusion, such as attachment to eating that being's flesh, hatred toward an enemy, or confusion, thinking that animal sacrifice is virtuous. (c) The desire to kill.

3. Action: Taking the life of a living being or causing or asking someone else to kill by weapons, poisons, or other forms of violence. This includes most cases of abortion, euthanasia, and assisted suicide.

4. Completion: That being dies before we do. Suicide is not a complete action.

Stealing: Taking what hasn't been freely given

1. Basis: Object belonging to another person.

2. Attitude: (a) Correctly identifying the object to be stolen. (b) Any of the three poisons, such as attachment to the object; animosity wishing to destroy the wealth of an enemy; ignorantly thinking that overcharging a customer, taking things from our employer, or cheating the government is fine. (c) The desire to take that object although it has not been freely given.

3. Action: Taking or asking someone else to take the object through force, stealth, or deception; includes not paying taxes, fees, tolls, and fares, and not returning objects we borrowed.

4. Completion: Moving the object and/or thinking that it is now ours.

Unwise and unkind sexual behavior

1. Basis: The partner of another person, someone who does not consent, is celibate, is a close relative, or a child. If you are in a relationship,

going outside that relationship. Having intercourse in a temple or monastery or near your teacher or the saṅgha.

2. Attitude: (a) Correctly identifying the person with whom you wish to have intercourse. (b) Any of the three poisons: with attachment, using others for your own sexual pleasure without caring for their feelings; angrily raping the partners or children of an enemy; ignorantly thinking sex is a high spiritual practice, that it's chic to have extramarital affairs, or that having protected sex isn't necessary when there is the possibility of sexually transmitted diseases.

3. Action: Meeting of the two organs.

4. Completion: Pleasure is experienced; climax is not necessary.

Lying

1. Basis: What is seen, heard, distinguished, and cognized, and what is not seen, heard, distinguished, and cognized. The person lied to is a human being other than oneself who is capable of understanding. Heaviest is lying to our spiritual teachers and parents.

2. Attitude: (a) Misrepresenting what we have seen, heard, distinguished, or cognized, or their opposites. (b) Any of the three poisons: with attachment, gaining something from that person or protecting our own reputation, angrily wanting to deceive, ignorantly thinking there is nothing wrong with lying. (c) The desire to make the other person believe what is false.

3. Action: Speaking, writing, or gesturing what we know to be untrue for personal gain, knowingly misleading others; heaviest is lying about our spiritual attainments. All four verbal actions are paths of actions whether we do them ourselves or tell others to do them.

4. Completion: The other person understands what we have said. If the other person doesn't understand, it is idle talk.

Divisive speech

1. Basis: People who are friendly or who are disharmonious.

2. Attitude: (a) Correctly identifying the people to be separated. (b) Any of the three poisons: with attachment, wanting a couple to split so you can be with one member or criticizing a competitor so you will get

the promotion or close a deal; with animosity or jealousy, wanting to stir up trouble; ignorantly causing disunity among those of another religion in order to convert them. (c) The desire to separate or cause friction between others.

3. Action: Causing disunity among friends or preventing those who are not harmonious from reconciling—it doesn't matter whether what we say is true or not. Worst is causing disunity in the saṅgha.

4. Completion: The other person understands what you have said; if they don't it is idle talk.

Harsh words

1. Basis: A sentient being who will be hurt by your words. Heaviest is abusing your spiritual teacher. Swearing at a machine is not included.

2. Attitude: (a) Correctly identifying the person you want to hurt. (b) Any of the three poisons: with attachment, criticizing others in order to be accepted by a group of people; angrily denigrating the enemy so that others will side with us or to rouse troops to fight; ignorantly thinking we are clever or witty. (c) The desire to speak harshly and make someone feel bad.

3. Action: Criticizing, insulting, ridiculing, maliciously teasing, verbally abusing, angrily blaming, humiliating someone privately or in front of others.

4. Completion: The other person understands what was said.

Idle talk

1. Basis: A topic without meaning or importance.

2. Attitude: (a) Knowing the topic we wish to speak about. (b) Any of the three poisons: with attachment, flattering and hinting to get something; angrily wanting to disturb someone; ignorantly wanting to pass the time. (c) The desire to speak this way.

3. Action: Gossiping, telling stories, joking without a good purpose, praying for terrible things to happen, wailing, teaching the Dharma to someone lacking interest or respect, reciting liturgies of other religions for no good reason, repeating jingles and slogans, grumbling, bickering over meaningless things, talking about entertainment, sports, politics, crime, and so forth without a good reason.

4. Completion: Saying the words out loud. It is not necessary that any-one hears or understands.

Covetousness

1. Basis: Possessions or wealth of another person. Worst is desiring offer-ings made to holy beings and the saṅgha.
2. Attitude: (a) Correctly identifying the object, (b) any of the three poi-sons, (c) the desire to make that object your own.
3. Action: Thinking "I will obtain this," and planning how to obtain it.
4. Completion: The determination to obtain the object. To be complete, five factors are necessary: being very attached to your possessions, wanting to accumulate more, longing to examine and experience the possessions of others, thinking that what another person has should be yours, and lacking integrity and not wanting to be free from the faults of covetousness.

Malice

1. Basis: A sentient being. Worst is malice toward holy beings and the saṅgha.
2. Attitude: (a) Correctly identifying the person you want to hurt, (b) any of the three poisons, (c) the wish that someone else suffer and experience problems.
3. Action: Thinking "I will make them suffer."
4. Completion: Deciding to inflict harm and planning how to do it. To be complete, five factors are required: animosity supported by the strong projection of negative qualities on the cause of the harm, impatience with the one harming you, resentment based on distorted attention on the cause of your anger, thinking "How wonderful if this person were harmed or suffered," and lacking integrity and not want-ing to be free from the faults of malice.

Wrong views

1. Basis: Something pertaining to the Dharma that is true and exists.
2. Attitude: (a) Perceiving something that exists to be nonexistent, (b) any

of the three poisons, (c) the desire to deny the existence of the Three Jewels, four truths, karma and its effects, and so forth.

3. Action: Adopting a wrong view. This has four types: (a) disparaging causes: thinking virtuous and nonvirtuous behavior don't exist, (b) disparaging effects: the results of this behavior don't exist, (c) disparaging activities concerning karmic seeds, rebirth, and taking spontaneous birth, and (d) disparaging existent phenomena: thinking buddhas, bodhisattvas, arhats, and so forth do not exist.

4. Completion: Deciding your wrong view is definitely correct. It must have five factors: confusion that doesn't understand phenomena, an argumentative attitude delighting in disparagement, a stubborn attitude due to reflecting on incorrect teachings, denying that the Three Jewels or karma and its effects exist, and lacking integrity and not wanting to be free from the faults of wrong views.

There are many other wrong views, but these are the worst because they undermine our roots of virtue and encourage us to do whatever we like without considering the destructive effects.

Although each of the ten can be initiated with any of the three poisons, killing, harsh words, and malice are completed exclusively with animosity. Stealing, unwise and unkind sexual behavior, and coveting are completed with attachment. Wrong views are completed with confusion. Lying, divisive words, and idle talk may be completed with any of the three afflictions.

According to the *Treasury of Knowledge*, some of the ten nonvirtues are karma (actions), some are karmic paths, some are afflictions, and some are more than one of these.[53] The mental factor of intention is *karma*. The intention to take life is the karma of killing and the intention to vent our anger through harsh speech is the karma of harsh speech. The three mental nonvirtues—covetousness, malice, and wrong views—are not karma; they are strong forms of the *afflictions* of attachment, animosity, and confusion, respectively. Karma (mental factor of intention) and afflictions are mutually exclusive. Afflictions are the cause of karma; they are forerunners that give rise to intentions. Strong attachment sparks the intention for unwise or unkind sexual behavior. Strong animosity provokes the intention to create disharmony between people through speaking divisively. Strong ignorant wrong views may instigate intentions to engage in any of the ten nonvirtues.

When the ten nonvirtues are done with all branches intact, they become *karmic paths* (*karmapatha*), indicating that they are conduits leading to future rebirths. They are also called karmic paths because they are either the cause of an intention or the path that intention travels to perform an action. The three mental nonvirtues are karmic paths because they cause an intention and because they lead to unfortunate rebirths. The seven nonvirtues of body and speech are karmic paths because they are the path that intention travels to carry out the intention and they are also the paths to unfortunate rebirths. These seven are also karma. The First Dalai Lama instructs (ELP 617):

> If one asks: Why are these ten called karmic paths? From the three of mind, the intention embarks on its path, so they are paths. The seven of body and speech are also karma, and because they are the paths on which the intention embarks, they are called karmic paths.

	KARMA	KARMIC PATH	AFFLICTION
Mental factor of intention	yes	no	no
Seven physical and verbal nonvirtues	yes	yes	no
Three mental nonvirtues	no	yes	yes

We commonly speak of the ten destructive actions and the ten constructive actions. However, technically, although all ten are karmic paths, not all of them are karma or action. The *Treasury of Knowledge* says, "Three are [only] paths, seven are [not only paths, but are] also actions." It also says, "Covetousness and so forth are not actions."

Encouraging or asking others to act destructively also creates destructive karma. If other factors are equal, the karma is heavier when we do the action ourselves because it requires more energy to overcome whatever hesitancy we may have had to do the action. Nevertheless, we create a complete karma when we ask someone to do the action and he or she does it. Leaders of companies, organizations, and governments need to be aware of this when they give instructions and set policies. Likewise, when we ask a family member or friend to lie on our behalf and that person does so, both of us create the destructive karma of lying. The same holds true for virtuous actions. Encouraging others to act constructively creates constructive karma for ourselves as well as for them. However, the virtue is heavier if we make an offering than if we ask someone else to do it for us.

Rejoicing at the harmful actions of others is tantamount to doing them ourselves. We can accumulate a great deal of destructive karma rejoicing in others' harmful deeds when we listen to the news, and great stores of merit are generated by rejoicing in the virtues of the buddhas, bodhisattvas, arhats, āryas, and all ordinary beings.

A person can accumulate the karma from eight of the ten nonvirtues simultaneously: at the same time he is coveting another's partner and having sex with her, the people whom he asked to kill, steal, lie, speak divisively, speak harshly, and talk idly are doing what he asked.

Because the motivation plays such an important role in the ethical dimension of an action, it is not always possible to distinguish a constructive or destructive action on the basis of the action alone. We may chat with colleagues at work for the purpose of establishing pleasant relationships with them. This is different from chatting with them in order to make ourselves look good, denigrate others, or waste time.

Instead of following every urge that enters our mind, it behooves us to be aware of what motivates us to act. We may be so charmed with a person or an object that we are oblivious to our intentions as we interact with them. Meanwhile attachment is rising in our mind and before we know it, we are coveting the object or the person's company. Similarly, while a colleague is giving us feedback about our work, we become defensive. Unaware that we've become angry, we do not notice our intention to speak harshly and soon we are astonished to find ourselves in a nasty argument with that person. Lacking mindfulness and introspective awareness of our intentions and afflictions, we find ourselves in difficult situations now and create destructive karma that will cause suffering in future lives. However, by repeatedly renewing our mindfulness of constructive actions and activating the introspective awareness that monitors what we are thinking, saying, and doing, we will be able to direct our body, speech, and mind with wisdom and kindness.

Taking and keeping precepts helps us to abandon nonvirtue by making us more mindful of how we would like to behave and how we are actually behaving. Holding precepts increases our conscientiousness and respect for ethical conduct. It also stops confusion in challenging situations because we reflect that previously, with a clear mind, we saw the disadvantages of this action and took a precept to abandon it.

Some actions have both constructive and destructive elements and bring mixed effects. For example, someone gives a donation to build a hospital for the poor with the thought that his name will appear on a plaque that lists donors. Although his motivation is nonvirtuous, the action benefits others. Alternatively, the thought could be virtuous but the action nonvirtuous: a teacher is motivated by affection and care for a student, but speaks harshly in order to motivate him to overcome his laziness. Some actions, such as sweeping the floor, that are done with an intention that is neither constructive nor destructive, bring neutral results.

The question also arises whether not helping someone can create negative karma. Here we must take into consideration the person's motivation as well as the situation. For example, two people are quarreling. One onlooker thinks, "My intervention could aggravate the situation," while another thinks, "Getting involved is very inconvenient for me." Neither of these people intervenes, but they create different karma.

Sometimes other people may become angry at us while, from our side, we had no intention of harming them. This even happened to the Buddha: Some villagers, upon seeing the Buddha and saṅgha enter their village to gather alms, were furious because they mistakenly thought the Buddha was simply living off their hard work. Although the Buddha was the object of their hostility, his action was not destructive. He had no intention to harm those people or to make them angry.

On the other hand, if someone deliberately antagonizes another person with the thought to upset him or willfully tries to make someone overly dependent and attached to him, his actions are destructive because a harmful intention was present.

There is much to ponder regarding the ten nonvirtues, and doing a review of our lives will enable us to identify habitual destructive actions that we need to purify and to prevent doing in the future.

REFLECTION

1. At this very moment you are creating the causes for what you will become and the events you will experience. What kind of future do you want to create for yourself?

2. Which actions do you need to engage in to bring about that future?

3. Which actions must you abandon?

4. Make a determination to set healthy and meaningful goals and to act in an ethical and kind manner in order to attain them.

Constructive Actions

The Buddha emphasized the disadvantages of poor ethical conduct and the benefits of good ethical conduct (DN 16.1.23–24):

> Householders, there are these five perils to someone of poor ethical conduct, of failure in ethical conduct. What are they? First, he suffers great loss of property through neglecting his affairs. Second, he gets a bad reputation for immorality and misconduct. Third, whatever assembly he approaches . . . he does so diffidently and shyly. Fourth, he dies confused. Fifth, after death, at the breaking up of the body, he arises in an unfortunate state, a bad fate, in suffering and hell. These are the five perils to someone of poor ethical conduct.
>
> Householders, there are these five advantages to someone of good ethical conduct and of success in ethical conduct. What are they? First, through careful attention to his affairs he gains much wealth. Second, he has a good reputation for morality and

good conduct. Third, whatever assembly he approaches . . . he does so with confidence and assurance. Fourth, he dies unconfused. Fifth, after death, at the breaking up of the body, he arises in a good place, a heavenly world. These are the five advantages to someone of good ethical conduct and of success in ethical conduct.

We restrain ourselves from acting harmfully to benefit ourselves and others, not by thinking that the Buddha commanded us to do so. For example, our doctor may advise us to have a low-fat diet. Even though we like food with a lot of fat, we follow his advice not out of duty but because we know it is for our long-term benefit. Abandoning destructive actions because we know their harm is like a clever animal who sees some food but does not eat it because he senses it may be a trap that will bring him suffering.

When a mosquito lands on your arm, instead of swatting it, shoo it away. This action of refraining from killing is constructive karma and is the cause for attaining a precious human life. I must admit, however, that sometimes mosquitoes really irritate me, and I'm tempted to slap them! Nevertheless, I restrain myself and later am happy that I did. Then I ask my attendant to please put better screens on the windows!

The ten paths of constructive actions are consciously restraining ourselves from engaging in the ten destructive ones. When faced with a situation in which we could lie, we remember its disadvantages and decide not to do it. Abstaining from a nonvirtuous action itself is virtuous karma. The Pāli tradition delineates three types of abstention that apply to the seven physical and verbal nonvirtues:

1. *Natural abstention* is restraining ourselves from nonvirtuous actions because we have learned as children to avoid them. Our parents taught us not to lie, and knowing that lying is not good, we developed the habit of speaking truthfully. While virtuous, this restraint is not necessarily stable. If we face strong peer pressure or lose mindfulness, we may act destructively.

2. *Abstention by adopting precepts* occurs by consciously and deliberately taking precepts to abstain from harmful actions. These precepts include the five lay precepts, monastic precepts, and the eight one-day precepts. Alternatively, we may make a strong determination to

restrain from the seven physical and verbal nonvirtues. Taking precepts reinforces natural abstention because when we are tempted to act harmfully, remembering the precepts and our preceptor strengthens our resolve to act virtuously.

3. *Abstention through eradication* is accomplished by attaining the ārya path—stream-enterer and above—and eradicating particular defilements. As we eliminate levels of defilement from our mind, they no longer cause us to transgress precepts.

The three mental paths of virtue are three virtuous mental factors when they are strongly developed. Noncovetousness is the mental factor of strong nonattachment. It is not just the absence of attachment but a mind that actively does not seek more and better. It temporarily frees the mind from greed and leads to generosity and the relinquishment of sensual desire. Nonmalice is the mental factor of strong nonhatred. This is not just the absence of hatred, but loving-kindness. Nonconfusion prevents and counteracts confusion. It is related to right view and wisdom and understands that our actions have an ethical dimension and bring results that we ourselves will experience.

The Buddha also describes the ten virtues as doing constructive actions (AN 10.211). Someone who abstains from killing "dwells compassionately toward all living beings." Abandoning divisive speech means "he unites those who are divided and encourages those who are in harmony." Someone who relinquishes harsh speech speaks words that are "gentle, pleasant to hear, endearing, heartwarming, courteous, agreeable to many folk, pleasing to many folk." Abandoning idle chatter, a person "speaks at the right time, in accordance with facts, and of matters that are beneficial . . . His talk is opportune, helpful, moderate, and meaningful." Someone who abandons maliciousness "has pure thoughts and intentions such as, 'May these beings be free from enmity, free from anxiety! May they be untroubled and live happily!'" In short, doing the opposite of the ten paths of destructive actions also constitutes practicing the ten paths of constructive actions. We mindfully save life, protect others' property, and promote fidelity in relationships. We speak truthfully, harmoniously, kindly, and at appropriate times. Our thoughts are generous, friendly, and wise.

The Pāli tradition further lists ten bases of meritorious deeds (*dasapuñña-kiriyavatthu*) to practice (CMA 209): generosity, ethical conduct, meditation, reverence, service, dedicating merit, rejoicing in others' virtue, listening to Dharma teachings, teaching the Dharma, and straightening out our views (developing correct views).

Contemplating the various harmful and wholesome actions enables us to develop wisdom that knows what to abandon and what to practice. This wisdom enables us to make wise decisions in our lives and eliminates the confusion of not knowing what is best to do. In doing so, it prevents problems and remorse.

Soon after the Buddha's son Rāhula became a monk, the Buddha explained to him that there are three phases to any action—the time before doing the action, the time of doing it, and the time after completing it—and counseled Rāhula to act only after repeated reflection, rather than impulsively (MN 61). Before beginning the action, the Buddha advised asking ourselves two questions that would enable us to decide wisely whether to do this action or not: (1) Will this action that I wish to do bring harm to myself, to others, or to both? What will be the most likely immediate result and long-term results of this action? Even if the action seems insignificant and won't adversely affect someone else, will it corrupt my mind in a way that will later lead my ethical conduct to degenerate? (2) Is this a nonvirtuous action that will bring painful results? Here the quality of our motivation is a crucial factor, so we should examine as honestly as we can what our actual intention is.

While doing the action, we should continue to hold these questions in our mind. If we see that the action will bring harm to ourselves or others or if we determine that it is nonvirtuous, we should stop immediately. It may seem strange to stop what we are saying in midsentence, but it is better than finishing the comment and having to deal with the painful consequences afterward.

After we have completed an action, we should review it with the two questions as our guide. If we realize in hindsight that it was nonvirtuous, we should reveal and confess it in our evening purification practice or tell a wise Dharma friend or our Dharma teacher. Then we should make a strong determination not to do that action again and undertake restraint. But if we realize that the action was constructive, we should rejoice, dwell happily, and continue training in that way.

The Weight of Karma

Not all constructive and destructive actions are equal in terms of the weight of the latencies they leave on our mindstream or the strength of the experiences they bring. Tsongkhapa cites five criteria that make destructive actions heavy:

1. *The strength of our attitude*—for example, lying with a strong wish to cause another harm—is heavier than acting with a weak intention.

2. *The method of doing the action* includes doing the action repeatedly, doing it ourselves, encouraging others to do it, delighting in it, planning it for a long time, and relishing having done it. An example is killing someone by first humiliating and torturing him.

3. *The lack of an antidote* makes a destructive action heavier. Examples include when the person does little if any constructive actions at other times, repeatedly engages in harmful actions, is not interested in avoiding harmful actions or purifying them once they have been committed, and has little sense of their own moral integrity or consideration for others. However, the destructive action of someone who tries to live ethically, is respectful to those worthy of respect, has knowledge of the Dharma, or has attained realization will be lighter because that person also has accumulated merit or will purify the nonvirtue.

4. *Holding wrong views* makes the action heavier than doing it with ordinary ignorance or confusion. Euthanizing an animal with the thought to put it out of its misery is not as heavy as doing it with the strong view that rebirth and karma and its effects do not exist. In the latter case, the person is philosophically convinced that a harmful action is without fault.

5. *The object of the action* is important. Criticizing our parents, spiritual teachers, those with Dharma realizations, and the poor or needy is much heavier than criticizing others. Our parents are strong objects for the creation of karma owing to their kindness in giving us life. Spiritual teachers are powerful objects because they lead us on the path, and the poor and sick are strong objects because of their need.

However, owing to the power of holy objects, any action done in relation to high bodhisattvas or images of buddhas and bodhisattvas has one aspect that can be the condition for attaining liberation. Killing a human being, a large animal, a fetus, relatives, or holy beings is heavier than killing others.

Generally speaking, of the seven physical and verbal nonvirtues, killing is the heaviest, with each successive nonvirtue being lighter than the previous one. This order is dependent on the amount of suffering the other sentient being experiences. Everyone cherishes his or her life more than anything else and suffers most when it is taken from them, while the suffering we experience from idle talk is minor. Of the three mental nonvirtues, wrong views are heaviest, then malice, and finally covetousness.

Although idle talk is the lightest of the three verbal nonvirtues, it is dangerous because it gives rise to so many other afflictions. When someone relates a story of either romance or war, both the storyteller and the listener generate attachment or anger, which in turn could provoke them to act with harm verbally and physically. For this reason, spiritual masters recommend that when with others, we should guard our speech, and when alone, we should guard our mind.

Other factors may make both constructive and destructive actions more powerful.

- *Frequency*—such as losing our temper often—creates heavy destructive karma, while repeatedly being patient with others creates strong virtue.
- *Regretting* harmful actions leads us to do purification, which lessens the power of the karmic seeds. However, regretting constructive actions decreases the power of the seeds of those actions.
- *Rejoicing* at both our harmful and helpful actions makes them more powerful.
- *A strong motivation* increases the strength of our actions. For this reason, acting when our mind is overwhelmed by jealousy, anger, or resentment is not wise. However, cultivating a strong motivation of compassion and bodhicitta each morning will positively affect all the virtuous actions we do that day.
- Constructive actions done by *those holding precepts* are more powerful

than those done by people without the precepts. The more precepts we hold, the stronger the results of our virtuous actions. A fully ordained monastic's generosity creates more powerful constructive karma than that of someone without precepts. The constructive actions of those holding bodhisattva's precepts are stronger, while virtuous actions done by those with all three ethical codes—prātimokṣa, bodhisattva, and tantra—are even greater.

- *Acting out of ignorance* is lighter than doing the action with awareness of the karmic consequences of our actions. Young children swatting insects without understanding that killing is harmful is not as heavy as the same action done by someone who knows that killing is nonvirtuous and either doesn't care or is overwhelmed by mental afflictions.
- *Mental illness* that obscures the mind lessens the strength of destructive actions. The Vinaya takes this into consideration when determining whether someone commits a full transgression of a root downfall such as killing a human being. A monastic who intentionally engages in and completes a root downfall is no longer a monastic and is expelled from the saṅgha. However, if a monastic suffering from severe mental illness does such an action, it is not considered a full transgression.
- The *general mental constitution* of a person influences the weight of an action as well as its results. If we put a lump of salt in a small cup of water, the water will be very salty and undrinkable, whereas if we put it in the river Ganges, it won't influence the water much. Similarly, when a person who is "undeveloped in body, virtuous behavior, mind, and wisdom . . . creates a trifling bad kamma, it leads him to hell," whereas when a person who "is developed in body, virtuous behavior, mind, and wisdom . . . creates exactly the same trifling bad kamma, it is to be experienced in this very life, without even a slight [residue] being seen, much less an abundant [residue]" (AN 3.100). Because of the great virtue in the latter person's mindstream, the destructive action does not grossly affect his character. He will experience an unpleasant result of the action in this life and there will be no further suffering residue to be experienced in future lives. The opposite occurs with a person of little virtue.

The question of the weight of naturally negative actions—such as killing and stealing—created by those with precepts can be looked at from different perspectives. Tsongkhapa said (LC 1:233):

> Therefore, the Buddha said that nonvirtues are light for the knowledgeable who regret their former nonvirtuous actions, restrain themselves from future nonvirtuous actions, do not conceal their negativities, and do virtuous actions as remedies for those nonvirtuous actions. However, nonvirtues are weighty for those who make a pretense of being knowledgeable and do not do these actions but belittle them and engage consciously in nonvirtuous actions.

Those living in precepts of any kind are continuously creating constructive karma as long as they are not transgressing a precept. Two people may be sitting in a room talking, one holding the precept to abandon killing, the other not. Neither of them is killing. The person with the precept is continuously creating the constructive karma of not killing because she is acting in accord with her virtuous intention to abandon killing, while the other person is not creating such karma. This is one advantage of living in precepts. However, if a person with precepts consciously engages in nonvirtuous actions and does not purify or have regret, the karma is heavier.

Understanding the factors that make an action more potent enables us to maximize the power of our virtue and inhibit the strength of our nonvirtue. Mindfulness of these factors induces deeper introspective awareness that monitors our thoughts, words, and deeds. Together this mindfulness and introspective awareness make our lives more vibrant and meaningful.

Without confidence in the law of karmic causality, it is extremely difficult to gain higher realizations on the path. Nāgārjuna told us (RV 5):

> Due to having faith [in karma and its effects], one relies on
>   the practices;
> due to having wisdom, one truly understands.
> Of these two, wisdom is foremost,
>   but faith must come first.

While the wisdom realizing emptiness is foremost in that it overcomes the ignorance that is the root of saṃsāra, we need to create the cause for a series of fortunate births in saṃsāra during which we can practice the path. Without belief in karma and its effects, we do not evaluate our actions and motivations and carelessly engage in many destructive actions that lead to unfortunate rebirths. In such births, we will be unable to meet the Dharma, let alone cultivate liberating wisdom. It will also be difficult to create virtue that will bring fortunate rebirths in the future. However, having even a general understanding and confidence in the functioning of karma and its effects gives us the ability to control our future by practicing virtue and abandoning nonvirtue.

Discerning Virtuous from Nonvirtuous Actions

Discerning virtue from nonvirtue can initially be difficult. Applying the above four criteria of the ten paths of nonvirtue to the ten paths of virtue is very helpful. Nāgārjuna's guideline regarding our motivation is also pertinent (RA 20):

> Attachment, animosity, confusion,
> and the karma that arises from them are nonvirtuous.
> Nonattachment, nonanger, nonconfusion,
> and the karmas that arise from them are virtuous.

Attachment has a specific meaning in Buddhist texts, where it is defined as a mental factor that, when referring to a polluted object, exaggerates its attractiveness and then wishes for and clings to it. "Polluted" means associated with ignorance and associated with cyclic existence. This includes our five psychophysical aggregates and the large majority of things around us. Attachment is afflictive, biased, and unrealistic, and actions done under the influence of sensual attachment are destructive. They lead to unhappiness in future lives and prevent our gaining spiritual realizations.

Sometimes it is difficult for us to distinguish attachment from genuine love and appreciation. One clue that attachment is present is when we initially think something is very wonderful and later find it boring or even disgusting. This indicates that initially we were exaggerating the attractiveness of the person, object, place, idea, and so forth. For example, when we see a new car in the showroom, it appears wonderful and we proudly show it off to our friends after we buy it. But after some time the car becomes uninteresting and we seek something new and exciting. This indicates we had an unrealistic view of the car and had exaggerated its ability to provide us continuous pleasure.

Anger is easier to recognize when it surges in our mind, but sometimes we are resistant to seeing that it is afflictive and motivates destructive karma. Instead we justify our anger as necessary to protect our own interests.

Confusion—ignorance about what is virtue and what is not—is also difficult to recognize. We easily believe our own or others' incorrect ideas about what to practice and what to abandon, and in the process engage in many damaging actions, thinking that they are virtuous. Only later do we see our lack of clarity involving ethical conduct.

Nonattachment, nonanger, and nonconfusion are not the lack of the three poisons, but mental factors that are their opposites. Nonattachment is a balanced, open attitude; nonanger is love; nonconfusion is wisdom. The three "nons" are virtuous mental factors and the actions motivated by them are also virtuous.

Observing our mind closely with mindfulness and introspective awareness, both in meditation and in daily life, helps us to recognize these mental states in our own experience. This takes time, but is very worthwhile because discerning virtue from nonvirtue in our own mind is essential to abandoning destructive karma and creating constructive karma.

Karma and Current Ethical Issues

Many ethical issues pertinent in the modern world have surfaced during my discussions with Dharma students and scientists, and people are interested in the Buddhist perspective on these. While some of these issues did not exist at the time of the Buddha due to lack of scientific knowledge, others did. Of those that did, some were of concern to ancient Indian society, others were not. Because Buddha and the great Indian sages did not tackle some of these ethical concerns directly, I will share my perspectives on them based on Buddhist principles.

Although several of these issues have become politicized, here I am regarding them solely as ethical issues. My intention is not to cause controversy but to encourage compassion for everyone involved in difficult situations. Only by listening and working together—not by hostile rhetoric or aggressive actions—can sensitive issues and difficulties be resolved.

As a human community we must think carefully and choose wisely what scientific and technological research to engage in for the betterment of sentient beings. We must reflect on the possible long-term consequences of medical and chemical research, knowing that the threats of biological and chemical warfare are real. What follows are some thoughts about specific issues.

Scientific research. Distinguishing the ethical status of an action simply by looking at the action itself is difficult because the actor's motivation is a key factor. A seemingly "beneficial" act done with a harmful intention produces suffering in the long term for the one who did it and usually harms others in the present. On the other hand, a forceful action may appear harmful, but if carried out with an altruistic motivation, it will be constructive. In the case of scientific research, not only the action but also the motivation must be taken into consideration.

Scientists must consider the long-term effects of their research on sentient beings and their environment. Pursuing scientific research simply out of curiosity to see how something operates or to invent interesting new devices is too simplistic a motivation. I do not know if scientists who researched atomic power sufficiently considered how governments could use the results of their work. Although scientists may expect good to come from their research, the actual outcome of their scientific investigation is not always clear. Scientists with a sincerely compassionate motivation and a sense of responsibility for the long-term implications of their research will make careful decisions about what to research.

Almost everything has advantages and disadvantages. Our concern should always be what will bring the greatest good to the greatest number of living beings. We should take the time to assess a situation as best as we can given our present knowledge and follow what is most beneficial, even if in the short term there are a few difficulties.

People often assume what is best for the economy, earns more income for their company, secures more political power, results in fame, or increases military might is most beneficial. These are not valid criteria for determining benefit; they are short-sighted and biased, and adhering to them could easily bring us—as individuals and as members of the human species—more suffering. We must consider that each and every sentient being wants happiness and freedom from suffering.

Genetic engineering. In one sense genetic engineering resembles already accepted procedures. Kidney, heart, and liver transplants are now common practice, and patients benefit tremendously from these. By extension, scientists could conceivably alter certain genetic components that are instrumental in causing diseases.

Much caution and forethought of all the implications are required, however. Just as a high degree of knowledge about possible outcomes of an organ transplant and ways to counteract damaging side effects is necessary before transplanting an organ, such forethought regarding the benefits and the byproducts of genetic engineering is necessary before proceeding with this research. This forethought involves not just a few people—such as a governmental commission or a committee of scientists—but all of us because genetic manipulation can potentially have an enormous effect on living beings. What could be the long-term effect on our bodies of eating genetically altered food? What could be the political, economic, social, and ethical ramifications of creating genetically designed children? As a human community we must discuss these questions and make wise decisions together.

Embryos from in-vitro fertilization. How to handle extra embryos after in-vitro fertilization has to do with how we define life. From a Buddhist viewpoint, sentient life—as distinct from mere biological life—involves the presence of consciousness. But when does consciousness enter the body? Most Buddhist texts agree that consciousness joins with the fertilized egg, but they don't specify if that occurs before or after the fertilized egg is implanted in the womb. However, once the sperm, egg, and consciousness are together and the cells start to multiply in the womb, a sentient being exists. We do not know if consciousness joins with an egg during in-vitro fertilization before it has been put in the womb.

Much discussion revolves around what to do with the excess fertilized

262 | THE FOUNDATION OF BUDDHIST PRACTICE

eggs after in-vitro fertilization that enables a childless couple to have a child. Should they be used for stem cell research? Should they be discarded? Given to another couple who wants to have a child? Kept indefinitely at a very low temperature? If those eggs have consciousness, do those sentient beings then suffer from cold? These questions are difficult to answer. I encourage doctors as well as couples to contemplate these issues before having in-vitro fertilization so that they do not suffer from confusion if faced with this situation.

Stem cell research. Research on stem cells harvested from human embryos could potentially bring cures for diseases and new ways to heal injuries. Genetic research could include tests to see if embryos had genetic defects that could later lead to debilitating diseases. But what is the effect of such research on the beings who inhabit those embryos? What kind of karma is created by doing this research? Will the knowledge derived from it bring happiness or may it create more misery and confusion? We need to investigate these issues and make wise decisions.

Some people accept that insects and animals have some form of sentience, but believe that since human beings have greater intellectual capabilities, they are superior. Others say that all sentient beings are similar in wanting happiness and not wanting suffering, and thus it is unsuitable for human beings to use animals for scientific research. Is it beneficial to harm some beings in order to devise ways of helping others? Unfortunately, we cannot ask the beings in the embryos or in the animal bodies if they agree to offer their lives for the potential benefit of others.

Cloning. Similar considerations about the presence of consciousness affect the issue of therapeutic cloning, in which scientists create a new human being with the same genes as another person, such that the clone's organs could be harvested and transplanted into the cloner. But Dolly, the cloned sheep, was a different sentient being with a different mindstream than her cloner. In the case of human beings, I don't think the clone would agree to donate his or her organs to the cloner or vice-versa. Unless we consider various ramifications and make wise, thoughtful decisions, we may become so enamored with science and technology that in the pursuit of happiness we create more problems.

Birth control and abortion. The presence of consciousness in a zygote also affects decisions regarding birth control and abortion. Birth control that inhibits the fertilization of the egg is fine. But once the egg is fertilized and a consciousness has entered, deliberately stopping the pregnancy is considered the destructive action of taking life. Situations such as the child being born severely disabled or the mother's life being at stake need special consideration. Although abortion in such cases still entails the taking of life, the motivation is different and usually involves regret and sadness, making the karma lighter.

Overpopulation is a genuine concern in our world. As a society and as individuals, we must be responsible for the future of our planet. Birth control that prevents conception rather than terminates pregnancy is best. Giving a child up for adoption is another worthy option. My hope is that we can inculcate a sense of responsibility in young people (and adults too), so that they will use their sexuality wisely. Overestimating the value of romantic love and rushing into sexual relationships often leave people emotionally hurt or facing an unwanted pregnancy. In general, we need to bring compassion to cases of unwanted pregnancy. Rather than judge and blame the people involved, we need to help them resolve the situation as best as possible.

Assisted suicide. It may happen that a family member has a terminal illness and, experiencing great pain, asks for help in terminating his or her life. Assisted suicide is difficult and complicated; interestingly, a somewhat similar situation arose during the Buddha's lifetime. A monk was meditating on the unattractiveness of the body. Misunderstanding the purpose of the meditation, which is to reduce lust, he grew so disgusted with his body that he was miserable day and night. He asked another monk to kill him to free him from his body. The other monk did, and when the Buddha heard about this, he established the precept to abandon taking life and encouraging death.

Making a decision to put someone out of their suffering is difficult when we do not know where he or she will be reborn. When we take rebirth into account, we see that assisted suicide does not stop all suffering.

I would encourage someone with a terminal illness to see herself as more than just her disease. She is still a whole person with great human potential. Spiritual practice can still go forward even when one is terminally ill. At the times her mind is clear, she can direct it toward cultivating love and compassion, even if she is suffering physically. Friends and relatives can encourage her to see that her life still has meaning and purpose even when her body is incapacitated or in pain.

On the other hand, someone may be in a coma with brain damage and no hope of recovery. Because he lacks proper mental functions, even if he is reminded of positive thoughts, the benefit is minimal or none. In addition, the family experiences great distress and society expends resources to keep the person alive. Such situations may be an exception, and it is understandable if the family allows the person to die naturally.

Suicide. Like other forms of taking life, suicide is considered killing. It is not a full karmic path, because the object of the action must be a person other than ourselves and the completion of the act means the victim dies first. Buddhism does not say a person who attempts suicide is evil and will be punished. However, it is a self-centered action that does not take into account the feelings of friends and family and how much they will suffer if one commits suicide.

Someone once told me that he longed for the peace of death because our world, with all its problems, is so difficult to bear. If we could be assured that in death we would find lasting happiness and peace, his wish might have some reason. However, we lack that guarantee. Death is not a cure for pain.

Meanwhile, because we are alive now, we can do something to resolve our difficulties and to contribute to the betterment of the world. The more we recognize the purpose and value of our precious human life, the more we will find meaning in our life and the more we will appreciate our good fortune to have this wonderful human brain and human heart. With these, we can practice the path to awakening, eliminating all problems. We need to cultivate a long-range perspective, patience, and confidence. With these, we can abandon despair, see the goodness around us, and know that we can make our life worthwhile.

The death penalty. Criminal actions that harm others create destructive karma. Using methods that are both wise and compassionate, as a society we must do our utmost to prevent it and to offer sympathy and support to families who grieve the loss of their loved ones or property. However, we must ask if executing the perpetrator dissipates the grief of the victims and their families.

Death is something that none of us wants. When it takes place naturally, it is beyond our control, but when death is willfully and deliberately inflicted, it is tragic. Whether death is caused illegally or legally—as in the case of the death penalty—negative karma is created. Even if we don't consider the karmic consequences in future lives, many disadvantages of the death penalty are evident now. A society may allow the death penalty in order to punish offenders, prevent them from reoffending, and deter other possible offenders. Research has shown, however, that executing offenders does not accomplish these aims.

I believe that human beings are not violent by nature. Unlike tigers, we are not naturally equipped with sharp teeth and claws for killing. The basic nature of each sentient being is pure. Human beings become violent owing to their afflictions, which exist in all of us. From this viewpoint, each of us has the potential to commit a crime as long as ignorance, hostility, attachment, and jealousy are within us. How, then, can we self-righteously condemn others as evil? Our own disturbing attitudes and emotions won't be overcome by executing others.

What is deemed criminal varies greatly from country to country. To use the death penalty as a punishment for such diverse actions is subjective and unreasonable. Furthermore, if we wish to deter criminal activity and prevent harmful activities, society must take care of children and ensure they receive a good education.

Executing human beings is an especially severe punishment because it is so final. A human life is terminated, and the executed person is deprived of the opportunity to change and to compensate for the harm he caused. However deplorable the act a person may have committed, everyone has the potential to improve and correct himself. I am a great admirer of Mahatma Gandhi's policy of *ahiṃsā,* or nonviolence. I appeal to those countries that employ the death penalty to observe an unconditional moratorium. At the same time, I encourage citizens and governments to give more support to education and to encourage a greater sense of universal responsibility for all beings in children and adults.

Vegetarianism. Eating meat involves the destructive action of killing even if we are not the butcher or fisherman. Being vegetarian is best, although it depends on our health. The Buddha specifically forbade his followers to eat meat in three circumstances (MN 55.5):

> Jivaka, I say that there are three instances in which meat should not be eaten: when it is seen, heard, or suspected [that the living being was slaughtered for one's consumption]... [I] say that there are three instances in which meat may be eaten: when it is not seen, not heard, and not suspected [that the living being was slaughtered for one's consumption].

Mahāyāna scriptures prohibit eating meat irrespective of those three situations, although there are a few exceptions.

In previous years, I would drive by poultry farms on the way to visit Tibetan settlements in South India. Hearing the chickens squawk in fear and seeing the horrible conditions in which they lived upset me greatly. When I heard that Tibetans ran these enterprises, I asked them to close them down and seek other employment. I am very happy that they have complied.

When I grew up in Tibet, the custom was to serve great amounts of meat during feasts and ceremonies. Thinking of so many animals being killed distressed me. In addition, it is unfitting for Buddhist practitioners who say they are practicing compassion to eat other beings' flesh. In Tibet and now in India I repeatedly said that this must stop, and now most monasteries do not serve meat during public gatherings. Similarly, only vegetarian food should be served at gatherings at Dharma centers. Otherwise, it is strange for people to hear teachings on compassion and then eat meat during the breaks between teachings!

Many people can be vegetarians without adverse consequences to their health. They take care of their diet and live in a place where they can procure healthy food. I would prefer to be a vegetarian. However, after some time of not eating meat, I fell ill with jaundice and traces of it remained as a chronic health problem. My doctors advised that, due to my strenuous schedule, I should eat meat. Although I aspire and would prefer to be totally vegetarian, now I must accept being a part-time vegetarian.

If those with health problems find it difficult to avoid eating meat, eating the flesh of large animals will prevent fewer living beings from dying. Eating small animals, such as shellfish and chicken, causes many beings to be killed for just one meal.

Neutering pets. From one perspective, spaying and neutering animals is seen as cruel. But from a broader perspective, when there are so many dogs and cats that they all suffer, don't have enough to eat, and spread disease to one another, then there may be a good reason to spay and neuter animals. This is now done in Dharamsala, where I live.

Sexual ethics. Sexual ethics falls within the general rubric of nonharmfulness, which is the fundamental principle in defining ethical conduct. The fundamental activity to abandon is adultery because it causes confusion and jealousy for the two people involved and for their families. The specific details of unwise and unkind sexual behavior are related to the culture and values of a particular society at a particular time.

In ancient times going to a prostitute was not considered sexual misconduct if the customer paid her properly. However, present societal values by and large consider prostitution exploitation of vulnerable people. Young girls are sold into prostitution and runaway teenagers are manipulated into it. Single mothers living in poverty turn to sex work to put food on the table for their children. It is not the women and children who are at fault here, but the pimps and johns who keep the system going with the excuse of helping them by providing income. If men's intention were to help women and children, then they would give them a safe place to live, an education, and job training. Prostitution is also a social issue rooted in poverty and lack of respect for other human beings.

If a person voluntarily chooses to earn their livelihood through sexual services and these services do not damage oneself or others in the short term or long term, the situation would not be considered sexual misconduct.

Gays and lesbians are widely accepted in Western societies, and there is increasing support of their equal rights in housing, employment, marriage, military service, participation in religion, and so on. In these societies, homosexuality would not be considered unwise and unkind sexual behavior when practiced in a respectful relationship and with protection against sexually transmitted disease. The main point, whether one is straight or gay, is not to hurt others either emotionally or physically through one's sexuality. Everyone is advised to avoid sexual relations that are manipulative, inconsiderate, or that could be emotionally or physically damaging to one or both parties. Safe sex with the use of condoms is a priority in upholding the Buddhist principle of nonharming.

Nowadays pornography is widespread, especially via the Internet. Material that reduces human beings to sexual objects harms both the viewer and the viewed. It stimulates undue lust that easily leads to inappropriate sexual behavior, especially in the case of child pornography. Instead of receiving love and support from adults, these young people are objectified and seen as the sexual playthings of lustful adults. Their self-esteem is severely damaged and they lose trust in adults. Spouses may be offended and lose respect for their beloved life partner who looks at pornography.

The state of mind that objectifies others and makes them into sexual objects for one's own pleasure is the opposite of the love and compassion we are trying to cultivate on the spiritual path. It inhibits opening our hearts toward others and destroys our happiness now and in the future.

11 | Results of Karma

THROUGH OUR INTENTIONS and our actions, we create our experiences. Each of us experiences the results of intentional actions we have done. The Buddha explains (AN 3.34):

> Whatever kamma an ignorant person [has done]
> born of attachment, anger, and confusion,
> whether what was fashioned by him be little or much,
> it is to be experienced right here:
> there exists no other site [for it].

Right here means in ourselves. We cannot transfer our karma to others so they experience the result, nor do we experience the result of others' actions. The results of our actions are concordant with their causes: if we create the cause for happiness, we experience happiness; if we create the causes for pain, that is what we will experience. The Buddha says (MN 136.6):

> Having done an intentional action by way of the body, speech, or mind [whose result is] to be felt as pleasant, one feels pleasure. Having done an intentional action by way of body, speech, or mind [whose result is] to be felt as painful, one feels pain. Having done an intentional action by way of body, speech, or mind [whose result is] to be felt as neutral, one feels neutral.

Experiencing the long-term results of our actions does not contradict the fact that our actions influence others here and now. Giving another person food, we temporarily cure his hunger as well as create the cause to have resources in our future lives. Dedicating virtuous actions for a dear one who is deceased may affect that person's rebirth in a positive way. Similarly, the Buddha's awakening was a result of his own efforts, but we also share the good fruits of his accumulation of merit over three countless great eons. In all these examples, one person's karma has not been transferred so that another person experiences its result. Rather, as sentient beings we are interdependent, and the actions of one person may activate the ripening of another person's karma.

The karmic result corresponds to the ethical nature of the action, which is primarily determined by the intention that motivated it. Actions done with a good motivation bring agreeable results for the person who does them, and actions done with destructive motivations bring miserable results in the long term. Actions may have immediate results that do not correspond with the ethical quality of the intention; these immediate results are not karmic results. For example, with the intention to help, Jeff gives some money to a friend. The next day someone steals the money, buys alcohol, and then injures someone in a car accident. Jeff's action was still a virtuous one, although it had an immediate, unintended suffering result.

Three Results of Karma

Our actions bring several results: some are immediate results, others are karmic results that ripen later. When we are angry and speak harshly to someone, we immediately feel uneasy and experience an unpleasant reaction from the other person. In addition, the mental action of malice and the verbal action of harsh speech leave karmic seeds (latencies) on our mindstream. After a few years, lifetimes, or even eons, those seeds will ripen in our experiencing unpleasant events.

The scriptures speak of three results that come about due to actions done with all four branches (basis, attitude, performance, completion) accomplished: the ripening result (vipākaphala), causally concordant result (niṣyandaphala), and environmental result (adhipatiphala).

To be a *ripening result* four factors are required: (1) The cause is either virtuous or nonvirtuous. (2) The result is connected with the continuum of sentient beings. (3) The result comes after the cause. (4) The result itself is neutral, neither virtuous nor nonvirtuous.[54]

An example of a ripening result is the human psychophysical aggregates—form, feeling, discriminations, miscellaneous factors, and consciousnesses—we appropriated in our present life. Their cause was virtuous karma and they are connected with the continuum of a sentient being. Our rebirth came after its karmic cause, and our body itself is neutral, neither virtuous nor nonvirtuous. Āryadeva says (CŚ 297):

> Suffering is a ripening
> and thus is not virtuous.
> Similarly, birth too is not virtuous,
> being a ripening [result] of actions.

Suffering arises due to nonvirtuous causes, but itself is neutral. Similarly, the body of a new life is a result of virtuous or nonvirtuous karma, but itself is ethically neutral. In general, a heavy destructive action brings rebirth as a hell being, a middle one brings rebirth as a hungry ghost, and a minor one results in rebirth as an animal.[55]

With the exception of the causally concordant behavioral result, all other results are neutral. How we respond to suffering and happiness and to the different situations in which they occur creates the causes for more future results. As causes, these actions may be virtuous, nonvirtuous, or neutral; they leave karmic seeds on our mindstream and these produce more rebirths and the experiences we encounter in them.

The *causally concordant result* is usually experienced when we are again born as a human. It is of two types: (1) The *causally concordant experiential result* is our experiencing circumstances similar to what we caused others to experience. Killing results in experiencing injury, illness, or a short life. Generosity brings resources. (2) The *causally concordant behavioral result* is the tendency to behave in the same way in the future. Someone who lies in this life will have the tendency to lie and deceive others in future lives, whereas someone who trains in truthful speech will readily speak truthfully in future lives.

Each nonvirtue also gives an *environmental result*, affecting the ambiance in which we live. The chart will help you see the results of the ten nonvirtues at a glance. The causally concordant behavioral result is not listed because it is the tendency to do that same action again.

ACTION	CAUSALLY CONCORDANT EXPERIENTIAL RESULT	ENVIRONMENTAL RESULT
Killing	Short life, poor health.	Place with strife and war. Food and drink aren't healthy, medicine is not potent.
Stealing	Poverty, our things are stolen or we don't have the power to use them.	Poor place with many dangers, droughts, or floods, poor harvests, natural disasters.
Unwise and unkind sexual conduct	Disagreeable or unfaithful spouse, marital disharmony.	Life in a dirty place with poor sanitation, a foul odor, and misery.
Lying	Others slander and deceive us, don't believe or trust us, accuse us of lying when we are telling the truth.	Place with disharmony in the workplace, deceitful people, corruption in society, and you feel afraid.
Divisive speech	Lack of friends, people don't like to be with us, we are separated from spiritual masters and Dharma friends, have a bad reputation.	Rocky, uneven land with cliffs, place where travel is difficult, dangerous.
Harsh words	We are insulted, blamed, and criticized even when we speak with a good intention; others misunderstand us.	Barren, dry place that is inhabited by uncooperative people and has thorns, sharp stones, scorpions, and dangerous animals.
Idle talk	People do not listen to our words or value what we say, others laugh at us.	Drab place with an unbalanced climate where fruit does not ripen at the proper time, wells go dry, flowers and trees don't blossom.
Covetousness	We have intense desires and cravings, can't complete projects or fulfill our wishes and hopes, our ventures fail.	Small crops; our property, belongings, and the environment constantly deteriorate; isolated and poor place.
Malice	We feel great hatred, fear, suspicion, guilt, paranoia, and fright for no obvious reason.	Place with epidemics, disputes, dangerous animals, and poisonous snakes; wars and calamities, unpleasant food.

ACTION	CAUSALLY CONCORDANT EXPERIENTIAL RESULT	ENVIRONMENTAL RESULT
Wrong views	We are very ignorant and dull mentally, have difficulty understanding the Dharma, take a long time to gain realizations.	Few crops, lack of a home and protector; natural resources are exhausted, springs go dry, polluted environment, chaotic society.

Nāgārjuna outlines the effects that will occur in future lives by engaging in harmful actions now. Some of these results may also occur in this life (RA 14–19).

> Due to killing one is born with a short life span;
> due to violence one encounters much torment;
> due to stealing one becomes impoverished;
> due to adultery one has enemies.

> By lying one becomes reviled;
> through speaking divisively, one loses friends;
> due to speaking harshly, one hears unpleasant sounds;
> from engaging in idle talk, one's words will be disregarded.

> Covetousness destroys one's desired objects;
> malice is said to bestow fear;
> wrong views lead to evil worldviews;
> consuming intoxicants brings mental confusion.

> Through not giving gifts one is poor;
> wrong livelihood results in getting tricked;
> arrogance leads to a lowly station;
> jealousy brings about unattractive appearance.

> From anger comes a bad complexion;
> stupidity from not questioning the wise.
> These are the effects when one is [reborn as] a human,
> but prior to all of them is a bad rebirth.

Such are widely known to be the ripening results
of these [actions] that are called the nonvirtues.
For all of the virtuous actions
there are the opposite effects.

REFLECTION

1. Reflect on your life, noting your habitual actions and any strong karmas you may have done.

2. One by one, consider what their ripening result, causally concordant results, and environmental result will be.

3. Be aware that through your choices and actions, you are creating the causes for your future.

4. Have the sense of your life being a conditioned event, and you are the one creating the conditions.

Sūtras and texts all agree on which actions are virtuous and which are not, although they may have slightly different presentations of their specific results. Also, some texts describe karma in a simplistic manner, as if only one action produced a complex situation. It is helpful to remember that the purpose of these statements is to give ethical direction to average people in ancient times and that the precise functioning of karma is a complex matter.

An action with all three parts complete—preparation (the branches of the basis and attitude), performance, and culmination—can produce all three results over a period of lives. The First Dalai Lama explains (EPL 623):

If one asks: What is the reason that all the karmas yield the three [results]?

In the case of killing, for example: by the preparation one causes another to suffer [which yields the ripening result], in the actual act one kills [which yields the causally concordant result], and subsequently one has extinguished [the victim's] vitality [which yields the environmental result]; therefore [each action] yields three types of fruit.

This does not mean that the preparation alone produces the ripening result and so forth, for a karma has to have all these branches complete to give rise to all these results. Linking parts of the action to specific results is a matter of emphasis.

One destructive action may bring many effects, and some effects may last for a long time. The same is true regarding constructive actions. In other cases, many karmas come together to make one effect.

Although karma and its effects have been presented primarily in terms of nonvirtuous actions, the same four branches are necessary to complete constructive actions and the same factors apply to make a constructive action heavy. The results of virtuous karma are the opposites of those for nonvirtuous actions. It is important for us to contemplate the ten virtues, the branches that make them complete, the factors that increase their strength, and the various results that come from them.

The *Shorter Exposition of Action* (*Cūḷakammavibhaṅga Sutta*, MN 135) speaks of pairs of opposite actions and their contrasting results. In each pair, the destructive action leads to an unfortunate rebirth and the constructive one to a fortunate rebirth. When we later are born human again, we will experience the causally concordant and environmental results of the action. Injuring sentient beings brings poor health and illness; refraining from causing injury brings good health. An angry and resentful character leads to being ugly; refraining from anger, hostility, and resentment—especially when criticized—results in being attractive. Envy and begrudging the achievements and honors of others lead to having little influence and people not listening to or paying attention to our words. Refraining from envy leads to gaining influence and respect. Stinginess leads to poverty; generosity brings wealth. Being obstinate and arrogant and not showing respect to those worthy of respect results in a lack of social status and educational and employment opportunities. Being free from obstinacy and arrogance and showing respect to those worthy of respect brings high status and many valuable opportunities. Being uninterested in discerning virtue from nonvirtue and what to practice from what to abandon on the path leads to being dull and stupid. Being interested in these, inquiring, and learning about them brings wisdom.

Is whatever we experience—pleasant, painful, or neutral—caused by previously created karma? Although karma is not always the direct cause of our experience, it is involved. The Buddha elucidates (SN 36.21):

> Bile, phlegm, and also wind,
> imbalance [of the three] and climate too,
> carelessness and assault,
> with kamma as the eighth.

Some painful feelings occur from imbalance in the three humors—bile, phlegm, wind, or all three together—while others have to do with change in climate, reckless behavior, or assault. We know this from our own experience, and it is considered true in the world. In saying this, the Buddha does not dismiss the role of karma in producing painful feelings. Rather, he rejects the claim that karma is the one and only direct cause for all painful feelings and affirms that karma plays a role in the feelings directly caused by the humors and external circumstances. Karma is given as the eighth cause of painful feelings, possibly indicating its dominant role when no physical disease or injury can be found as the immediate cause of a person's pain. The Abhidharma explains that all painful physical feelings are due to karma, although they are not necessarily produced only by karma.

Our motivation influences the result of our actions. Even fabricated bodhicitta is a powerful motivation for engaging in the ten constructive karmic paths. Tsongkhapa explains (LC 1:239):

> The *Sūtra on the Ten Grounds* says that those who have cultivated these ten [virtues] through fear of [the dangers of] cyclic existence and without [great] compassion, but following the words of others, will achieve the fruit of a śrāvaka. There are those who are without [great] compassion or dependency on others, and who wish to become buddhas themselves. When they have practiced the ten virtuous [paths of] actions through understanding dependent arising, they will achieve the state of a solitary realizer. When those with an expansive attitude cultivate these ten

through [great] compassion, skillful means, great aspirational prayers, in no way abandoning any living being, and focusing on the extremely vast and sublime wisdom of a buddha, they will achieve the ground of a bodhisattva and all the perfections. Through practicing these activities a great deal on all occasions, they will achieve all the qualities of a buddha.

The Ripening of Karmic Seeds

Our mindstream is home to countless karmic seeds. Our future rebirth is not due to the sum total of all these seeds, but to whichever seed or seeds ripen just prior to our death. Cooperative conditions—such as our present thoughts and emotions and the events around us—influence which karmic seeds ripen in the present. Just as a daisy seed will not grow into a daisy without proper fertilizer, heat, and water, karmic seeds will not ripen without certain conditions being present in our lives. A virtuous mental state enables seeds of constructive actions to bear results, while nonvirtuous thoughts and emotions fertilize the seeds of nonvirtuous karma. Drinking and taking recreational drugs establishes conditions in life that facilitate the ripening of the seeds of destructive actions.

Vasubandhu commented on which karmic seed is most likely to ripen at the time of death (ADKB):

> Actions cause fruition
> in cyclic existence—first the heavy,
> then the proximate, then the habituated,
> then what was done earlier.

In general, heavy karma will ripen before lighter karma. If two heavy karmas are equal in weight, the one whose potential was reinforced nearer to the time of death will ripen first. If the potentials are equal, the action that is more habitual will ripen first. If the person is equally habituated to both actions, the one that was done first (earlier) will ripen.

The Pāli commentator Buddhaghosa describes the order in which karma producing rebirth ripens at the time of death in a slightly different order (Vism 19.15). Heavy karma, be it virtuous or nonvirtuous, will ripen first.

The heaviest virtuous karma is the attainment of one of the dhyānas; the heaviest nonvirtuous karmas are the five actions of immediate retribution: killing one's mother, father, or an arhat, wounding a buddha, and causing a schism in the sangha.

If there is not an exceptionally heavy karma, an action done very habitually will ripen. Paying attention to our habitual behaviors is important. Having a regular daily meditation practice, making offerings, praising others, and reflecting on the four immeasurables are good habits to develop. Habitually lying to others, losing our temper, and cheating others become strong karmic forces that will propel us into an unfortunate rebirth if they ripen at death.

In the absence of a habitual karma, a death-proximate karma—an action that is vividly remembered just before death—will ripen. The memory is so strong that it pushes the mind in that direction.

Reserve karma is any other karma not included above that is strong enough to bring a rebirth. In the absence of any of the above three, a karma that has been done often will ripen at the time of death and project the next rebirth.

The ripening of one karmic seed temporarily prevents the ripening of another. The ripening of the seed of a heavy karma means the seed of a lighter karma cannot ripen at that time. When a karma to be reborn in the formless realm ripens, all karmic seeds that could bring painful results are temporarily unable to ripen because beings in the formless realm do not experience feelings of pain. Those seeds remain on the person's mindstream until suitable conditions manifest for them to ripen. Similarly, when a karmic seed to be reborn as a hungry ghost bears its result, karmic seeds to receive wealth are temporarily blocked from ripening. These seeds are not destroyed or lost, but will ripen later when appropriate conditions are present.

Our karma will definitely bring results unless the seeds are inhibited from ripening. When the four opponent powers are applied to nonvirtues sincerely and diligently, those seeds will become unable to bear a result or will ripen in minor suffering. Similarly, when strong anger or wrong views manifest in our mind, they impair the ability of seeds of virtue to ripen: these seeds will either not be able to ripen or will bring only a minor result. In both these cases, the karmic seeds have not been totally eradicated: they are still present, but like damaged seeds, they are unable to bring their full results. If the purification or the anger is very strong, the potency of the karmic seed is so damaged that even when appropriate conditions are present, it will not bear any result, just as a burned seed cannot grow even when water, fertilizer, and sunshine are present. However, only direct, nonconceptual realization of emptiness fully removes seeds of destructive karma.

When cooperative conditions are not present, karmic seeds may exist in someone's mindstream but be impeded from ripening. For example, someone on the fortitude stage of the path of preparation has not yet abandoned the seeds for unfortunate rebirths, but these seeds cannot ripen into such rebirths because of the power of this person's inferential realization of emptiness.

The *Questions of Upāli Sūtra* (*Upāliparipṛcchā Sūtra*) speaks of a case in which a monastic with pure behavior holds malice toward another monastic with pure conduct. It says his "great roots of virtue are diminished, thoroughly reduced, and completely consumed." *Diminish* means that the result of great virtue becomes less and the duration of its happy result is shorter, but not all the good effects are stopped. *Reduce* means it can bring only a small pleasant result, and *consume* indicates that a result cannot ripen at all.

On the other hand, the *Teaching of Akṣayamati Sūtra* (*Akṣayamatinirdeśa Sūtra*) says that one of the benefits of dedicating merit for awakening is that the merit will not be consumed until awakening is attained, just as a drop of water that has flowed into the ocean will not be consumed. The *Array of Stalks Sūtra* (*Gaṇḍavyūha*) states that bodhicitta and virtues associated with it cannot be extinguished by afflictions or polluted actions.

How are we to understand these seemingly inconsistent passages? Saying that merit dedicated for awakening will not be consumed until awakening is attained means that this merit will not finish bearing its effects until then. However, that does not mean that anger and wrong views cannot damage it. Although they cannot destroy the merit completely, they can interfere with when, how, and for how long it ripens. Nevertheless, the results of that merit, although impeded, will not finish until awakening has been attained. Anger can render merit that has not been dedicated for awakening incapable of bearing any result. For this reason, dedicating our merit for full awakening is extremely important.

Saying that bodhicitta and the virtues associated with it cannot be extinguished by afflictions or polluted actions means that afflictions and karma cannot harm bodhicitta to the same extent that bodhicitta can harm them. It does not mean that afflictions and destructive karma cannot damage our bodhicitta and the virtues associated with it at all. Anger can harm our bodhicitta in two ways: we will not be able to generate new paths quickly but will have to again accumulate the merit that produces them, and we will experience the undesirable effects of nonvirtue.

In addition to anger and wrong views, in the *Compendium of Training (Śikṣāsamuccaya)* Śāntideva points out other actions that damage the virtues of one following the bodhisattva path: staying with householders who have strong attachment to material possessions and entertainment, boasting about spiritual attainments we do not have, and abandoning the Dharma by neglecting the Buddhadharma and making up our own version of the Buddha's teachings. These actions also impede our progress along the path, even if we do virtuous practices. Studying this text as well as Nāgārjuna's *Compendium of Sūtras (Sūtrasamuccaya)*, which also discusses the bodhisattva path, is very helpful.

Contemplating how the ripening of karma can be affected by counteracting forces makes us more conscientious. This, in turn, strengthens our mindfulness and introspective awareness in daily life. We become aware that getting angry is completely counterproductive. This increases our inner strength to set anger aside, just like a person seeing a delicious-looking sweet quickly puts it down upon hearing that it is laced with poison.

Since karma influences our experience of happiness and suffering, its ripening strongly influences our feeling aggregate. Although we often discuss karma ripening as the four effects discussed above, the reason we find some results desirable and others not is because of the experiences of happiness or misery they bring us. The situations we encounter in life as well as the pleasant, unpleasant, and neutral feelings we experience in them are related to our previous actions.

While encountering people who criticize us is due to our destructive karma of harsh speech, sometimes we hear criticism where there is none. In this case our feeling of being hurt is due to our misinterpretation of the event. As we become more familiar with the practice of mind training, which encourages us to view situations from more positive perspectives, the experience of mental pain declines. In fact, if we practice well, even if people wish to hurt our feelings we won't feel hurt.

We may find that certain emotions or intentions easily and frequently arise in our minds. This is a result of habits in previous lives. Someone who angers easily has a strong habit with this emotion. Should the anger grow to become physical violence, the physical deed may be related to previous karma, since the causally concordant behavioral result of violence is the tendency to do the action again.

Some children like to kill insects or torment animals. This is another instance of a causally concordant behavioral effect of killing. Other children naturally help others from a young age, even though their parents did not explicitly teach them. This behavior, too, is a causally concordant behavioral result. In addition, these children were habituated with certain emotions—anger or compassion—in previous lives.

We can apply our understanding of karma when watching the news or hearing of the good and bad experiences of others. Here we reflect on the types of actions people have done that created the causes for their present pleasurable and miserable experiences. In a natural disaster, many people lose their lives and property. What kind of actions could have caused this? Many first-responders and neighbors come to their aid and there is an outpouring of donations to help them resettle. What actions caused them to receive this help? What will be the long-term results for the people who offered aid? This is a very practical way to contemplate karma and apply our understanding to our lives.

When doing this, as noted above, do not fall into a wrong understanding of karma and its effects by thinking that others deserve to suffer or are morally inferior because they are suffering. Suffering comes as a result of our actions, not as a reward or punishment for them. Since all of us have created destructive karma in this and previous lives, judging others as morally inferior and ourselves as superior is absurd. A person and his actions are different. The action may be harmful, but the person is not evil—each of us has the potential to become a fully awakened buddha.

Some people question, "Is helping suffering people interfering with their karma?" Such thinking is foolish. Compassion is the appropriate response to misery, and we should always reach out to aid those who are suffering. The notion of karma must never be used to justify oppression or apathy in the face of problems that can and must be corrected. If we remain idle, we create the karma to not receive help when we are in misery.

REFLECTION

1. Think of some of the good circumstances you have in your life, for example, health, sufficient wealth, family, education, friends, hobbies, satisfying work, opportunities to hear Dharma teachings, connection with the monastic saṅgha, and so on.

2. Think of the types of actions you must have engaged in during previous lives to create the causes for these excellent circumstances.

3. Rejoice at the virtue you created and make a strong determination to engage in virtuous activities in this life to make preparation for good future lives where you will be able to continue your Dharma studies and practices.

Definite and Indefinite Karma

Some actions are definite (*niyata karma*) to produce a result unless that karmic seed is impeded from ripening; others are indefinite (*aniyata karma*) in that their producing a result is not certain. *Levels of Yogic Deeds* (*Yogācārabhūmi-śāstra*) explains (LC 1:240):

> Karma whose results are definite to be experienced are actions that are consciously done and accumulated. Karma whose results are not definite to be experienced are actions that are consciously done but not accumulated.

Definite karma are actions that have been done (*kṛta*) and accumulated (*upacita*); their results are certain to be experienced unless they are purified in the case of destructive actions or impeded by anger or wrong views in the case of constructive actions. *Done* means we consciously thought about or set something into motion physically or verbally. *Accumulated* means that we had an intention to act. All virtuous and nonvirtuous mental actions are accumulated. No one can force us to engage in mental actions.

It is not certain that results will be experienced from actions that have not been both done and accumulated. The four possibilities between done and accumulated are given below, together with examples.

Karma done but not accumulated are the ten following actions. They are not certain to bring results; their motivation is weak or has changed since the time the action was done. Almost all other actions aside from these ten are accumulated karma. Here we can see the great impact motivation has on our actions and their results.

1. *Actions done in dreams.* We dream of making offerings to the Buddha or of killing an enemy. If, upon waking, we rejoice at virtuous actions in a dream, we create virtuous mental karma; if we regret them, the karma is nonvirtuous. Rejoicing at destructive actions in a dream creates nonvirtuous mental karma; regretting those actions and making a strong determination not to do them in waking life is virtuous mental karma.

2. *Actions done unknowingly.* Believing the art supplies on the table are for everyone to use, we take them without knowing that they in fact belong to a particular person.

3. *Actions done unconsciously.* We accidentally step on an insect without any conscious intention.

4. *Actions done without intensity or continuity.* We off-handedly utter a few words of idle talk or chit-chat for a short time.

5. *Actions done mistakenly.* Someone wishes to steal a book, but steals a box instead; someone intends to praise one person, but mistakenly praises another.

6. *Actions done forgetfully.* We tell a friend that we will not share his comments with others, but forgetting that we said this, we tell others.

7. *Actions done unwillingly.* Someone has no wish to kill another person but is forced at gunpoint to do so.

8. *Actions that are ethically neutral.* Walking, sweeping, reading, driving, cycling, eating, sleeping.

9. *Actions eradicated through regret.* Although in general we speak truthfully, we lie to someone and later have strong regret.

10. *Actions eradicated with a remedy.* Seeing the disadvantages of killing, we no longer wish to go fishing, hunting, or take the life of any living being and take a precept to abandon killing. Alternatively, we weaken worldly attachments by attaining dhyānas or eradicate the seeds of those destructive actions by direct perception of emptiness.

Karma that is both done and accumulated are the main causes producing a rebirth and are not included in the ten above. In general, their four branches are complete and their result is certain to be experienced. These karmas have six characteristics (EPL 652):

1. The action is done deliberately, not impulsively or coercively against our will.
2. All parts of the action are complete. This eliminates situations such as trying to kill someone, but only injuring them, or thinking to attend Dharma teachings, but not going.
3. We do not regret the action afterward.
4. No antidote is applied to purify the karma.
5. We rejoice at having done the action.
6. The result is certain to be experienced.

Although actions with all four branches complete are definite karmas, they may not be strong enough to propel a rebirth. For example, the motivation is very weak or the action insignificant. *Karma that is not done but accumulated* is, for example, plotting for a long time to rob someone and then deciding against it, or dreaming of helping others and rejoicing when we wake up. *Karma that is neither done nor accumulated* is having no intention to cause an accident, but almost hitting another vehicle when driving.

Definite actions are certain to bring results unless we apply counterforces to them. *Definite* does not mean that events are predetermined or fated and therefore there is no purpose exerting energy to oppose them. Purifying destructive karmas by means of the four opponent powers is effective in lessening or stopping the result.

When Karma Ripens

In terms of when karma ripens, definite karma may bear results in this life (*dṛṣṭa dharma karma*), the very next life (*upapadya*), or lives subsequent to that (*aparaparyāya*). Karma that is the second of the twelve links will ripen in the next life or one after that. Actions that ripen in this life are those that are very strong owing to the special qualities of the field—for example, holy beings—or the strength of our intention. *Levels of Yogic Deeds* lists four pairs of actions that may ripen in the same life as they are created:

1. Nonvirtuous actions done with strong attachment to our body and virtuous actions done with strong disinterest in our body.
2. Nonvirtuous actions done with great malice toward others and virtuous actions done with heartfelt compassion for them.
3. Nonvirtuous actions done with deep malice and lack of respect for the Three Jewels or our spiritual mentors and virtuous actions done with deep confidence and regard for them.
4. Nonvirtuous actions done with intense animosity toward those who have been kind to us, such as parents and teachers, and virtuous actions done with an intense wish to repay their kindness.

In general, the results of heavy constructive and destructive karmas may be experienced in the same life in which they are created, whereas karmas that are slightly less heavy are likely to be experienced in the very next life. Karmas that are not as heavy as those are experienced in lives after that.

The Pāli Abhidharma also discusses karma that ripens in this life, in the next life, and in lives subsequent to that, and adds another option, karma that becomes defunct.[56] *Karma that ripens in this life* brings its result in the same life in which it was created. If such karma fails to encounter cooperative conditions for its ripening, it becomes defunct and does not ripen at all. *Karma that ripens in the very next rebirth* must produce its result in the next life. If it does not meet the conditions to ripen then, it becomes defunct. *Karma that ripens in subsequent lives* is karma that ripens whenever suitable conditions come together in any life subsequent to the next one. This karma becomes defunct only with the attainment of final nirvāṇa, when an arhat passes away. Contrary to the description in the Sanskrit tradition, the Pāli Abhidharma says that in order of its strength, karma that ripens in subsequent lives is the strongest, followed by karma that ripens in the next life, with karma that ripens in this life being the weakest.

Defunct karma is not a specific class of karma but describes karma that could have ripened but does not owing to a lack of appropriate conditions. For example, karmic seeds remaining on the mindstreams of arhats become defunct when they die and enter nirvāṇa without remainder.

How is the idea of "defunct" karma reconciled with the Buddha's explanation that the results of our actions will definitely be experienced? The Buddha says (AN 10.217):

> I declare, monastics, that actions willed, performed, and accumulated will not become extinct as long as their results have not been experienced, be it in this life, in the next life, or in subsequent future lives. As long as these results of actions willed, performed, and accumulated have not been experienced, there will be no making an end to suffering, I declare.

This statement applies to karmas that are capable of yielding results (*vipakarahakamma*). Within the certainty that destructive actions will produce misery, never happiness, and constructive actions will lead to happiness, never suffering, there is some flexibility as to how, when, and if a karma ripens. Just as undamaged seeds that have the capability to grow will sprout when planted in fertile soil with sufficient water, so too will seeds of constructive and destructive karmas bring their results when planted in the mindstream of an ordinary being.

Nevertheless, as a conditioned phenomenon, the ripening of karma can be affected by other forces. If this were not the case and karmic seeds could never be modified, we could never reach the end of duḥkha because the karma to be experienced would be endless. The Buddha elaborates (AN 3.34):

> [However,] once greed, hatred, and confusion have vanished, that action is thus abandoned, cut off at the root, made barren like a palm-tree stump, obliterated so that it is no more subject to arise in the future.
>
> It is like seeds that are undamaged, not rotten, unspoiled

by wind and sun, capable of sprouting and well-embedded: if a person were to burn them in fire and reduce them to ashes, then winnow the ashes in a strong wind or let them be carried away by a swiftly flowing stream, those seeds would be radically destroyed, fully eliminated, made unable to sprout, and would not be liable to arise in the future.

When ordinary beings later become arhats, their polluted karma—be it virtuous or nonvirtuous—may still ripen as pleasant or unpleasant experiences when they are alive. When they pass away and attain nirvāṇa without remainder, all polluted karma becomes defunct.

Other circumstances can also render karma defunct. The *Book of Analysis* (*Vibhaṅga*) explains that there are certain cases in which a constructive or destructive karma will not bring a result. Four factors may prevent this.

1. The *realm of rebirth*. A destructive karma is due to ripen in the next existence as an unfortunate rebirth, but the person creates a powerful constructive karma that causes her next life to be in a fortunate rebirth. Blocked from ripening, that destructive karma "dries up" and does not ripen.

2. The *person's physical body or possessions*. A constructive karma in the person's mindstream has the tendency to ripen in a particular rebirth, but the person has a weak body or lacks the requisites to sustain his life. The situation of his body and possessions inhibits the constructive karma from ripening.

3. *The time*. A constructive karma has the tendency to ripen in a certain rebirth but the person is born in a time of war, drought, or economic depression. Since the cooperative conditions for the ripening of this constructive karma are not present at that time, the karma loses its effectiveness and does not ripen.

4. *Personal effort*. Someone may have a destructive karma on her mindstream that is due to ripen in premature death, but she makes wise choices, behaves ethically, puts herself in good situations, and cultivates friendships with ethical people. As a result, the destructive karma lacks the conducive circumstances to ripen. However, if she drinks and drives, she provides ample opportunity for that destructive karma to ripen. Although we do not have much control over the

288 | THE FOUNDATION OF BUDDHIST PRACTICE

first three factors, by living wisely here and now we can influence
which karmic seeds in our mindstreams will ripen.

How Karma Functions

With respect to how karma functions, the Pāli Abhidharma describes four
types (CMA 200): productive, supportive, obstructive, and supplanting
karmas. *Productive karmas* are the virtuous or nonvirtuous intentions that
produce the aggregates of a rebirth. This includes the body and mind at the
first moment of the new life as well as mental states and aspects of the body,
such as the sense faculties, that develop later on.

Supportive karma does not produce its own result but supports the production or duration of the result of another karma by creating conducive
circumstances for the other karma to ripen. After a virtuous karma results
in our having a fortunate rebirth, supporting karma could extend our life
span, prolong a disease caused by a nonvirtuous karma, or lengthen the
time that we experience happiness or misery.

Obstructive karma also does not produce its own result but interferes
with the ripening of another karma, making its result weak or shorter in
duration. If we had created the constructive karma to receive an inheri-
tance, obstructive karma would prevent us from claiming it. If we had created the destructive karma to have a severe illness, obstructive karma could
mitigate the effect so that we have a mild stomachache instead.

Supplanting karma is virtuous or nonvirtuous karma that cuts off the
ripening of a weaker karma and ripens in its place. Unlike obstructive
karma, supplanting karma does not simply interfere with the ripening of
another karma but actually ripens instead of it. A destructive karma may be
about to ripen at the time of death, but through a change of circumstances
a stronger supplanting constructive karma ripens instead. A particular
karma may perform any of these four functions at different times.

The Benefits of Contemplating Karma and Its Effects

Contemplating karma and its effects helps us to see ourselves, our experiences, and our lives as dependent on a variety of factors: they arise
and cease due to causes and conditions. They are neither random nor

predetermined—both of those positions contradict conditionality. This awareness of conditionality prepares us to later study the twelve links of dependent origination that describe how we are born into saṃsāra and how to free ourselves from it. It also prevents us from slipping into nihilism when we study and meditate on the emptiness of inherent existence: the fact that people and things arise and change due to causes and conditions assures us that they exist.

When we experience adversity, life seems unfair and we ask, "Why me?" When we have knowledge of how the law of karma and its effects operates we understand that we created the causes for our experiences. The mind-training teachings suggest that we reflect on the karmic causes of our problems because it helps us to accept responsibility for our actions and stop blaming others for our unhappiness. Recalling that we have acted destructively humbles our arrogance and leads us to change our attitudes and behavior.

Our mindstream resembles a garden with a variety of seeds planted in it. Depending on which seeds are watered, particular plants will grow at that time. The other seeds are still in the ground; they will ripen whenever the proper amount of water, fertilizer, and heat are present. Similarly, karmic seeds from numerous actions we have done in previous lives and this life are on our mindstream. Our present thoughts and actions act like water and heat causing specific seeds to ripen. Gambling waters the seeds of destructive karma, making it easier for us to have financial problems. Speaking with kindness will water seeds of virtuous karma, making it easier for them to bear their results.

The maturation of karma is not fatalistic; we have some ability to influence which seeds ripen. We also see that our lives are not the sum total of all actions we have ever done, but depending on which karmic seeds ripen we can go from a good situation to an unpleasant one and back again quickly. We also get a sense of the incredible swirl of countless causes created in previous lives that come together to bring about just one event in our lives. The intricacy and complexity of the functioning of karma and its effects is far more than we can currently grasp. Nevertheless, learning the general and specific characteristics of karma and its results aids us in making wise decisions.

Once we break our leg, we cannot unbreak it, although we can work skillfully with the situation to minimize the pain. Similarly, once karmic seeds have ripened, we cannot undo their results. Understanding this, we will accept unpleasant events in our lives rather than rail against them and make effort to create constructive karma when dealing with difficult situations. If we give way to anger and the wish to retaliate against the driver of a car that rear-ended us, we compound our misery in the present and create more destructive karma, the result of which we will have to experience in the future. However, if we remain calm and speak respectfully to the person, we avoid creating more causes for suffering.

In short, Buddhaghosa indicates the strong role karma plays in our lives (Vism 19.18):

> Kamma-result proceeds from kamma,
> result has kamma for its source,
> future becoming springs from kamma,
> and this is how the world goes around.

12 | The Workings of Karma

O UR ACTIONS CAN BE classified in several different ways. Learning these enriches our understanding of karma and its effects, which, in turn, helps us to be more mindful of thoughts, words, and deeds.

Projecting and Completing Karma

Projecting and completing karma are differentiated by the types of results they bring. *Projecting karma* ripens in rebirth in a saṃsāric realm with the five aggregates of a desire-realm or form-realm being or the four aggregates of a formless-realm deva. It is the second of the twelve links of dependent origination. *Completing karma* determines the specific attributes or experiences in that life. The projecting karma of ethical conduct leads the mind to be born with human aggregates, and the completing karma of speaking kindly to others makes the body attractive.

All four branches must be complete for an action to become projecting karma, but this is not necessary for a completing karma. In births resulting from either virtuous or nonvirtuous projecting karma, we can experience the results of either virtuous or nonvirtuous completing karma. The chart gives some examples of possible results.

	VIRTUOUS PROJECTING KARMA	NONVIRTUOUS PROJECTING KARMA
Virtuous completing karma	Human life with eight freedoms and ten fortunes	Pampered pet
Nonvirtuous completing karma	Human life lived in poverty	Beasts of labor

While projecting karma determines the type of body we appropriate—human, animal, and so forth—completing karma affects such factors as the genetic predispositions of the body and whether those predispositions are activated.

Vasubandhu says that a projecting karma produces only one rebirth and only one rebirth arises from a projecting karma, whereas Asaṅga states that one projecting karma can produce one or many rebirths and many karmas can produce one or many rebirths.

The results of many completing karmas are experienced in one life. Someone may be born in a war-torn country because of one nonvirtuous completing karma, but receive shipments of food, medicine, and clothing resulting from virtuous completing karma. Circumstances in our lives may frequently change depending on the completing karma that ripens at any particular time.

Collective and Individual Karma

Sentient beings are social and often act together. We belong to various groups and work, play, practice Dharma, and raise the next generation together. As such, we experience common results together. Asaṅga's *Compendium of Knowledge* discusses various possibilities of how this occurs.

Some actions are done collectively by a large group; they result in experiences shared by everyone in that group, such as living in the same country or experiencing a natural disaster. Collective karma is also created in small groups: The people attending Dharma teachings or a soccer game create collective karma. All the participants will experience a similar result in a future group situation.

We also create individual karma when we are part of a group; this results in experiences that are not shared by others. Everyone at a Dharma teaching creates virtuous group karma because the purpose of the gathering is virtuous. Within that group, one person listens attentively and thinks, "These teachings are important and I want to practice them." Another person with a wandering mind thinks, "I wonder what's for lunch?" In the future, these two people will find themselves in a similar agreeable situation but will experience it differently because of the individual karma they created. Similarly, as the result of collective karma they created together, many people may be in a place plagued by an epidemic, but owing to individual karma, some will fall ill while others won't.

It is important to be heedful of the groups that we choose to join and the purposes for which they are established because we reap the result of the collective actions of that group that correspond to the purpose of the group. The First Dalai Lama says (EPL 614):

> If one asks: In the course of a war and so forth, if one person kills another, does the karmic path arise only for that single person?
>
> No. In a war and so forth, since they are all there with the same purpose of killing, they all have the karmic path in the same way as the killer.

While sitting in a crowd of thousands who have gathered to hear His Holiness teach, I (Chodron) marvel at the opportunity to be part of a group that has formed for the purpose of developing compassion and attaining awakening. The collective karma created by this group is very different from a group whose purpose is to increase the value of a company's stock.

Sometimes without choice we find ourselves part of a group whose purpose or activities we do not agree with. For example, we may be the citizen of a state that employs capital punishment. If we do not endorse this activity, we do not create this particular collective karma. Being clear and aware of our intentions in such situations is extremely important so that we can skillfully guide our creation of karma.

Naturally Nonvirtuous Actions and Proscribed Actions

Karma is also divided into naturally nonvirtuous (*prakṛti-sāvadya*) actions and actions proscribed by the Buddha (*prajñaty-avadya*). Those that are naturally nonvirtuous—such as the ten nonvirtues—are so-called because they are done with a nonvirtuous motivation, their nature is nonvirtuous, and they have the potential to produce suffering results. Whoever does them—whether that person is monastic or lay—creates nonvirtue (*akuśala*) and negativity (*pāpa*) and will experience unpleasant results.[57]

Actions proscribed by the Buddha are those regulated by precepts, such as the prātimokṣa precepts of monastics. Some of these actions are not naturally nonvirtuous and do not necessarily involve an afflictive motivation; they may also be done with a neutral or constructive motivation. Examples are singing, dancing, watching entertainment, wearing perfumes, ornaments, and cosmetics, eating after midday, and handling money.

When those who hold monastic precepts transgress a precept, they commit an offense or downfall (*āpatti*) by engaging in an action proscribed by the Buddha. To purify this, they must confess and apply the appropriate method as prescribed in the vinaya. For this reason, it is very important for monastics to attend a poṣadha rite with four or more fully ordained monastics. Depending on the gravity of the offense, the way of making amends differs. Someone committing a remainder offense must enter a period of penance in which he or she temporarily relinquishes monastic privileges. A monastic who obtains an article by wrong livelihood must relinquish the article. Minor offenses are purified by confessing them to another monastic who is free from that transgression.

If the transgressed precept regulates an action that is naturally nonvirtuous, such as killing an animal or telling small lies, the monastic creates negativity and needs to apply the four opponent powers to purify this karma in addition to amending the offense by confessing to the saṅgha.

Even if the action itself is not naturally negative, people engaging in it—whether they hold precepts or not—may still create negativity if they have a nonvirtuous intention while doing the action. A monastic who handles money with contempt for the precepts creates negativity as well as an offense that must be confessed to the saṅgha. Similarly, when monastics motivated by attachment or anger eat in the evening, they must rectify both the negativity as well as the offense. If they eat after noon under circumstances in which the Buddha allowed them to eat—for example, the monastic is ill, working for the saṅgha, or traveling—there is no offense or negativity. If none of those extenuating circumstances apply and the monastic eats because she sees the food as medicine to keep her body healthy so she can practice the Dharma, there is an offense but no negativity.

In brief, in a case where the offense also creates negativity—such as a monastic lying—the negativity and the offense are one nature but nominally different. As such, they are purified by different methods. When offenses have been confessed to the saṅgha with the prescribed ritual, they are said to have been purified. However, the negativity can only be purified through sincere application of the four opponent powers. On the other hand, if the person purifies the negativity by engaging in the four opponent powers, but does not confess the offense and make amends to the saṅgha and attend poṣadha, the offense remains and obscures the mind. Until the person confesses and makes amends, he is not fit to carry out certain monastic activities such as giving ordination. If the person is not conscientious, these offenses may later lead him to engage in negativities or create further offenses.

Intention Karma, Intended Karma, and Mental Karma

Karma is of two types, intention karma (*cetanā-karma*) and intended karma (*cetayitvā karma*). Vasubandhu explains (ADK):

> Karma gives rise to the diversity of the world.
> It is [of two kinds], intention [karma] and what it produces
>   [intended karma].
> Intention is mental karma:
> [the intended karma] it produces is physical and verbal karma.
> These [physical and verbal karmas] consist of perceptible and
>   imperceptible [karma].

Intention karma is mental karma, specifically the mental factor of intention. Once a strong intention has arisen in the mind, physical and verbal actions—intended karma—follow. Physical and verbal actions may be either perceptible karma (*vijñapti*) that reveals the person's intention or imperceptible karma (*avijñapti*) that does not. For example, when strong malice is present in our mind, the mental factor of intention that accompanies it is mental karma. That intention to harm another person leads us to speak spitefully to him; our voice uttering the snide comment is perceptible verbal karma. The harsh tone of our voice reveals our intention to hurt him.

Asaṅga says (ADS):

> What is mental karma? It is a mental action that conditions the mind; it consists of meritorious, demeritorious, and immutable [actions].

Mental karma (*manas karma*) is the mental factor of intention, which accompanies a primary mind and is included in the fourth aggregate (miscellaneous factors). When the mental factor of intention accompanies a primary mental consciousness that is also accompanied by a virtuous mental factor, such as faith or love, it becomes constructive karma. That intention is mental karma and intention karma.

Similarly, the intention that accompanies a primary mental consciousness that is also accompanied by a nonvirtuous mental factor, such as attachment, resentment, or discouragement (which is a form of laziness), is destructive karma. The intention is mental karma and intention karma, and the nonvirtuous mental factor is an affliction.

Intentions—intention karmas—produce intended karmas (*cetayitvā karma*), which are physical and verbal actions. Motivated by the intention that shares the same primary mental consciousness as attachment, someone engages in the verbal intended karma of lying in order to get what he wants. Motivated by the intention that shares the same primary mental consciousness as vengeance, someone may kill another person who speaks divisively about her to ruin her reputation.

A strong mental intention that instigates lying and a strong mental intention that abandons lying are both the mental factor of intention and intention karma. The former is accompanied by a nonvirtuous mental factor such as anger, the latter by a virtuous one such as integrity. When either intention is accompanied by the other branches that form a complete karmic path, it becomes the second link of dependent origination and has the power to propel a rebirth in cyclic existence. The physical or verbal actions that are brought about by these mental karmas are intended actions.

Physical and Verbal Karma, Perceptible and Imperceptible Forms

All Buddhist schools agree that karma is connected to our intentions. Sautrāntikas, Cittamātrins, and Svātantrikas say that all karma of body, speech, and mind is the mental factor of intention. The mental factor of intention that motivates an action is intention karma, and the mental factor of intention at the time of doing the physical or verbal action is intended karma.

For them both intention karma (mental karma) and intended karma (physical and verbal actions) are intentions.

Vaibhāṣikas say that karma can be of two kinds: intention karma, which is the mental factor of intention, and intended karma, which is karma of body and speech. The karmas of body and speech are of two types: perceptible forms (*vijñapti*) and imperceptible forms (*avijñapti*). *Perceptible physical karma* is "the shape of the body when it is motivated by an intention and is moving, for example, when prostrating or killing... perceptible verbal karma is the sound of the voice," for example, when lying or speaking kindly. The shape of the body and the sound of our voice are forms, and they "are perceptible forms in that they enable others to understand our motivation" for doing the action (EPL 558–59). Perceptible forms may be virtuous, nonvirtuous, or neutral.

Imperceptible forms are subtle forms that are not perceivable by the sense faculties and that arise only when a person has a strong intention. They are either virtuous or nonvirtuous. Neutral actions lack the powerful intention necessary to bring forth an imperceptible form. Imperceptible forms continue to exist no matter if the person is conscious, sleeping, or engaged in other actions. An example is monastic precepts.

Imperceptible forms are obscure phenomena, established by reliable cognizers depending on authoritative scripture. Chim Jampelyang in *Ornament of Abhidharma* (*mngon pa'i rgyan*) quotes a sūtra that establishes their existence:

> All forms are subsumed in three types of form: (1) forms that are visible and obstructive, (2) forms that are invisible but obstructive, and (3) forms that are invisible and nonobstructive.

An example of *visible and obstructive forms* is a table. It can be perceived by the eye consciousness and obstructs the space it occupies so that other things cannot occupy that space at the same time. Examples of *invisible but obstructive forms* are sounds, tastes, and odors; they cannot be seen by the eye but are obstructive. The sound of people laughing is obstructive because it prevents our hearing someone who is whispering. An example of *invisible and nonobstructive forms* is imperceptible forms. Vaibhāṣikas assert that only imperceptible forms are examples of the third type of forms, whereas Prāsaṅgikas include other phenomena such as dream objects.[58]

The *Treasury of Knowledge* speaks of three types of imperceptible forms: ethical restraints, antirestraints, and other imperceptible forms.

1. Ethical restraints (*saṃvara*) constrain us from afflictive activity. They are of three types: prātimokṣa restraints, concentration restraints, and unpolluted restraints. (a) Prātimokṣa restraints are of eight types: the precepts of male and female fully ordained monastics, training nuns, male and female novices, male and female lay followers with the five precepts, and lay followers with the eight one-day precepts. When we take the precept not to kill, steal, and so forth, an imperceptible form arises in us that acts like a dam that helps us restrain from doing that destructive action. These ethical restraints remain until they are completely broken, voluntarily relinquished, or we die. (b) The concentration restraint is possessed by beings who have meditative stability arising from concentration. (c) The unpolluted restraint is possessed by āryas in meditative equipoise. When āryas are in meditative equipoise, their right speech and right action—two factors of an ārya's eightfold path—are imperceptible forms that are unpolluted by ignorance.

2. Antirestraints (*asaṃvara*) are the opposite of restraining from destructive actions. They arise due to someone's strong intention to act destructively and remain until that person gives up that profession and its motivation or until he dies. Examples are the antirestraints of a butcher or exterminator.

3. Other imperceptible forms arise by depending on holy objects, making firm promises, and acting with strong reverence or other positive motivations. The *Scripture on Discernment* (*Vinayavibhaṅga*) describes seven virtues derived in relation to substances (*aupadhika puṇya kriyā vastu*) that are meritorious imperceptible forms: offering a residence to the saṅgha, offering a prayer hall to the saṅgha, offering cushions or seats for the prayer hall, offering food regularly to the saṅgha, offering food to travelers and guests, offerings useful items to the sick and to medical professionals, and offering food to the saṅgha at the monastery if it is difficult for the monastics to go on alms round because of inclement weather. The Buddha praised these

virtues as being "of great fruit, highly beneficial, splendid, and enormous in nature." The merit of those who offer these will "unceasingly increase at all times, whether they are walking, sitting, sleeping, or waking."

Our intention in making these seven offerings is that others will use them to create merit. Whenever they do so, we accumulate a virtuous imperceptible form. This imperceptible form continues until we die, unless it vanishes because we have strong afflictions or the prayer hall and so forth is destroyed. At our death the imperceptible form is lost, but its having-ceased (*naṣṭa*) goes on to future lives.[59] When suitable conditions arise, it will ripen and bring its happy result.

Another example of the third type of restraint is the imperceptible form that arises when we ask someone to perform a constructive or destructive physical or verbal action. For example, a military commander accumulates the karma of killing by ordering his soldiers to kill the enemy. Although he does not kill with his own hands, he accumulates the nonvirtuous imperceptible form of killing each time one of his soldiers kills. The military commander will experience the suffering result of these actions of killing, as will the soldiers. When we tell friends and relatives to give donations to those in need, charities, and temples, we accumulate virtuous imperceptible forms when they make the offerings.

Vasubandhu cites the above two situations—creating merit through certain material objects and accumulating karma when we order or ask others to perform an action—as reasons to prove the existence of imperceptible forms. Without imperceptible forms, our merit from offering the seven substances could not increase if later our mind were in a nonvirtuous or neutral state. Without the existence of imperceptible forms, we could not accumulate nonvirtue if our mind were in a virtuous state at the time someone we told to steal goes out and robs. This is because we cannot accumulate destructive karma when our mind is in a virtuous state and cannot accumulate merit when our mind is in a nonvirtuous state.

Furthermore, while in meditative equipoise on emptiness on the path of seeing, āryas possess all branches of the eightfold path. If there were no imperceptible forms, they could not possess right speech, right action, and right livelihood at that time. Also, the fact that precepts and ethical restraints are imperceptible forms enables them to act as a dam that impedes transgressions.

While the explanation of imperceptible forms is found in the *Treasury of Knowledge*, a text expressing Vaibhāṣika and Sautrāntika tenets, many Tibetan scholars say it is also accepted by Prāsaṅgikas. To support this, they point to a passage in the *Discrimination of the Five Aggregates*, a text attributed to Candrakīrti that describes imperceptible forms as "any form that is a phenomena source that is neither visible nor obstructive and can only be perceived by the mental consciousness, such as ethical restraints, antirestraints..."[60]

By saying that physical and verbal karmas are the mental factor of intention, Sautrāntikas, Cittamātrins, and Svātantrikas have difficulty explaining what physical actions are and how physical movement of the body is karma. The Prāsaṅgika presentation is more aligned with conventions. They say that in the action of prostrating, there is the physical karma that is a perceptible form—the form of the body moving. In addition, there is an intention that motivates that action, and that intention is the mental karma of prostrating. All tenet schools agree that the second link of dependent origination is the mental factor of intention (when the other branches of a karmic path are complete). The karma of harsh words or the karma of saving someone's life is the mental factor of intention that motivates those actions; this intention leaves the karmic potential that brings forth a new rebirth.

According to Vaibhāṣikas and Prāsaṅgikas, imperceptible forms belong to the aggregate of form but are forms for mental consciousness (*dharmāyatanarūpa*). As such, they are included in the phenomena source (*dharmāyatana*), not the form source (*rūpāyatana*).

I have a theory to explain why Vaibhāṣikas and Prāsaṅgikas agree that physical and verbal actions are form, whereas the other schools say they are intention. Vaibhāṣikas are not very analytical; they understand things according to worldly conventions and the perceptions of ordinary people. In worldly conventions, we say, "I heard her speak the truth. We saw him beat the dog." On the basis of these ordinary conventions, we speak of physical and verbal actions as things that we see and hear—as forms.

Sautrāntikas, Cittamātrins, and Svātantrikas posit things on the basis of their being objective phenomena that exist from their own side. The originator of the Svātantrika school, Bhāvaviveka, said in the *Blaze of Reasoning*:

We also actually impute the term "self" to [the mental] consciousness conventionally . . . because [the mental] consciousness takes rebirth, it is said that it is the self.[61]

All schools who accept rebirth say that the self transmigrates. People who are unable to posit phenomena as existing by mere designation usually posit the mind—specifically the mental consciousness—to be the self, since it, and not the body, is what transmigrates. Within the mental consciousness, only the mental factor of intention can be pointed to as being karma. Why? When these people analyze actions while considering them to be objectively existent, they see that unless an intention is involved, an action cannot be karma. A boulder rolling downhill is action, but not karma. Thus they point to the mental factor of intention as the karma and not the physical and verbal actions per se.

According to Prāsaṅgikas, if we analytically search for something that objectively exists beyond the conventional norm, we cannot find anything. They thus accept things as existing merely by convention, and conventionally we say we perceive physical and verbal actions through our senses. For this reason, Prāsaṅgikas accept physical and verbal karmas to be form.

Gloomy and Bright Karmas and Their Effects

The Buddha spoke of four kinds of karma (MN 57.7):[62]

> There are these four kinds of karma declared by me after I had realized them for myself by direct knowledge. What four? There is gloomy karma with gloomy results; there is bright karma with bright results; there is karma that is gloomy and bright with gloomy and bright results; there is karma that is neither gloomy nor bright, with neither gloomy nor bright results, which leads to the destruction of karma.

1. Nonvirtue is *gloomy karma with gloomy fruition*. It is afflictive by nature and produces disagreeable results in one of the three unfortunate states. Born there, afflictive contact arises, leading to afflictive painful feelings such as feelings experienced in the hell states.

2. *Bright karma and bright fruition* is virtue included in the form realm. The mental states of beings in this realm are either virtuous or neutral; their nonvirtuous mental factors have been temporarily suppressed, so their actions do not produce the duḥkha of pain.[63] Form-realm beings do not experience unpleasant feelings. Bright karma is created in a mindstream that is not mixed with negative thoughts; it brings a pleasant result that is unmixed with suffering in that being's mindstream.

3. *Gloomy-bright karma with gloomy-bright fruition* is the virtue of the desire realm. While this karma is bright in that it is virtuous, it arises in a mindstream that also has nonvirtuous thoughts, making it gloomy-bright virtue. It yields pleasant results, but the mindstream in which it ripens also experiences painful feelings, making its result gloomy-bright. Human beings, some beings in the unfortunate states, such as pet animals, and some devas experience this.

4. *Unpolluted karma* is neither gloomy nor bright. Cyclic existence is perpetuated by polluted karma. Wise ones, who have realized emptiness directly, do not create polluted karma and free themselves from uncontrolled rebirth. Vasubandhu says (EPL 675, n 118):

> Unpolluted karma causes the termination and the elimination of those three [types of] karma... Since it is contrary to entering into [the process of cyclic existence, unpolluted karma] is not included within the [three] realms; therefore is has no fruition [in saṃsāra].

In the consciousness that is an ārya's true path realizing emptiness nondually, the mental factor of intention is unpolluted karma. Arhats and pure-ground bodhisattvas also create unpolluted karma when they engage in other activities in post-meditation time. Such karma is unpolluted in that it is not created under the influence of ignorance; it is never nonvirtuous and does not generate causes for rebirth. It is the remedy to the above three types of karma, leads out of cyclic existence, and gives rise to true cessations and nirvāṇa. Until arhats leave their body, they will experience the results of previous karma, some of which may be painful. However, they do not react to pain by generating more afflictions, and thus do not accrue new karma.

Unpolluted karma also refers to the subtle intention that arhats and bodhisattvas on the pure grounds must generate for their physical, verbal, and mental actions owing to the presence of cognitive obscurations in their mindstreams. Unpolluted karma and the latencies of ignorance give rise to the mental body of arhats and bodhisattvas on the pure grounds. Buddhas do not have unpolluted karma because they have eliminated the cognitive obscurations. Being effortless and spontaneous, their actions are called awakening activities (T. 'phrin las). These compassionate actions are a special type of activity that is effective because of buddhas' great virtue. Their ability to successfully use awakening activities to benefit sentient beings depends on the accumulation of merit by those sentient beings and their karmic connection with the buddhas.

In terms of highest yoga tantra, the mind of someone experiencing the fourth-stage actual clear light has the mental factor of intention, which could be considered unpolluted mental karma. When this person emerges from the actual clear light, he or she immediately manifests a pure illusory body, which is unpolluted in the sense that the mind associated with it is free from afflictive obscurations. This illusory body is considered a physical phenomenon, so perhaps its actions could be considered unpolluted karma of the body and speech.

Purifying Destructive Karma

With only a superficial glance, we may believe our actions are basically virtuous, but if we closely observe our physical, verbal, and mental activities we may find that our motivations for constructive action are often weak, the actions are done hurriedly or distractedly, and we forget to dedicate the merit. Constructive actions require much effort on our part, like a tired donkey carrying a heavy load uphill. On the other hand, when faced with circumstances in which acting negatively could bring immediate benefit to our selfish aims, we easily engage in destructive actions, like water flowing downhill. We have strong habits with such behavior from previous lives. Understanding this, mindful observance of our ethical standards and purification of past misdeeds becomes imperative to avoid pain and to secure happiness.

The *Sūtra Showing the Four Dharmas* (*Caturdharmanirdeśa Sūtra*)

304 | THE FOUNDATION OF BUDDHIST PRACTICE

reveals an excellent practice for purifying all destructive actions—the four opponent powers—which were described briefly in chapter 6 (LC 1:252):

> Maitreya, when a bodhisattva mahāsattva possesses these four powers, they will overcome any negativities they have done and accumulated. What are they? They are the power of regret, the power of the antidote, the power of resolve, and the power of reliance.

First learn to accurately assess your actions, accept responsibility for your misdeeds, admit them, and regret them. Strong regret is the key to purification, for without it there is no motivation to counteract negativities. Regret is not guilt, so do not despise yourself thinking that the more you berate yourself the more you atone for your misdeeds.

Make an effort to understand how you became involved in these negativities by reflecting, "Was my interpretation of the situation accurate or was it skewed by my self-centeredness? What was my motivation? How were my body, speech, and mind involved in this action? Do I engage in this action often? Did I rejoice afterward?" Then contemplate, using your Dharma knowledge, how you could think about and deal with a similar situation should it happen in the future. Such in-depth reflection will help you to uncover destructive emotional, verbal, and physical behaviors, and by understanding these, you can begin to change them.

In chapter 2 of *Engaging in the Bodhisattvas' Deeds*, Śāntideva proposes many points to reflect on that evoke our regret. If we were to die at this moment, the seeds of these harmful actions would be on our mindstream, so alarmed at the prospect of experiencing an unfortunate rebirth, we should regret our nonvirtues and turn to the Three Jewels for guidance. Engaging in destructive actions out of attachment for friends and family is futile, considering that we will have to separate from them, and our destructive karma will continue with us into our next life. Misdeeds bring frightening results in this and future lives, so this is no time to be complacent. In this way, express regret (BCA 2.28–29):

> Since beginningless cyclic existence,
> in this life and in others,

unknowingly I committed negativities
and caused them to be done [by others].

Overwhelmed by the mistakes of ignorance,
I rejoiced in what was committed,
but now, seeing these mistakes,
from my heart I confess them to the Protectors.

Second, perform virtuous actions as an antidote to your misdeeds. Although all virtuous actions fulfill this, six practices in particular are recommended:

1. Recite, study, or contemplate sūtras, especially the Perfection of Wisdom Sūtras (Prajñāpāramitā Sūtras) and the *Sūtra of the Golden Light* (*Suvarṇaprabhā Sūtra*).
2. Meditate on emptiness by contemplating Nāgārjuna's teachings or the *Heart Sūtra*.
3. Recite mantras containing the names of the buddhas, such as the Vajrasattva mantra.
4. Make buddha images and statues, create altars and shrines, and build stūpas or monasteries.
5. Make offerings to the buddhas and bodhisattvas.
6. Recite the names of buddhas, for example, the names of the thirty-five buddhas.

Prostrating to these buddhas with reverence for their excellent qualities while reciting their names is especially powerful. Meditation on bodhicitta—even for a few minutes—and engaging in actions motivated by bodhicitta have the power to purify the seeds of destructive karma created over eons. Other remedial actions are making donations to charities, monasteries, or spiritual practitioners; doing volunteer work in a hospital, Dharma center, or other health facility; and printing Dharma books for free distribution.

Third, make a strong determination to abandon such actions in the future. This fortifies your inner strength to oppose habitual destructive ways of thinking and acting and to change your ways; it is like making New Year's resolutions, only you should keep these! If you cannot resolve to

306 | THE FOUNDATION OF BUDDHIST PRACTICE

abandon certain actions forever, resolve to avoid them for a certain period of time. During that time, be very conscientious to avoid the action. This will give you confidence, and then you can extend the time some more.

Fourth, reestablish good relationships with the objects of our destructive actions—holy objects such as the Buddha, Dharma, and Saṅgha, or our spiritual mentors, or sentient beings. By taking refuge, we reaffirm our connection with the Three Jewels and our spiritual mentors. By generating bodhicitta, we replace the negative intentions that caused us to harm others with positive feelings toward them.

The order of the four opponent powers may vary according to the specific purification practice you do. In Prostrations to the Thirty-Five Buddhas, first you take refuge and generate bodhicitta, then prostrate as the remedial action, followed by generating regret and resolve to avoid repeating the actions. In the Vajrasattva practice the order is taking refuge and generating bodhicitta, regret, reciting Vajrasattva's mantra as the remedial action, and resolving not to do the action again.

As ordinary beings we don't know where we will be reborn, and the time between this life and an unfortunate rebirth is one breath. If we don't purify our misdeeds and work hard to prevent an unfortunate rebirth before we die, it may be a long time before we have the opportunity to practice the Dharma again.

It's important to do purification before the seeds of harmful actions ripen; once a cup is broken, we cannot unbreak it. Similarly, doing pūjās after a suffering result has occurred cannot undo the present suffering, although it will create virtue that could reduce future suffering. The efficacy of the pūjā depends on a variety of factors, including the potency of the karmic seeds that are about to ripen.

Making specific predictions about the extent to which negativities have been reduced or eliminated is difficult and depends on many factors, such as the intensity of the regret, the sincerity of our resolve to refrain from repeating the action, the concentration with which we did the remedial behavior, and the sincerity of our refuge and bodhicitta. It also depends on whether we did the four opponent powers over a long or short period of time and whether all four opponent powers were applied or only some.

Although purification done by ordinary beings does not remove karmic seeds from the mindstream, it weakens them so that their results will be less intense or will last for a shorter period of time. Instead of experiencing a car accident, we may trip and stub our toe. Rather than suffering from domestic disharmony for years, we may endure it for only some weeks or months. Instead of being born in an unfortunate state, we may fall ill in this life. Understanding this, we will not become upset when we fall ill or encounter unpleasant situations. Instead we will think, "How fortunate that a powerful destructive karma is now ripening. Compared to the intense suffering I would have experienced for a long time had it ripened in an unfortunate rebirth, I can manage the current misery." Seeing the situation in this way protects our mind from creating more negative karma by angrily reacting to problems. It enables our mind to remain unperturbed by this comparatively small suffering that will soon end.

Purification can also prevent the coming together of the cooperative conditions for a karma to ripen. Purification may "burn" the karmic seeds so that they do not bring a result, but only by realizing emptiness directly is the potency to produce unfortunate rebirths completely eliminated. It is good to seal purification practices, as well as all our virtuous practices, by contemplating emptiness and dependent arising. We do this by reflecting that the I who created the destructive action, the action itself, its karmic seed, and so forth arise dependently and yet are empty of inherent existence. Similarly, the person doing the purification practice, the action of purifying, and the karmic seeds that are purified lack inherent existence but exist dependently. Although all the factors involved in creating nonvirtue and in purifying negativities lack inherent existence, they still exist and function on the conventional level, and so purification is important.

Doing the four opponent powers repeatedly may bring certain signs of purification or the reduction of the strength of the seeds of destructive actions. We may repeatedly dream of being with our spiritual mentor or the saṅgha, or in a temple. Dreaming that we walk on a mountain or see the rising of the sun or moon may also indicate purification. This does not mean that every dream involving these is a sign of purification; dreams are due to a variety of factors. Changes in daily life occurrences also indicate purification. Whereas previously our mind was often unclear and heavy, now we are more attentive when listening to Dharma teachings or studying. We understand the meaning more easily and have deeper meditation experiences. Our mind is less resistant to the Dharma and integrating the Dharma in our lives becomes much easier.

While purification is always possible and advisable, avoiding destructive actions is better. We may glue a cup back together, but it's better not to have broken it to start with. However, when strong negative emotions, mental obscuration, lack of mindfulness or conscientiousness, or carelessness overpower us and we act negatively, it's important not to despair but to remember that we can purify these actions, and then put energy into doing so. This not only aids our spiritual practice but also helps us psychologically by reducing guilt and making us more honest with ourselves.

Being indolent in purifying our nonvirtue only harms us. I find it amusing, yet sad, that although some people call themselves Buddhists, they heed the advice of fortune tellers more than the teachings of the omniscient Buddha. The Buddha warned us that suffering will come from our harmful actions, yet we ignore this and think there is no need to exert so much energy to purify our karma by doing the four opponent powers. But if a fortune teller tells us that we will fall ill unless we do a particular antidotal activity, we are eager to follow his instructions. It should not be like this!

Creating Our Future

Contemplating karma and its effects makes us question if doing something simply because it feels good in the moment or brings us temporary benefit is wise. Drinking liquor may make us temporarily feel good, but we also say and do many foolish things. Initially certain actions may benefit our self-centered aims, but their karmic consequences in the long run will bring suffering. On the other hand, waking up early in the morning to do our meditation practice may be uncomfortable now, but it brings so many beneficial results later. Being honest in business may initially bring less profit, but it will result in greater security and wealth later.

The Buddha suggested that we consider the long-term karmic effects of our actions in order to evaluate if we are creating the causes for the kind of future we want to have. Reflecting deeply and in detail about the effects of karma will increase our motivation to become more mindful and conscientious regarding our behavior, speech, and thoughts. Such reflection also gives us a more expansive view of how things operate. Instead of simply considering the immediate effects of our actions, strong as they may be, we begin to care about even more potent effects that can ripen years or even lifetimes in the future.

The Buddha outlined excellent advice for how to make a decision or tackle a difficult situation: if an action brings both long- and short-term benefits, do it. If it brings long-term benefit, but temporary discomfort, doing it is still worthwhile. But if it brings immediate happiness yet causes suffering as the long-term karmic effect, then avoid it. If it brings misery now and in the future, definitely avoid it.

These teachings on karma are not theoretical; they relate to our daily life activities when we continually engage in actions that become the causes for pain or for happiness and awakening. Although understanding the detailed workings of karma and explaining them by reasoning alone is difficult, accepting the natural law of karma and its results is supported by more valid reasons and fewer logical inconsistencies than other explanations. Knowing this, be confident in thinking, "Having attained a precious human life, I have the potential and the responsibility to create the causes for happiness, and I will do this."

Who Creates Constructive Karma?

Scriptures say that the demarcation between Dharma and non-Dharma actions is the presence or absence of the eight worldly concerns. They further say that Dharma motivations begin with the aspiration for a good rebirth, followed by the determination to be free from cyclic existence and attain liberation, and culminate in bodhicitta.

However, people can create constructive karma without believing in rebirth or having a Dharma motivation. For example, at the time of the Buddha, an old man wanted to become a monk, but Śāriputra could not determine if he had created enough merit to receive ordination. The Buddha, with his supernormal power that sees the karma of all sentient beings, observed that in a previous life, the old man had been a fly on a piece of cow dung that floated in water around a stūpa. Although this tiny insect did not have the motivation to take a human rebirth and become a monk, through contact with this holy object he accumulated the merit that enabled him to be ordained. Such merit is called the "root of virtue concordant with liberation," which arises when sentient beings have contact with powerful holy objects.[64] This is a unique kind of dependent arising wherein the object becomes powerful owing to the buddhas' and ārya bodhisattvas' inconceivable collection of merit and to their altruistic aspiration that anyone who even sees, hears, thinks about, or contacts them receives benefits that will ripen in awakening.

Non-Buddhist practitioners who develop very high states of meditative concentration also create constructive karma that brings fortunate rebirth in the form and formless realms in their next lives, where they experience the bliss that arises from deep states of samādhi.

Many human beings act with kindness. They may know nothing about karma or future lives yet feel compassion for those who are suffering and help them motivated by genuine care. They work hard without getting angry or complaining; they are honest and respect those worthy of respect. Some care for the ill and elderly, others teach children or work to prevent global warming. Some seek protection for wildlife and endangered species, others strive for human rights. Such actions create merit leading to a good rebirth.

Mother Teresa was not Buddhist; she did not necessarily accept rebirth, although she probably aspired to be born in heaven. Her dedication to the welfare of the poor was extraordinary, and the actions she did to care for them were certainly virtuous. She created much merit that will certainly bring happy results.

The law of karma and its results functions whether someone believes in it or not. Similarly, whether someone believes that gravity exists or not, she still walks on the ground because of its power. Someone who does not know what constitutes nonvirtue may still engage in destructive actions and experience their painful results even if he does not consider his actions unethical.

Secular ethics is a useful guideline for those who do not adhere to any spiritual path and want their daily actions to be beneficial. Their main aim is their own interests in this life, but they consciously focus on not harming others when fulfilling this aim. In this way, even if not all of their daily actions are virtuous, at least they will be neutral and some will be virtuous. Animals, too, create constructive and destructive karma. Their ignorance, however, hinders them from deliberately refraining from harmful acts and engaging constructive ones.

Needless to say, someone who gives a gift to bribe another person is not practicing generosity. Similarly, harming one living being in order to give to another is not the practice of generosity, nor is giving weapons the practice of generosity.

In the early years of the Communist Party in China, some of its members had a real sense of altruism and dedicated their entire lives to improving the welfare of the peasants and the poor. This was virtuous. Unfortunately, they were biased, and with hatred destroyed the lives and possessions of the educated and the wealthy. These Communist officials had two contradictory emotions: compassion for the poor and animosity toward the rich. These mutually opposed emotional states constitute two separate mental states; one motivates virtuous activities, the other nonvirtuous actions. They create different karma depending on which mental state motivates them to act at a particular time and what act they do. Such situations are not unique to Communist officials. We see this happens quite often in our own lives as well.

The Complexity of Karma

Some accounts of karmic events are puzzling. For example, Śāntideva relates the story of Śāriputra relinquishing bodhicitta. Śāriputra was a bodhisattva on the path of accumulation, whose bodhicitta was not stable. Once, another person returned Śāriputra's generosity with ingratitude, provoking Śāriputra to give up bodhicitta. Scriptures say that after generating bodhicitta, if someone relinquishes it, he is reborn as a hell being. Yet Śāriputra achieved arhatship in that life.[65] How can this be explained? Śāntideva responds by saying that the complex workings of karma are beyond our understanding; only the buddhas' wisdom comprehends it fully.

Another story says that Nāgārjuna died from decapitation as a result of karma he created in a previous life when he accidentally cut off the head of an ant with a scythe. Explaining this story in the context of the general Buddhist understanding of karma is difficult, considering that one sūtra says that Nāgārjuna was a highly realized bodhisattva. He was renowned as a great practitioner and teacher of *Guhyasamāja Tantra*, and in *Ocean of Reasoning*, Tsongkhapa spoke of him having fully developed bodhicitta and wisdom realizing emptiness. If such an outstanding person as Nāgārjuna with these magnificent qualities was unable to achieve buddhahood in a single lifetime, then the teaching in the *Guhyasamāja Tantra* that attaining awakening in a single lifetime is possible must be a fairy tale. In this light, we see that the story about him being decapitated because of having inadvertently killed an ant cannot be taken in a literal or ordinary way.[66]

In the *Sublime Continuum*, Maitreya said that the Buddha, while not wavering from absorption in emptiness, appears in diverse emanations. From this perspective, Śākyamuni Buddha was an emanation body. Emanation bodies come from the enjoyment body, and this, in turn, is a manifestation of the truth body. Therefore, the Buddha was awakened before he appeared in our world in the form of the prince from Kapilavastu. All the activities and events in his life were in fact demonstrations done intentionally to teach us. From this perspective, it could be that Nāgārjuna was already a buddha and the story of his death was a demonstration done to teach us.

The law of karma and its effects is very subtle, and its intricacies are beyond our understanding; only an omniscient buddha is able to know these fully. Since the Buddha is not present here and now, we cannot ask him for clarification regarding the subtle aspects of karma. Buddhaghosa says (Vism 19.17):

> The succession of kamma and its result...is clear in its true nature only to the Buddha's knowledge of kamma and its result, which knowledge is not shared by disciples.

Vasubandhu agrees (ADKB):

> Nobody but the Buddha understands in its entirety karma, its infusion, its activity, and the fruit that is obtained.[67]

When discussing karma and how it ripens, the number of complications is enormous. Unfortunately, my head is too small for this vast expanse of knowledge. Now I see the truth in Milarepa's statement, "I don't know about the complex issues of *Parchin* (lit. "crossing to the other shore"; it explains the bodhisattvas' paths and practices), but if you can move from saṃsāra to nirvāṇa, then you have indeed gone to the other shore. I don't know about the complications of Vinaya (lit. "taming," and refers to monastic precepts and rites), but if this very crude mind of yours is tamed, then this is Vinaya."

Creating the Causes for Higher Rebirth, Liberation, and Awakening

Nāgārjuna sets out the aims of the spiritual path (RA 3–4):

> That [disciple] first [practices] the Dharma of higher rebirth;
> afterward comes the highest good,
> because, having obtained higher rebirth,
> one proceeds in stages to the highest good.

> Here, [we] maintain that higher rebirth is happiness,
> and highest good is liberation.
> In brief, the method for attaining them
> is summarized as faith and wisdom.

Can people who are not Buddhist create constructive karma for higher rebirth and the highest good of liberation and awakening? For an action to become the cause for upper rebirth, it is not necessary that the person doing it have the motivation to attain that state, but for an action to become the cause for the ultimate spiritual aims of liberation and awakening, the person must have the intention to attain those states.

Candrakīrti says that ethical conduct is a cause for higher rebirth, liberation, and full awakening (MMA 24):

> For common beings, those born from the word [śrāvakas],
> those set toward solitary awakening, and
> those conqueror's heirs [bodhisattvas], a cause of the highest good
> and higher rebirth is none other than proper ethical conduct.

Tsongkhapa comments in *Illuminating the Thought*, a commentary to Candrakīrti's *Supplement*, that this does not exclude other virtuous actions from being causes of higher rebirth and highest good.

There are, however, many other causes that are not ethical conduct. Thus this means that to achieve special higher states and the highest good, a definite relation with ethical conduct is necessary. If ethical conduct is forsaken, there is no way that these can be accomplished.[68]

There are three causes for a precious human life: (1) *Observance of pure ethical conduct* entails, at the least, avoiding the ten destructive paths of actions and practicing the ten constructive ones. It is the projecting cause that makes us take rebirth as a human being. (2) *The cultivation of other virtuous qualities* is the practice of generosity, fortitude, meditation, and so on. It brings conducive circumstances for Dharma practice: done with proper motivation, generosity is the cause for wealth; ethical conduct brings good health, long life, and good relationships; fortitude produces an attractive appearance; joyous effort enables us to be able to attain our goals. Concentration maintains our positive motivation, and wisdom enables us to choose qualified spiritual mentors and understand the Dharma correctly. (3) *Powerful dedication prayers* direct our constructive karma to ripen in a precious human life. Having these good circumstances in future lives will enable us to continue on the path to awakening with ease. Planting the karmic seeds to have them is done in this life.

Without living ethically and observing karma and its effects, a fortunate rebirth is not possible. The First Dalai Lama says (EPL 655):

> As it says in (Āryadeva's) *The Four Hundred*: "By ethical conduct one goes to a high rebirth; by the view one goes to the supreme state." For the purpose of obtaining higher rebirths, ethical conduct is foremost.

To attain liberation, in addition to renunciation of saṃsāra and the determination to attain nirvāṇa, we must have the wisdom realizing emptiness. Renunciation and the aspiration for nirvāṇa give us the motivation to practice the path of cleansing the mind of ignorance, which is the root of saṃsāra. The wisdom realizing emptiness is the actual realization that overcomes ignorance. The Buddha's teachings describe how to cultivate renunciation and wisdom realizing emptiness; we should examine if other paths contain these teachings.

To attain buddhahood, two critical factors are required: bodhicitta and the wisdom realizing emptiness. As above, the wisdom realizing emptiness is necessary to cleanse the mind of all ignorance, which keeps us bound in cyclic existence, and its latencies, which inhibit the mind from knowing all existents. Bodhicitta gives us the aspiration and energy to create the vast merit necessary to attain full awakening. Here, too, the Buddhadharma teaches us how to cultivate these two factors, and we need to examine if other paths also contain these teachings.

When we speak of higher spiritual goals such as liberation and awakening, the meaning of "Dharma" becomes more specific. It must be the teachings and the path that lead to nirvāṇa and awakening. In this context, actions motivated by attachment to rebirth in cyclic existence and actions done without the correct understanding of emptiness are not suitable.

The attainment of full awakening requires the bodhicitta motivation. After all, how could there be a buddha who lacks compassion and the altruistic intention? In *Bodhisattva Grounds* (*Bodhisattva Bhūmi*), Asaṅga says that someone who has fully dedicated his or her body, speech, and mind for the welfare of sentient beings continuously holds the thought to do all actions totally for the benefit of all sentient beings. With such an intention, she has no fault or infraction in the bodhisattva training and she creates great virtue. Śāntideva says (BCA 1.18–19):

> And for those who have perfectly seized
>   this mind,
> with the thought never to turn away
> from totally liberating
> the infinite forms of life,
>
> from that time hence,
> even while asleep or unconcerned,
> a force of merit equal to the sky
> will perpetually ensue.

316 | THE FOUNDATION OF BUDDHIST PRACTICE

Kedrup, one of Tsongkhapa's foremost disciples, once praised Tsongkhapa, saying, "Your simple act of breathing accumulates enormous virtue." I don't think this means that Tsongkhapa has bodhicitta manifest in
his mind each time he breathes, thinking, "I inhale to become a buddha for
the benefit of sentient beings." Rather, all of his actions—including eating,
sleeping, and so on—are motivated by or associated with powerful bodhicitta. Nāgārjuna says (RA 483):

> Like the earth, water, wind, and fire,
> medicinal herbs, and the trees in the wilderness,
> may I always freely be an object of enjoyment
> by all beings as they wish.

If someone conjoins bodhicitta with the wisdom directly realizing reality, he or she is on the path to fulfilling the collections of merit and wisdom
and becoming a buddha.

A Deeper Perspective on Causality

Karma and its effects is sometimes taught in simple terms to new audiences
in order to communicate the importance of ethical conduct. As a result,
some people may think about karma and its effects in a very simplistic way,
as in "I hit you this life and you will hit me in the next life." As we've seen,
the effect of an action is dependent on many conditions and factors. In
this light, it is important to view karma and its effects within the broader
perspective of dependent arising and emptiness.

Dependent arising is the innermost treasure of the Buddha's teaching.
By understanding it, practitioners are able to gradually accomplish their
temporary and ultimate aims. Happiness in saṃsāra—including higher
rebirth—comes about by understanding the dependent arising of karma
and its effects. This understanding forms the basis for adopting the ethical
conduct of restraining from destructive actions and engaging in constructive ones.

However, understanding dependent arising in terms of karma and its
effects—or causal dependence in general—is not the complete understanding of dependent arising. Animals also understand cause and effect to some

extent. If we investigate the meaning of causal dependence further, how do we account for the fact that a cause produces an effect? Why is one event dependent on certain other specific events and not on others? This points to a deeper way to understand cause and effect. If cause and effect existed inherently, they would have a fixed essence; they would be self-enclosed entities that could not interact with other things. For cause and effect to function, things must be interrelated, and thus the very nature of things must be dependent. Having the nature of dependence, one thing can produce another, and a cause and its effect are related.

Causes do not depend on their effects in a temporal sense—we know that causes precede the effects that depend on them—but they do depend on effects in terms of their identity. Without there being a potential effect, something cannot be identified as a cause. The very identity of something as a cause depends on its effect; cause and effect are defined in terms of each other. Because they are mutually dependent, they do not possess an inherent essence. They exist in dependence on term and concept; they exist by dependent designation. If they had any findable nature, they could not be related as cause and effect. Nor could their identity be mutually defined in terms of each other.

In this way, understanding dependent arising in terms of cause and effect leads to the deeper understanding of phenomena as empty of inherent existence and to the understanding that phenomena are mutually dependent and exist by dependent designation. Comprehending this will enable us to counteract ignorance and attain liberation.

The Path of the Initial-Level Practitioner: A Conclusion

This completes the topics of the path in common with the initial-level practitioner. As a preliminary to the path in common with the middle-level practitioner and the path of the advanced practitioner, it cannot be omitted or ignored. This practice is said to be "in common with" the initial-level practitioner in that we do not seek good rebirths as an end in themselves. Our final aim is full awakening; we keep this bodhicitta motivation in mind from the first step on the path until the last.

Cherish your precious human life and the possibilities it grants you, and be aware that it is hard to obtain and does not last long. Train yourself to catch your proclivities for the eight worldly concerns and use awareness of your mortality to make wise choices about how to use your time and resources. Contemplate karmic causality to encourage yourself to create the causes for happiness and abandon the causes for suffering. By properly meditating on these topics and integrating them into your life, you will create a strong foundation for the practices to come and make your life meaningful.

Notes

1. In the Pāli tradition, the four seals are not mentioned in the context of distinguishing a teaching as Buddhist. However, there is overlap between the first three seals and three characteristics of saṃsāric phenomena found in the Pāli suttas, and the peaceful state of nirvāṇa is certainly spoken of in the Pāli suttas.

2. *Treasury of Knowledge* and *Lamrim Chenmo* consider unintentional actions such as accidentally stepping on an insect to be a type of karma whose result is not definite to be experienced.

3. In some cases ignorance (*avidya*) and confusion (*moha*) are synonymous, both referring to not understanding or misapprehending the ultimate nature of reality. In other cases, as is the situation here, confusion refers to not understanding or misunderstanding karma and its effects, and ignorance refers to not understanding or misapprehending the ultimate nature of reality.

4. Jeffrey Hopkins, *Maps of the Profound* (Ithaca, NY: Snow Lion Publications, 2003), 948. For more on the Prāsaṅgika view of reliable cognizers, see 947–55.

5. Candrakīrti's list of four reliable cognizers differs from the list that Dharmakīrti set forth, which is commonly taught in Mind and Awareness (*Lorig*) courses in Tibetan monastic universities. What constitutes each type of reliable cognizer differs as well. Usually people first learn the seven types of awarenesses according to Dharmakīrti's presentation, where reliable cognizers are of two types: direct and inferential. Inferential reliable cognizers are of three types: factual inferential cognizers, inferential cognizers based on renown, and inferential cognizers based on belief. Dharmakīrti also asserts a fourth direct cognizer—apperception. In this book we are following Candrakīrti's presentation.

6. These four reliable cognizers were commonly accepted in ancient India by both Buddhist and non-Buddhist schools. In addition to direct perceivers and inferential cognizers, which the Vaiśeṣika school accepted, the Sāṃkhya school added reliable cognizers depending on scripture and the Nyāya school added reliable cognizers using an example or analogy.

7. Comprehended objects are objects cognized or known by a reliable cognizer.

8. Chokyi Gyaltsen, *Presentation of Tenets* (*Grub mtha'i rnam bzhag*), http://www .glensvensson.org/uploads/7/5/6/1/7561348/presentation_of_tenets.pdf.

9. This is according to Jamyang Shepa's *Great Exposition of Buddhist and Non-Buddhist Views on the Nature of Reality*. Chokyi Gyaltsen says there are two divisions of direct reliable cognizers: nonconceptual and conceptual. The two presentations come to the same point.

10. Some people may initially have difficulty accepting the Buddha being a credible person as a valid reason for accepting a scriptural statement. Dharmakīrti agrees that this is not an indisputable reason. While we can prove the possibility of awakening by inference, we ordinary beings do not have the ability to know incontrovertibly that a specific individual is indeed awakened. Still, examining the Buddha's qualities enables us to make an informed decision to give credence to his statements.

11. Translated by John Dunne.

12. Yojana is a Vedic measurement.

13. See the story of the Kālāmas in *Approaching the Buddhist Path*, 126.

14. In philosophical texts, consciousness is equivalent to knower (T. *rig pa*) and awareness (T. *blo*). The meaning of *rigpa* in Dzogchen is different, and both *rig pa* and *blo* can be translated into English in several ways.

15. Absorption without discrimination (*asaṃjñāsamāpatti*) and absorption of cessation (*nirodhasamāpatti*) are not minds but are designations for states where consciousness does not function because something temporarily inhibits its arising. According to Vasubandhu, the mental consciousness is not present at this time.

16. T. W. Rhys-Davids, *The Questions of King Milinda* (New York: Dover Publications, 1963).

17. In the Sanskrit tradition, life faculty (*jīvitendriya*) is classified as an abstract composite. As the state of living, it is the basis for consciousness and warmth.

18. According to the Pāli Abhidhamma, mindfulness accompanies only a virtuous mind.

19. These three understandings are also called the "three wisdoms." Many scholars say that serenity is necessary for the understanding arising from meditation to be present. For example, the wisdom arising from meditation on emptiness arises together with the union of serenity and insight on emptiness, not before.

20. "View of a personal identity" is also translated as "view of the transitory collection" or "view of the perishing aggregates," which are more literal translations of the Tibetan term. Here "aggregates" and "collection" refer to the five psychophysical aggregates. They are perishing and transitory because they change in each moment. According to the lower schools, the aggregates are the observed object of the view of a personal identity, whereas according to the Prāsaṅgikas, the aggregates are the basis of designation of the I, and the mere I is the observed object of the view of a personal identity. The lower schools say the view of a personal identity grasps the person to be self-sufficient and substantially existent.

21. Translators from Pāli often translate this term as "view of rules and rites" and explain it as meaning dogmatic clinging to ethical precepts and religious observances.

22. This term has also been translated as "meaning generality" and "mental image."

23. There are three types of conceptuality—a conceptual consciousness apprehending: (1) A sound generality. The reverberation of the sound "pot" is in our mind, although we don't know what it refers to. (2) A conceptual appearance (meaning generality). An image of the pot appears to our mind, although we don't know the term "pot." (3) The sound generality and conceptual appearance suitable to be mixed. We associate the conceptual appearance of pot and the term "pot." We may think by using the sound of words, pictures, or both. Correct conceptual consciousnesses are determinative knowers—they think, "This is such and such."

24. Elizabeth Napper, *Traversing the Spiritual Path*, ed. Jeffrey Hopkins (UMA Institute for Tibetan Studies, http:/uma-tibet.org, January 2016), 204.

25. According to Dr. Jeffrey Hopkins, his teacher Geshe Gedun Lodro said that from the viewpoint of a conceptual appearance being the opposite of what is not the object, it is permanent. However, from the perspective of a conceptual appearance being a mental creation, it is a functioning thing; for example, when we visualize a meditational deity, the conceptual appearance of the deity has an effect on our mind.

26. All Mahāyāna practitioners practice the Perfection Vehicle, including those who also practice the Vajra Vehicle. Here the Perfection Vehicle and the Vajra Vehicle are considered to be separate branches of the Mahāyāna in order to illustrate some of their differences.

27. Matthieu Ricard, *On the Path to Enlightenment* (Boston: Shambhala Publications, 2013), 150.

28. Maitreya's text is written from the Yogācāra-Svātantrika Madhyamaka viewpoint. Here the higher training in wisdom realizes the selflessness of persons—the lack of a self-sufficient, substantially existent person. The seventh quality refers to realizing the two types of selflessness of phenomena as asserted by the Cittamātrins. According to the Prāsaṅgikas, both the third and seventh qualities refer to realizing the emptiness of inherent existence of persons and phenomena.

29. Thomas Cleary, trans., *Entry into the Realm of Reality* (Boston: Shambhala Publications, 1989), 151.

30. The English translation of the section on "Relying on the Teacher" is twenty-three pages long. Only half of one page is dedicated to the topic of seeing our spiritual mentors as the Buddha.

31. T. *dmigs pa'i yul du byas nas bsgom pa*. Its object is a "content object."

32. T. *ngo bor skyes nas bsgom pa*. Its object is an "aspect object."

33. Tenzin Gyatso and Thubten Chodron, *Approaching the Buddhist Path* (Boston: Wisdom Publications, 2017), chap. 11.

34. Thupten Jinpa, trans. http://www.tibetanclassics.org/html-assets/WorldTranscendentHym.pdf.

35. Translated by Geshe Dadul Namgyal.

36. Translated by Geshe Dorje Damdul.

37. Olivia Goldhill, "A Civil Servant Missing Most of His Brain Challenges Our

Most Basic Theories of Consciousness," Quartz Media, http://qz.com/722614/a--civil-servant-missing-most-of-his-brain-challenges-our-most-basic-theories-of-consciousness/.

38. Dr. Ian Stevenson is a noted exception. See his book *Cases of the Reincarnation Type* (Charlottesville: University of Virginia Press, 1975).

39. In the case of visual perception, scientists also speak of the aspect of the object appearing on the retina.

40. Also see Sara Boin-Webb, trans., *Abhidharmasamuccaya: The Compendium of the Higher Teaching (Philosophy) by Asaṅga* (Fremont, CA: Asian Humanities Press, 2001), 85.

41. Damdul Namgyal, "Sutra in Response to a Query over What Happens after Death: A Review," http://thubtenchodron.org/2008/08/dialog-regarding-rebirth/.

42. The eight freedoms are found in Nāgārjuna's *Letter to a Friend* (*Suhṛllekha*), and the ten fortunes are from Asaṅga's *Śrāvaka Grounds* (*Śrāvaka Bhūmi*).

43. Tsongkhapa notes that ordinary beings born in the formless realm, and desire-realm gods who are always distracted by sense pleasures, are in unfree states because they lack the opportunity to create virtue.

44. Thomas Cleary, trans., *The Flower Ornament Scripture* (Boston: Shambhala Publications, 1993), 1218.

45. The eight worldly concerns are also mentioned in the *Mañjuśrī-buddhakṣetraguṇavyūha Sūtra*.

46. H. H. the Dalai Lama, *Mind in Comfort and Ease* (Boston: Wisdom Publications, 2007), 114, 116–17.

47. Glenn Mullin, trans., *Gems of Wisdom from the Seventh Dalai Lama* (Ithaca, NY: Snow Lion Publications, 1999), 43.

48. Jan Nattier, *A Few Good Men: The Bodhisattva Path According to The Inquiry of Ugra* (*Ugraparipṛcchā*) (Honolulu: University of Hawai'i Press, 2003), 246–47.

49. Andrew Olendzki, trans., "Dhammapada," Wikiquote.org, https://en.wikiquote.org/wiki/Dhammapada.

50. *Lord of death* is anthropomorphizing mortality.

51. For a more detailed explanation of His Holiness's views on the interface of evolution and karma, see *The Universe in a Single Atom: The Convergence of Science and Spirituality* (New York: Morgan Road Books, 2005).

52. Garma C. C. Chang, ed., *A Treasury of Mahāyāna Sūtras: Selections from the Mahāratnakūta* (University Park: The Pennsylvania State University Press, 1983), 244.

53. LC 1:227.

54. Cittamātrins and below say that the cause of a ripening result must be either polluted virtue or nonvirtue, whereas Mādhyamikas assert that the causes of a ripening result and that result itself may also be unpolluted virtue accumulated by ārya bodhisattvas. They cite a buddha's signs and marks as an example; they are the virtuous ripening results of the unpolluted uninterrupted paths of the ten grounds. (Causes for a buddha's signs and marks may also be created while we are ordinary beings, as explained in the *Precious Garland* and the *Ornament*.) Similarly,

Mādhyamikas say that the unpolluted ripening results of ārya bodhisattvas— their being born wheel-turning monarchs and lords of certain realms—come from unpolluted causes created on the bodhisattva path.

55. The *Sūtra on the Ten Grounds* reverses the last two results.

56. Defunct karma corresponds with indefinite karma—karma that is not certain to ripen or whose time of ripening is uncertain—in the Sanskrit tradition.

57. Negativity includes the ten nonvirtues, other destructive actions, and nonvirtuous mental states. Negativity and nonvirtuous karma are not synonyms. For example, anger is a negativity but is not a nonvirtuous action because it is an affliction.

58. Only Vaibhāṣikas and Prāsaṅgikas accept imperceptible forms, but the way they assert them differs. Vaibhāṣikas say they are substantially established, whereas the Prāsaṅgikas do not. The other tenet schools do not accept imperceptible forms.

59. A having-ceased is the potential that brings the result of that action. It will be explained in a later volume.

60. Not all scholars agree that Candrakīrti is the author of this text. Also, not all Tibetan scholars agree that Prāsaṅgikas accept imperceptible forms.

61. Jeffrey Hopkins, *Tsong-kha-pa's Final Exposition of Wisdom* (Ithaca, NY: Snow Lion Publications, 2008), 41.

62. These four are also mentioned in the First Dalai Lama's Abhidharma commentary (EPL 607–8).

63. Even Brahmā's arrogance—due to his mistakenly thinking that he created the universe—is neutral.

64. This special root of virtue is described in the scriptures in the context of differentiating virtue concordant with liberation, which is a synonym for the path of accumulation, and the root of virtue concordant with liberation, which is created owing to the power of the holy object and becomes a cause for liberation. Whereas virtue concordant with liberation requires that the person has the aspiration for liberation, the root of virtue concordant with liberation does not.

65. The great twentieth-century Theravāda meditator Ajahn Mun in Thailand had taken the bodhisattva ethical restraints in a previous life and relinquished them in this life. Yet he is said to have attained arhatship in this life.

66. Karma is defined as intention. Some stories—such as this story about the cause of Nāgārjuna's death—suggest that karma may be accrued even when no intention is present. We cannot say with complete conviction that these stories are false, because the subtle workings of karma are beyond our comprehension. In some cultures, such startling stories play an important role in helping people to understand the importance of conscientiously observing karma and its effects.

67. William S. Waldron, "How Innovative Is the Ālayavijñāna?" [n.d.], http://www.middlebury.edu/media/view/440169/original/waldron_how_innovative_is_alayavijnanao.pdf.

68. Jeffrey Hopkins, trans., *Compassion in Tibetan Buddhism* (Ithaca, NY: Snow Lion Publications, 1985), 200.

Glossary

abstract composites (viprayukta-saṃskāra). Impermanent phenomena that are neither forms nor consciousnesses.

actual clear light (of the fourth stage). A stage on the completion stage of highest yoga tantra in which all winds have been dissolved in the indestructible drop at the heart and the fundamental, innate clear light mind directly perceives emptiness.

afflictions (kleśa). Mental factors that disturb the tranquility of the mind. These include disturbing emotions and wrong views.

afflictive obscurations (kleśāvaraṇa). Obscurations that mainly prevent liberation; afflictions and their seeds.

aggregates (skandha). The four or five components that make up a living being: form (except for beings born in the formless realm), feelings, discriminations, miscellaneous factors, and consciousnesses.

analytical meditation (vicārabhāvanā, T. dpyad sgom). Meditation done to understand an object.

appearing object (T. *snang yul*). The object that actually appears to a consciousness. The appearing object of a conceptual consciousness is a conceptual appearance of something.

apprehended object (muṣṭibandhaviṣata, T. 'dzin btangs kyi yul). The main object with which the mind is concerned, that is, the object that the mind is getting at or understands. Synonymous with engaged object.

arhat. Someone who has eliminated all afflictive obscurations and attained liberation.

ārya. Someone who has directly and nonconceptually realized the emptiness of inherent existence.

bardo (antarābhava). The intermediate state between one life and the next.

basis of designation. The collection of parts or factors in dependence on which an object is designated.

bodhicitta. A main mental consciousness induced by an aspiration to bring about the welfare of others and accompanied by an aspiration to attain full awakening oneself.

bodhisattva. Someone who has spontaneous bodhicitta.

causally concordant behavioral result. Karmic result in which our action is similar to an action we did in a previous life.

causally concordant experiential result. Karmic result in which we experience circumstances similar to what we caused others to experience.

causally concordant result. The karmic result that corresponds to its cause. It is of two types: the result similar to the cause in terms of our experience and the result similar to the cause in terms of our habitual behavior.

cognitive faculty (indriya). The subtle material in the gross sense organ that enables perception of sense objects; for the mental consciousness, it is previous moments of any of the six consciousnesses.

cognitive obscurations (jñeyāvaraṇa). Obscurations that mainly prevent full awakening; the latencies of ignorance and the subtle dualistic view that they give rise to.

collection of merit (puṇyasaṃbhāra). A bodhisattva's practice of the method aspect of the path that accumulates merit.

comprehended object (prameya, T. gzhal bya). That which is the object known or cognized by a reliable cognizer.

conceived object (T. zhen yul). The object conceived by a conceptual consciousness; synonymous with the apprehended or engaged object of a conceptual consciousness.

conceptual appearance (artha-sāmānya). A mental image of an object that appears to a conceptual consciousness.

conceptual consciousness (kalpanā). A consciousness knowing its object by means of a conceptual appearance.

conceptual fabrications. False modes of existence and false ideas imputed by the mind.

consciousness (jñāna). That which is clear and cognizant.

consequence (prasaṅga). A statement used in debate to show the other person the contradiction present in his or her belief.

conventional existence (saṃvṛtisat). Existence.

conventional truths (saṃvṛtisatya). That which is true from the perspective of grasping true existence.

cyclic existence (saṃsāra). The cycle of rebirth that occurs under the control of afflictions and karma.

death (maraṇabhava). The last moment of a lifetime when the subtlest clear light mind manifests.

definite karma. Actions that are consciously done and accumulated (there was an intention to act) whose results are definite to be experienced.

definitive sūtra (nītārtha sūtra). Sūtras that mainly and explicitly teach ultimate truths.

dependent arising (pratītyasamutpāda). This is of three types: (1) causal dependence—things arising due to causes and conditions, (2) mutual dependence—phenomena existing in relation to other phenomena, and (3) dependent designation—phenomena existing by being merely designated by terms and concepts.

desire realm (kāmadhātu). One of the three realms of cyclic existence; the realm where sentient beings are overwhelmed by attraction to and desire for sense objects.

deva. A being born as a heavenly being in the desire realm or in one of the meditative absorptions of the form or formless realms.

dhyāna. A meditative stabilization in the form realm.

direct reliable cognizer (pratyakṣa-pramāṇa). A nondeceptive awareness that knows its object—an evident phenomenon—directly, without depending on a reason.

duḥkha. Unsatisfactory experiences of cyclic existence.

Dzogchen. A tantric practice emphasizing meditation on the nature of mind, practiced primarily in the Nyingma tradition.

eight worldly concerns (aṣṭalokadharma). Material gain and loss, disrepute and fame, blame and praise, pleasure and pain.

emanation body (nirmāṇakāya). The buddha body that appears as an ordinary sentient being to benefit others.

emptiness (śūnyatā). The lack of inherent existence and true existence.

enjoyment body (saṃbhogakāya). The buddha body that appears in the pure lands to teach ārya bodhisattvas.

environmental result. The result of karma that influences what environment we live in.

evident phenomena (abhimukhī). Phenomena that ordinary beings can perceive with their five senses.

existent (sat). That which is perceivable by mind.

extreme of absolutism (śāśvatānta). The extreme of eternalism; believing that phenomena inherently exist.

extreme of nihilism (ucchedānta). The extreme of nonexistence; believing that our actions have no ethical dimension; believing that nothing exists.

five actions of immediate retribution (ānantaryakarma). Killing one's mother, father, or an arhat, wounding a buddha, and causing a schism in the saṅgha.

form body (rūpakāya). The buddha body in which a buddha appears to sentient beings; it includes the emanation and enjoyment bodies.

form realm (rūpadhātu). The saṃsāric realm in which beings have bodies made of subtle material; they are born there due to having attained various states of concentration.

formless realm (*ārūpyadhātu*). The saṃsāric realm in which sentient beings do not have a material body.

four seals (*caturmudrā*). Four views that make a philosophy Buddhist: all conditioned phenomena are transient, all polluted phenomena are duḥkha, all phenomena are empty and selfless, nirvāṇa alone is true peace.

four truths of the āryas (*catvāry āryasatyāni*). The truth of duḥkha, its origin, its cessation, and the path to that cessation.

full awakening (*samyaksaṃbodhi*). Buddhahood; the state in which all obscurations have been abandoned and all good qualities developed limitlessly.

Fundamental Vehicle. The path leading to the liberation of hearers and solitary realizers.

grasping inherent existence. Grasping persons and phenomena to exist truly or inherently. Synonymous with grasping true existence.

grasping true existence (true grasping, *satyagrāha*). Grasping persons and phenomena to exist truly or inherently.

hell being (*nāraka*). A being born in one of the unfortunate classes of beings who suffer intense physical pain as a result of their strong destructive karma.

highest yoga tantra (*anuttarayogatantra*). The most advanced of the four classes of tantra.

hungry ghost (*preta*). A being born in one of the unfortunate classes of beings, who suffers from intense hunger and thirst.

ignorance (*avidyā*). A mental factor that is obscured and grasps the opposite of what exists. There are two types: ignorance regarding ultimate truth and ignorance regarding karma and its effects.

impermanence (*anitya*). The transient quality of all compositional phenomena and functioning things. Coarse impermanence can be known by our senses; subtle impermanence is something not remaining the same in the very next moment.

inattentive awareness. A consciousness that doesn't ascertain its object, even though that object is appearing to it.

inferential reliable cognizer (anumāna-pramāṇa). An awareness that knows its object—slightly obscure phenomena—nondeceptively, purely in dependence on a reason.

inherent existence (svabhāva). Existence without depending on any other factors; independent existence.

interpretable sūtra (neyārtha sūtra). A sūtra that speaks about the variety of phenomena and/or cannot be taken literally.

karma. Intentional action; it includes intention karma (mental action) and intended karma (physical and verbal actions motivated by intention).

karmic seeds. The potency from previously created actions that will bring their results.

latencies (vāsanā). Predispositions, imprints, or tendencies.

liberation (mokṣa). The state of freedom from cyclic existence.

Mahāmudrā. A type of meditation that focuses on the conventional and ultimate natures of the mind.

meditative equipoise on emptiness. An ārya's mind focused single-pointedly on the emptiness of inherent existence.

mental direct reliable cognizers. Nondeceptive mental awarenesses that know their objects by depending on another consciousness that induces them.

mental factor (caitta). An aspect of mind that accompanies a primary consciousness and fills out the cognition, apprehending particular attributes of the object or performing a specific function.

mind (citta). The part of living beings that cognizes, experiences, thinks, feels, and so on. In some contexts it is equivalent to primary consciousness.

mindstream (cittasaṃtāna). The continuity of mind.

mistaken awareness. An awareness that is mistaken in terms of its appearing object.

monastic. Someone who has received monastic ordination; a monk or nun.

Mount Meru. A huge mountain at the center of our world system, according to ancient Indian cosmology.

nirvāṇa. The state of liberation of an arhat; the emptiness of a mind that has been totally cleansed of afflictive obscurations.

nonabiding nirvāṇa. A buddha's nirvāṇa that does not abide in either cyclic existence or personal liberation.

nonconceptual consciousness. A consciousness that knows its object directly, not by means of a conceptual appearance.

nonduality. The nonappearance of subject and object, inherent existence, conventional truths, and conceptual appearances in an ārya's meditative equipoise on emptiness.

nonexistent (asat). That which is not perceivable by mind.

observed object (ālambana, T. dmigs yul). The basic object that the mind refers to or focuses on while apprehending certain aspects of that object.

permanent (nitya). Unchanging, static. It does not mean eternal.

permanent, unitary, independent self. A soul or self (*ātman*) asserted by non-Buddhists.

person (pudgala). A living being designated in dependence on the four or five aggregates.

polluted (āsava). Under the influence of ignorance and its latencies.

powa. A practice for transferring the consciousness at the time of death so that it will take a precious human life or be reborn in a pure land.

Prāsaṅgika Madhyamaka. The Buddhist philosophical tenet system whose views are most accurate.

prātimokṣa. The different sets of ethical precepts for monastics and lay followers that assist in attaining liberation.

primary consciousness (vijñāna). A consciousness that apprehends the presence or basic entity of an object; they are of six types: visual, auditory, olfactory, gustatory, tactile, and mental.

pure land. Places created by the unshakable resolve and merit of buddhas where all external conditions are conducive for Dharma practice.

reliable cognizer (pramāṇa). A nondeceptive awareness that is incontrovertible with respect to its apprehended object and that enables us to accomplish our purpose.

reliable cognizer based on an example. Inferential cognizers that realize their object by understanding that it is similar to something else.

reliable cognizer based on authoritative testimony. An inferential cognizer knowing very obscure phenomena that cannot be established through direct perceivers or other inferential reliable cognizers, but only by depending on the authoritative testimony of a trustworthy source, such as a credible person or scripture.

ripening result (vipākaphala). The karmic result that is a rebirth; the five aggregates a being takes.

Sautrāntika. A Buddhist tenet school that espouses Fundamental Vehicle tenets. It is considered higher than the Vaibhāṣika school.

scriptural authority. Relying on a scripture that has met three criteria that deem it reliable.

self (ātman). Refers to (1) a person, or (2) inherent existence.

self-grasping (ātmagrāha). Grasping inherent existence.

self-sufficient substantially existent person (T. *gang zag rang rkya thub pa'i rdzas yod*). A self that is the controller of the body and mind. Such a self does not exist.

sense direct reliable cognizers. Incontrovertible awarenesses that know their objects—sights, sounds, smells, tastes, and tangible objects—directly by depending on a physical cognitive faculty.

sentient being (sattva). Any being with a mind, except for a buddha.

six perfections (ṣaḍpāramitā). The practices of generosity, ethical conduct, fortitude, joyous effort, meditative stability, and wisdom that are motivated by bodhicitta.

slightly obscure phenomena (*parokṣa*). Phenomena that can initially be known only by using factual inference.

solitary realizer (*pratyekabuddha*). A person following the Fundamental Vehicle who seeks liberation and who emphasizes understanding the twelve links of dependent arising.

śrāvaka (hearer). Someone practicing the Fundamental Vehicle path leading to arhatship who emphasizes meditation on the four truths of the āryas.

stabilizing meditation (T. *'jog sgom*). Meditation to focus and concentrate the mind on an object.

superknowledge (*abhijñā*). Special powers gained through having deep states of concentration.

Svātantrika Madhyamaka. A philosophical tenet system that is not as accurate as the other branch of Madhyamaka, the Prāsaṅgika.

syllogism (*prayoga*). A statement consisting of a subject, predicate, and reason, and in many cases, an example.

taking and giving (T. *tong len*). A meditation practice for cultivating love and compassion that involves visualizing taking on the suffering of others, using it to destroy our self-centered attitude, and giving our body, possessions, and merit to others.

tathāgata. A buddha.

thesis (*pratijñā*). What is to be proven—the combination of the subject and the predicate—in a syllogism.

thing (*bhāva*). Something that performs a function.

three criteria for existent phenomena. It is known to a conventional consciousness; its existence is not invalidated by another conventional reliable cognizer; it is not invalidated by a mind analyzing emptiness.

three criteria of a correct inference or syllogism. Presence of the reason in the subject, pervasion or entailment, and counterpervasion.

true cessation (*nirodhasatya*). The cessation of a portion of afflictions or a portion of cognitive obscurations.

true existence (satyasat). Existence having its own mode of being; existence having its own reality.

true grasping. See "grasping true existence."

truth body (dharmakāya). The buddha body that includes the nature truth body and the wisdom truth body.

twelve links of dependent arising. A system of twelve factors that explains how we take rebirth in saṃsāra and how we can be liberated from it.

two truths (satyadvaya). Ultimate truths and veil (conventional) truths.

ultimate bodhicitta (paramārthabodhicitta). Direct nonconceptual realization of emptiness in the continuum of an ārya bodhisattva.

ultimate truth (paramārthasatya). The ultimate mode of existence of all persons and phenomena; emptiness; objects that are true and appear true to their main cognizer.

unfortunate states (apāya). Unfortunate states of rebirth as a hell being, hungry ghost, or animal.

unpolluted (anāsrava). Not under the influence of ignorance.

unreliable awareness. An awareness that does not correctly apprehend its object and cannot help us accomplish our purpose. These include correct assumers, inattentive perceivers, doubt, and wrong awarenesses.

Vaibhāṣika. A Buddhist tenet school that espouses Fundamental Vehicle tenets. It is considered the lowest tenet school.

veiled truths (saṃvṛtisatya). Objects that appear true to ignorance; objects that appear to exist inherently to their main cognizer, although they do not; synonymous with conventional truths.

very obscure phenomena (atyantaparokṣa). Phenomena that can be known only by relying on the testimony of a reliable person or a valid scripture.

view of a personal identity (view of the transitory collection, *satkāyadṛṣṭi*). Grasping an inherently existent I or mine (according to the Prāsaṅgika system).

Vinaya. Monastic discipline.

white appearance, red increase, and black near attainment. Three subtle minds that manifest after coarser minds have been absorbed and before the subtlest clear light mind arises.

wrong or erroneous awareness (viparyaya jñāna). A mind that is erroneous with respect to its apprehended object, and in the case of conceptual cognizers with respect to its conceived object.

yogic direct reliable cognizers. Nondeceptive mental consciousnesses that know their objects by depending on a union of serenity and insight.

Recommended Reading

Berzin, Alexander. *Wise Teacher, Wise Student*. Ithaca, NY: Snow Lion Publications, 2010.

Boin-Webb, Sara, trans. *Abhidharmasamuccaya: The Compendium of the Higher Teaching (Philosophy) by Asaṅga*. Fremont, CA: Asian Humanities Press, 2001.

Chodron, Thubten. *Don't Believe Everything You Think*. Boston: Snow Lion Publications, 2012.

_____. *Good Karma: How to Create the Causes of Happiness and Avoid the Causes of Suffering*. Boulder, CO: Shambhala Publications, 2016.

_____. *Working with Anger*. Ithaca, NY: Snow Lion Publications, 2001.

The Dhammapada: The Path of Truth. Translated by the Venerable Balangoda Ananda Maitreya. Revised by Rose Kramer. Berkeley, CA: Parallax Press, 1995.

Dhargyey, Geshe Ngawang. *An Anthology of Well-Spoken Advice*. Dharamsala: Library of Tibetan Works and Archives, 2001.

Dreyfus, Georges B. J. *Recognizing Reality: Dharmakīrti's Philosophy and Its Tibetan Interpretations*. Albany: State University of New York Press, 1997.

Dunne, John D. *Foundations of Dharmakīrti's Philosophy*. Boston: Wisdom Publications, 2004.

Gehlek, Nawang. *Good Life, Good Death: Tibetan Wisdom on Reincarnation*. New York: Riverhead Books, 2001.

H. H. Tenzin Gyatso, the Fourteenth Dalai Lama. *An Open Heart*. Boston: Little, Brown, 2011.

_____. *Beyond Religion*. Boston: Houghton Mifflin Harcourt, 2011.

_____. *Healing Anger*. Ithaca, NY: Snow Lion Publications, 1997.

_____. *How to See Yourself as You Really Are*. New York: Atria Books, 2007.

_____. *The Four Noble Truths*. London: Thorsons, 1997.

_____. *The Good Heart*. Boston: Wisdom Publications, 1996.

_____. *The Joy of Living and Dying in Peace*. London: Thorsons, 1998.

_____. *The Universe in a Single Atom*. New York: Morgan Road Books, 2005.

_____. *Transforming the Mind: Teachings on Generating Compassion*. London: Thorsons, 2000.

H. H. Tenzin Gyatso, the Fourteenth Dalai Lama, and Thubten Chodron. *Buddhism: One Teacher, Many Traditions*. Boston: Wisdom Publications, 2014.

Hopkins, Jeffrey. *Cultivating Compassion*. New York: Broadway Books, 2001.

_____. *Maps of the Profound*. Ithaca, NY: Snow Lion Publications, 2003.

_____. *Meditation on Emptiness*. Boston: Wisdom Publications, 1996.

Jinpa, Thupten. *Essential Mind Training*. Boston: Wisdom Publications, 2011.

MacKenzie, Vicki. *Reborn in the West: The Reincarnation Masters*. New York: First Marlowe and Company, 1996.

Newland, Guy. *Introduction to Emptiness*. Ithaca, NY: Snow Lion Publications, 2008.

Perdue, Daniel. *The Course in Buddhist Reasoning and Debate*. Boston: Snow Lion Publications, 2014.

Pruden, Leo M., trans. *Abhidharmakośabhāṣyam of Vasubandhu*. vol. 2. Berkeley, CA: Asian Humanities Press, 1991.

Rabten, Geshe. *The Mind and Its Functions*. Switzerland: Editions Rabten Choeling, 1981.

Rato, Khyongla. *My Life and Lives*. New York: Penguin, 1991.

Rinchen, Geshe Sonam, and Ruth Sonam, eds., trans. *How Karma Works: The Twelve Links of Dependent-Arising*. Ithaca, NY: Snow Lion Publications, 2006.

Rinpochay, Dilgo Khyentse. *Enlightened Courage: An Explanation of the Seven-Point Mind Training*. Ithaca, NY: Snow Lion Publications, 2006.

Rinpoche, Anyen. *Dying with Confidence*. Boston: Wisdom Publications, 2010.

Rinpochay, Lati, and Elizabeth Napper. *Mind in Tibetan Buddhism*. Ithaca, NY: Snow Lion Publications, 1968.

Rinpoche, Patrul. *The Words of My Perfect Teacher*. Boston: Shambhala Publications, 1998.

Rogers, Katherine Manchester. *Tibetan Logic*. Ithaca, NY: Snow Lion Publications, 2009.

Sonam, Ruth, trans. *Āryadeva's Four Hundred Stanzas on the Middle Way*. Ithaca, NY: Snow Lion Publications, 2008.

Sopa, Geshe Lhundup, and Jeffrey Hopkins. *Cutting Through Appearances: Practice and Theory of Tibetan Buddhism*. Ithaca, NY: Snow Lion Publications, 1989.

Sopa, Geshe Lhundup, and David Patt. *Steps on the Path to Enlightenment*, vol. 1, *The Foundation Practices*. Boston: Wisdom Publications, 2004.

_____. *Steps on the Path to Enlightenment*, vol. 2, *Karma*. Boston: Wisdom Publications, 2005.

Tegchok, Geshe Jampa. *Transforming Adversity into Joy and Courage*. Ithaca, NY: Snow Lion Publications, 2005.

Thurman, Robert. *Infinite Life*. New York: Riverhead Books, 2004.

Tillemans, Tom J. F., and Gene Smith. *Scripture, Logic, Language: Essays on Dharmakīrti and His Tibetan Successors*. Boston: Wisdom Publications, 1997.

Tsering, Geshe Tashi. *Buddhist Psychology*. Boston: Wisdom Publications, 2006.

Yeshe, Lama. *Life, Death, and after Death*. Boston: Lama Yeshe Wisdom Archives, 2011.

Index

to ordinary beings and āryas, distinctions in, 19–20
as permanent, 52
reflecting on, 224, 226, 227
in sealing dedication of merit, 150
as ultimate nature, 14
understanding, benefits of, 219
understanding phenomena and, 54
Engaging in the Bodhisattvas' Deeds (*Bodhicaryāvatāra*, Śāntideva), 145, 194–95, 304
enjoyment body, 156–57, 218–19, 312.
    See also buddha bodies, three
environmental result, 271, 272–73, 275
epistemology, xvii, 17, 21
equal taste, 143
equanimity
    eight worldly concerns and, 200
    mental factor of (*upekṣa*), 65
    See also four immeasurables
Essence of Eloquence (Tsongkhapa), 73
ethical conduct, xviii, 253
    benefits of, 202, 313–14
    Buddhist views on modern, 259–68
    as cause of favorable rebirth, 188–89, 205
    confusion and, 259
    correct view and, 120–21
    in daily life, 157
    importance of, 316
    karmic results of, 270, 314
    levels of, 122
    mindful observance of, 303
    perils and advantages of, 250–51
    precepts and, 249
    projecting karma of, 291
    secular presentation of, 3–4, 310
    in seeking others' approval, 195
    of spiritual mentors, 124–26
    in tantra, 121, 122
    in three vehicles, 83–84
    at time of death, benefit of, 219
    virtue and nonvirtue in, 235–36
    wealth and, 192–93

ethical restraints (*saṃvara*), 298
euthanasia, 242, 254
evident phenomena, 18
    Candrakīrti's view, 23, 24, 25
    death and impermanence as, 47
    as examples, 32, 33
    to highly realized beings, 36
    previous lives as, 173
    and scriptural authority, determining, 34, 41–42
existents (*sat*), 51, 52, 169
Explanatory Tantra Vajramālā, 138
extremes, view of (*antagrāhadṛṣṭi*), 66

F

factual inferential cognizers, 18–19, 30–31, 37, 43, 44–45, 319n5
failure, aversion to, 196–97
faith
    based on reasoning, 128
    as cause of favorable rebirth, 188
    common and uncommon, 104
    cultivating, 224–25
    of disciples, 112
    gaining, 158
    in karma, 216, 231, 257, 308
    mental factor of, 54, 296
    realization and, 137
    in serenity, 45
    in spiritual mentors, 86, 94, 103–4, 105, 106, 114
    in Three Jewels, 141
    types of, 64, 140
    See also blind faith
fame, 193–95, 206
family, 176, 200–201
fear, 175, 216, 217–18, 221, 224, 237, 272, 273
feelings, 10, 27, 46, 55, 56, 61
Fifty Verses of Relying on a Spiritual Master (*Gurupañcāśikā*, Aśvaghoṣa), 90, 125
five actions of immediate retribution, 186, 278

animosity and, 246
as intention, 300
karma of, four branches, 244
karmic results of, 270, 272, 273, 280
refraining from, 252
having-ceased (naṣṭa), 299, 323n59
heart cakra, 150, 220
Heart Sūtra, 54, 305
hell beings/hell states, 184, 214, 215,
216, 271, 301, 311
highest yoga tantra
conduct in, 120
death process in, 218–20
gurus in, 90, 108
master-disciple relationship in, 123
mind, view of in, 166
sexual union in, 122
sleep, transforming in, 156–57
unpolluted mental karma in, 303
holy objects, 146, 255, 298–99, 306, 310,
323n64
homosexuality, 267
human potential, 187, 201–2, 232, 263
humors, three, 276
hungry ghosts, 154, 184, 214, 215, 216,
271, 278

I

idle talk, 239–40, 244–45, 246, 252,
255, 272
ignorance, 14, 131, 305, 319n3
of animals, 215, 310
definition of, 66
duḥkha and, 9
eradicating, 12, 13
karma and, 10, 319n3
karmic weight and, 254, 256
overcoming, 258, 314–15, 317
as polluted, 258
Prāsaṅgika view of, 11–12
unpolluted karma and, 302
Illuminating the Thought
(Tsongkhapa), 313–14
illusory body, 203, 227, 303

imagination, 110, 140, 144, 163
imperceptible forms (avijñapti), 58,
295, 297, 300, 323n58, 323n60
impermanence, 7–9, 13, 16
of causes, 169, 232
coarse, 47
conceptual and nonconceptual consciousness and, 72
of eight worldly concerns, 197
of mind, 163
as object of meditation, 132, 133
to ordinary beings and āryas, distinctions in, 19–20
reflecting on, 9, 205, 206–7, 217, 226
reliable cognizers of, 17
subtle, factual inferential cognizers
of, 18–19
three kinds of wisdom in realizing,
30–31
inattentive awareness, 22, 24, 26
India, 4, 5, 7
Indian Buddhism, 21, 319nn5–6
inference, 19–20, 22
inferential cognizers (anumāna), 22,
24, 26
in analytical meditation, 132–33
in authoritative testimony, 35–36
Candrakīrti's view of, 23, 25
correct assumptions and, 44–45
deterioration of, 31
Dharmakīrti's view of, 319n5
meditation and, 45–47
purpose of, 27–28
variant views on, 31–32
inherent existence, 10, 11–12, 42–44,
132
Inquiry of Ugra Sūtra (Ugraparipṛcchā), 200–201
insects, 262, 311
insight
attachment to, 99
breath in, 139
inferential cognizers and, 45, 46
into selflessness, 9

About the Authors

THE DALAI LAMA is the spiritual leader of the Tibetan people, a Nobel Peace Prize recipient, and an advocate for compassion and peace throughout the world. He promotes harmony among the world's religions and engages in dialogue with leading scientists. Ordained as a Buddhist monk when he was a child, he completed the traditional monastic studies and earned his geshe degree (equivalent to a PhD). Renowned for his erudite and open-minded scholarship, his meditative attainments, and his humility, Bhikṣu Tenzin Gyatso says, "I am a simple Buddhist monk."

Peter Aronson

BHIKṢUṆĪ THUBTEN CHODRON has been a Buddhist nun since 1977. Growing up in Los Angeles, she graduated with honors in history from UCLA and did graduate work in education at USC. After years studying and teaching Buddhism in Asia, Europe, and the United States, she became the founder and abbess of Sravasti Abbey in Washington State. A popular speaker for her practical explanations of how to apply Buddhist teachings in daily life, she is the author of several bestselling books, including *Buddhism for Beginners*. She is the editor of Khensur Jampa Tegchok's *Insight into Emptiness*. For more information, visit sravastiabbey.org and thubtenchodron books.org.

Also Available by the Dalai Lama from Wisdom Publications

Buddhism
One Teacher, Many Traditions

The Compassionate Life

Essence of the Heart Sutra
The Dalai Lama's Heart of Wisdom Teachings

The Good Heart
A Buddhist Perspective on the Teachings of Jesus

Imagine All the People
A Conversation with the Dalai Lama on Money, Politics, and Life as it Could Be

Kalachakra Tantra
Rite of Initiation

The Life of My Teacher
A Biography of Kyabjé Ling Rinpoche

Meditation on the Nature of Mind

The Middle Way
Faith Grounded in Reason

Mind in Comfort and Ease
The Vision of Enlightenment in the Great Perfection

MindScience
An East-West Dialogue

Practicing Wisdom
The Perfection of Shantideva's Bodhisattva Way

Science and Philosophy in the Indian Buddhist Classics, vol. 1
The Physical World

Sleeping, Dreaming, and Dying
An Exploration of Consciousness

The Wheel of Life
Buddhist Perspectives on Cause and Effect

The World of Tibetan Buddhism
An Overview of Its Philosophy and Practice

Also Available from Thubten Chodron

Insight into Emptiness
Khensur Jampa Tegchok
Edited and Introduced by Thubten Chodron

"One of the best introductions to the philosophy of emptiness I have ever read."—José Ignacio Cabezón

Practical Ethics and Profound Emptiness
A Commentary on Nagarjuna's Precious Garland
Khensur Jampa Tegchok
Edited by Thubten Chodron

"A beautifully clear translation and systematic explanation of Nagarjuna's most accessible and wide-ranging work. Dharma students everywhere will benefit from careful attention to its pages."
—Guy Newland, author of *Introduction to Emptiness*

Buddhism for Beginners

Cultivating a Compassionate Heart
The Yoga Method of Chenrezig

Don't Believe Everything You Think
Living with Wisdom and Compassion

Guided Meditations on the Stages of the Path

How to Free Your Mind
Tara the Liberator

Living with an Open Heart
How to Cultivate Compassion in Daily Life

Open Heart, Clear Mind

Taming the Mind

Working with Anger